Children's Well-Being: Indicators and Research

Volume 28

Series Editor

Asher Ben-Arieh, Paul Baerwald School of Social Work & Social Welfare
The Hebrew University of Jerusalem
Jerusalem, Israel

This series focuses on measurements and indicators of children's well-being and their usage, within multiple domains and in diverse cultures. It presents measures and data resources, analysis of data, exploration of theoretical issues, and information about the status of children, as well as the implementation of this information in policy and practice. By doing so it explores how child indicators can be used to improve the development and the well-being of children.

The series provides an international and applied perspective by bringing in a variety of analytical models, varied methodologies, and discussions on wide-ranging social policy regimes. This is a companion to the journal *Child Indicators Research* and is an exclusive channel for book publication in the field of measures and indicators of children's lives. The diverse and international advisory board of experts in the field ensures a thorough review of proposals and manuscripts in this series.

The series accepts high-quality, high-impact, and academically sound scientific monographs and contributed volumes. Volumes that add novel insights into the child indicators field are especially encouraged.

Ziba Vaghri • Roberta Ruggiero • Gerison Lansdown
Editors

Children's Rights-Based Indicators

Strengthening States' Accountability to Children

Springer

Editors
Ziba Vaghri
GlobalChild Program of Research
University of New Brunswick
Saint John, NB, Canada

Roberta Ruggiero
Centre for Children's Rights Studies, Faculty of Law
University of Geneva
Geneva, Switzerland

Gerison Lansdown
School of Law
University College Cork
Cork, Ireland

ISSN 1879-5196 ISSN 1879-520X (electronic)
Children's Well-Being: Indicators and Research
ISBN 978-3-031-71596-9 ISBN 978-3-031-71594-5 (eBook)
https://doi.org/10.1007/978-3-031-71594-5

This work was supported by Canadian Institutes for Health Research

This Springer imprint is published by the registered company Springer Nature Switzerland AG
The registered company address is: Gewerbestrasse 11, 6330 Cham, Switzerland

Foreword of the Chairpersons of the Committee on the Rights of the Child (2006–2021)

The United Nations Convention on the Rights of the Child—the most widely ratified human rights treaty in the world—entered into force in 1990. This was a major milestone, but only the beginning of the long journey towards greater respect for the rights of children and adolescents.

Over thirty years of reporting from the States Parties to the Committee on the Rights of the Child have revealed many gaps between the promise of the Convention and the reality on the ground for children. As with other human rights treaties, the full realization of children's rights under the Convention remains a challenge. This book comprises part of a significant body of work by an international team of experts that has been encouraged and supported by the United Nations Committee on the Rights of the Child and its seven successive chairpersons since its inception.

As the past Chairs of the Committee, we have borne witness to the fact that—despite progress in many areas—there is still insufficient understanding of what the rights of children entail and how to interpret and implement them. There is an urgent and pressing need for tools that can facilitate a better understanding of the specific measures that are needed in respect of legislative and policy development and how to measure progress in their implementation in terms of the realization of the rights of children. This publication is part of a line of efforts to facilitate a better understanding of that process. It is the outcome of outstanding work that we have all supported during our tenure as the chair of the UN CRC Committee and have worked with this team and guided their work.

Building on the success of and momentum of the authors' first book *Monitoring State Compliance with the UN Convention on the Rights of the Child: An Analysis of Attributes,* this book offers a comprehensive set of structural, process and outcome indicators for every right in the Convention to measure State compliance and performance on their implementation. As a result, we believe that the information presented in this book will be of benefit not only to children but also to States, advocates, policymakers, service providers and academics in all 196 countries that are States Parties to the Convention on the Rights of the Child.

Chairpersons of the Committee on the Rights of the Child:

Jaap Egbert Doek, 2001–2007
Yanghee Lee, 2007–2011
Jean Zermatten, 2011–2013
Kirsten Sandberg, 2013–2015
Benyam Dawit Mezmur, 2015–2017
Renate Winter, 2017–2019
Luis Ernesto Pedernera Reyna, 2019–2021

Preface

My daughter learned "The Garden Song," by David Mallett, in her preschool, and taught it to me. The musical mention of inch-by-inch progress, working hard, and believing in reaching the desired outcome struck a chord with me, a single mother of two who was going through her doctoral training at the time. Every parent can relate to how hectic mornings can be when getting children dressed, fed, and ready for school. After we and our bags all made it to the car, sometimes with breakfast on the go, singing "The Garden Song" together on the drive to school became a morning ritual:Inch by inch, row by row,
We are gonna make this garden grow
All it takes is work and hope[1]

Like a start-of-day meditation, singing together calmed the children and provided me with the needed fuel to push through another long and onerous day.

Completing my graduate training while raising two children was, undoubtedly, an inch-by-inch journey for me. I can't help drawing the analogy between that process and the process of arriving at the point of writing this book. Looking back, I have spent close to two decades of my professional life on a series of projects that each contributed to a few inches of moving forward and finally culminating in the GlobalChild platform and indicators and now this book—another inch-by-inch journey of my life.

Steps along the way included a series of offshoot projects and studies that brought opportunities for collaboration with a vast number of high-profile child rights and child development experts and advocates, as well as children, from across the world, and ongoing consultation with the United Nations Committee on the Rights of the Child (the Committee, hereafter) for over a decade (2008–2021). However, the genesis of this magnificent inch-by-inch journey was earlier.

In the early 2000s, I was exposed to governments in different regions of the world and recognised that challenges implementing and monitoring the United Nations Convention on the Rights of the Child (CRC) were universal, regardless of the development level of the State Party. Common complaints were:

[1] "The Garden Song," © 1975 David Mallett. Lyrics used by permission. The actual third line, as I learned much later, is "All it takes is a rake and a hoe," however my daughter learned this different third line.

- Difficulties deciphering the articles
- Knowing what needs to be in place to promote a certain right
- How to measure if progress has been made for a given right
- What needs to happen for children as evidence of success in fulfilling a right.

Between 2007 and 2012, I had the good fortune of being a member of the General Comment 7 (GC7) indicators team, an international team commissioned by the Committee that was working to operationalise *General Comment No. 7 (2005): Implementing Child Rights in Early Childhood*. Through this project, we created seventeen indicator sets for rights relevant to early childhood,[2] and tested them in Tanzania and Chile, and later in the province of British Columbia in Canada.

Regrettably, and in part due to the sudden and unfortunate passing of the GC7 project lead Professor Clyde Hertzman, this project did not get us to where we wanted to go. However, it clearly illustrated the effectiveness of using indicators to present a clear picture of the rights of children within a given state. As the person who was spearheading the pilots of GC7 indicators, in 2012, in one of the last meetings of the GC7 indicators team, I suggested operationalising the entire CRC as the way of moving forward and building upon what we learned from the GC7 indicators project.

Responses from most of the GC7 team were a mixture of dismissal and "not possible," largely due to the perceived enormity of such a task. After all, it had taken us close to 5 years to create indicators for one General Comment. Operationalising forty-one articles and the amount of research needed to go into that appeared to be a daunting task (and it was!). However, the idea stayed with me and the response I gave to the teammates about the enormity of the task was: "If this is an enormous task, then we just need to assemble an enormous team to do it!" That is what we exactly did when the time arrived.

I recall two people who spoke in favour of such an undertaking. One was the late Professor Hertzman, a brilliant Canadian scholar who, from that point onward, had encouraged the idea whenever I brought it up in our internal meetings or personal conversations. The other supporter was Professor Lothar Krappmann, the German member of the Committee on the Rights of the Child (2003–2011), who had played an instrumental role in building the indicators of GC7, also known as the Early Childhood Rights Indicators. Krappmann believed this was a daunting but much-needed task. I remain grateful for having not one but two mentors and supporters of their calibre.

In 2012, the UN Office of the High Commission on Human Rights (OHCHR) published the seminal book, *Human Rights Indicators, A Guide to Measurement and Implementation*. Through the members of representatives of different UN agencies in the GC7 indicators teams, we had already obtained the SPO framework of indicators (Structural, Process, and Outcome-related) years before publishing that book, and we had used the framework proposed in building the GC7 indicators.

[2] Early Childhood Rights Indicators (ECRI) or indicators of GC7 (2010). Available at: https://ecri.globalchildnetwork.com/index.php/content/overview.

Indeed, discussions about developing and using indicators had been underway for decades. However, publishing that book brought the use of indicators to the forefront of the attention of UN agencies and human rights stakeholders, and the popularity and utility of indicators in monitoring human rights were recognised and validated.

Around the same time, the government of Canada made a significant commitment to the improvement of global maternal and child health and development. Under that favourable ambience, in 2015 I returned to Canada after a year in Geneva and a short-term employment as the Technical Officer of Early Childhood Development at the World Health Organization headquarters. My time in Geneva and experiencing the life of an expat (as short as it was), led to many subsequent steps in my career, among them revitalising the idea of developing a full set of indicators for the entire CRC. The first order of business for me upon returning home was submitting a proposal to the Canadian Institutes of Health Research (CIHR), a prominent federal funder in Canada, requesting funds for 5 years to build GlobalChild, the world's first comprehensive child rights monitoring platform. GlobalChild was presented as a rights-based approach to promoting child development in Canada and beyond.

Relying on the resounding "Yes" and generous funding from the CIHR, in 2016 I flew to Geneva and invited Hon. Jean Zermatten, the former chair of the UN CRC Committee, with whom I had spoken previously about the vision of GlobalChild, to chair the steering committee of this global project and help me build a team. Jean graciously accepted my invitation. We embarked on the critical task of recruiting an international team of scholars and advocates to realise this vision of GlobalChild. This was the enormous team that I envisaged!

The team comprised four different structures with sophisticated governance in place:

- Steering Committee
- Indicators Development Team (the authors of this book)
- Reference Group
- Secretariate (my research programme at the university).

More information on these structures and their responsibilities are provided in Chap. 1.

By the fall of 2016, the international team was in place, funding was secured, and work was underway to realise the vision of GlobalChild that I had proposed 4 years earlier—the work that was initially supported by Hertzman and Krappmann only and was now embraced by a large group of child rights experts.

Throughout this work, I was the principal investigator in the eyes of the funders of the project and the Vice-chair of the Steering Committee in the eyes of the team, and gradually became the face of GlobalChild. However, in every presentation and every forum I have been determined to give face to the impressive team that was pushing the project. Similarly, it is my hope that the reader of this publication understands that my co-authors and I take credit only for the inches we contributed towards this inch-by-inch process, but there were so many more contributors.

It's been quite a journey, personally and professionally, for all of us. It is our intention and our desire that this work brings incremental but transformative changes, not only in the way we perceive children's rights but also, and more importantly, in the way children experience them: an inch-by-inch but fruitful growth.

Saint John, NB, Canada Ziba Vaghri

Acknowledgements

This book builds upon years of research that became possible because of the generous funds of the Canadian Institutes for Health Research (CIHR) granted to Dr. Ziba Vaghri

Canadian Institutes of Health Research   Instituts de recherche en santé du Canada

Contents

1 **Introduction** ... 1
Ziba Vaghri, Roberta Ruggiero, and Gerison Lansdown

Part I

2 **Methodology: A Human Rights-Based Framework for Monitoring Compliance with the CRC** ... 9
Gerison Lansdown, Ziba Vaghri, and Roberta Ruggiero

Part II

3 **Measuring Progress: Evaluating the Use and Added Value of Indicators for Children's Rights Compliance** ... 21
Roberta Ruggiero, Gerison Lansdown, and Ziba Vaghri

Part III Children's Rights Indicator Sets

4 **General Principles** ... 33
Ziba Vaghri, Roberta Ruggiero, Gerison Lansdown, Adem Arkadas-Thibert, and Christian Whalen
Article 2—Non-discrimination ... 34
Article 2—Guidance ... 36
Article 3—The Best Interests of the Child ... 39
Article 3—Guidance ... 42
Article 6—The Right to Life and Optimum Development ... 44
Article 6—Guidance ... 45
Article 12—The Right to Be Heard ... 47
Article 12—Guidance ... 50

5 **Civil and Political Rights** 57
Ziba Vaghri, Roberta Ruggiero, Gerison Lansdown, Adem Arkadas-Thibert, and Christian Whalen
Article 7—Right to Birth Registration a Name, Nationality, and to Know and Be Cared for by Parent As Far as Possible 58
Article 7—Guidance 60
Article 8—Right to Preservation of Identity 60
Article 8—Guidance 62
Article 13—Freedom of Expression 63
Article 13—Guidance 64
Article 14—Freedom of Thought, Conscience, and Religion 66
Article 14—Guidance 67
Article 15—Freedom of Association and Assembly 68
Article 15—Guidance 70
Article 16—Right to Privacy 72
Article 16—Guidance 73
Article 17—Right to Information 75
Article 17—Guidance 77

6 **Family Environment and Alternative Care Rights** 81
Ziba Vaghri, Roberta Ruggiero, Gerison Lansdown, Adem Arkadas-Thibert, and Christian Whalen
Article 5—The Right to Parental Guidance Consistent with the Evolving Capacities of the Child 83
Article 5—Guidance 85
Article 9—The Right Not to Be Separated from Parents 88
Article 9—Guidance 89
Article 10—The Right to Family Reunification 91
Article 10—Guidance 93
Article 11—The Right to Protection from Illicit Transfer and Non-return of Children Abroad 95
Article 11—Guidance 96
Article 18—Rights Concerning Parental Responsibility 97
Article 18—Guidance 99
Article 20—The Rights Concerning Children Deprived of their Family Environment 101
Article 20—Guidance 103
Article 21—Adoption 105
Article 21 –Guidance 107
Article 25—The Right to Periodic Review 109
Article 25—Guidance 110

7 **Disability, Health, and Welfare Rights** 111
Ziba Vaghri, Roberta Ruggiero, Gerison Lansdown,
Adem Arkadas-Thibert, and Christian Whalen
Article 23—The Rights of Children with Disabilities 113
Article 23—Guidance 115
Article 24—The Right to Health. 120
Article 24—Guidance 123
Article 26—The Right to Benefit from Social Security 130
Article 26—Guidance 132
Article 27—The Right to a Standard of Living Adequate for Physical,
Mental, Spiritual, Moral and Social Development 134
Article 27—Guidance 136
Article 33—The Right to Protection from Illicit Use of Narcotic
Drugs and Psychotropic Substances 139
Article 33—Guidance 141

8 **Education, Leisure, and Cultural Activities Rights** 145
Ziba Vaghri, Roberta Ruggiero, Gerison Lansdown,
Adem Arkadas-Thibert, and Christian Whalen
Article 28—The Right to Education 146
Article 28—Guidance 150
Article 29—The Aims of Education 158
Article 29—Guidance 160
Article 30—Culture, Religious and Linguistic Rights of Minority or
Indigenous Children 162
Article 30—Guidance 163
Article 31—The Rights to Rest, Play, Recreation, and Cultural and
Artistic Activities 165
Article 31—Guidance 167

9 **Measures to Protect Children from Violence** 171
Ziba Vaghri, Roberta Ruggiero, Gerison Lansdown,
Adem Arkadas-Thibert, and Christian Whalen
Article 19—The Right to Protection from all Forms of Violence 172
Article 19—Guidance 176
Article 37—Prohibition of Torture, Capital Punishment and
Arbitrary Deprivation of Liberty. 182
Article 37—Guidance 186
Article 39—The Right to Physical and Psychological Recovery 191
Article 39—Guidance 193

10 Protection Measures from Exploitation 197
Ziba Vaghri, Roberta Ruggiero, Gerison Lansdown, Adem Arkadas-Thibert, and Christian Whalen
Article 32—The Right to Protection from Economic Exploitation and Hazardous Activities 198
Article 32—Guidance 200
Article 34—The Right to Protection from all Forms of Sexual Exploitation and Sexual Abuse 204
Article 34—Guidance 206
Article 36—The Right to Protection from Other Forms of Violence ... 210

11 Protection Measures for Children in Vulnerable Situations 213
Ziba Vaghri, Roberta Ruggiero, Gerison Lansdown, Adem Arkadas-Thibert, and Christian Whalen
Article 22—The Right to Protection for Refugee and Asylum-Seeking Children 215
Article 22—Guidance 216
Article 35—Prevention of Abduction, Sale and Trafficking.......... 219
Article 35—Guidance 221
Article 38—The Right to Protection from Armed Conflict 222
Article 38—Guidance 225
Article 40—The Rights in a Juvenile Justice Setting 226
Article 40—Guidance 231

12 General Measures of Implementation 235
Ziba Vaghri, Roberta Ruggiero, Gerison Lansdown, Adem Arkadas-Thibert, and Christian Whalen
Article 1—Definition of a Child 236
Article 4—General Measures of Implementation.................. 237
Article 4—Guidance 240
Articles 42 and 44.6—Making the Convention and the States Parties Compliance Widely Known among Children and Adults 241
Articles 42 and 44.6—Guidance.............................. 242

Glossary for Part III 245

Appendix for Part I 259

References 263

Chapter 1
Introduction

Ziba Vaghri, Roberta Ruggiero, and Gerison Lansdown

The Convention on the Rights of the Child (CRC) is the first legally binding treaty specifically addressing the human rights of children. In the 35 years since its adoption, it has garnered ratification from 196 member states of the United Nations, marking its commitment to safeguarding and promoting children's rights worldwide. Since its adoption, the CRC has led to notable changes for children worldwide. It has been instrumental in building recognition of children as rights holders rather than mere subjects of adult protection (Gadda et al., 2021; Tobin, 2019; Vuckovic-Sahovic et al., 2012). From an almost universal banning of capital punishment for children to providing safe spaces for the participation of children in important national forums, such as children's parliament in some countries,[1] and

[1] For examples, see *Children's Parliaments and Children's Councils in World Vision Programmes* at https://www.wvi.org/sites/default/files/Children's%20Parliaments%20and%20Children's%20Councils%20in%20WV%20programmes.pdf and Launch of the CP4Europe child participation web-platformathttps://www.coe.int/en/web/children/-/launch-of-the-cp4europe-child-participation-web-platform.

Z. Vaghri
GlobalChild Program of Research, University of New Brunswick, Saint John, NB, Canada

R. Ruggiero (✉)
Centre for Children's Right Studies, Faculty of Law, University of Geneva, Geneva, Switzerland
e-mail: Roberta.ruggiero@unige.ch

G. Lansdown
School of Law, University College Cork, Cork, Ireland

Z. Vaghri et al. (eds.), *Children's Rights-Based Indicators*, Children's Well-Being: Indicators and Research 28,
https://doi.org/10.1007/978-3-031-71594-5_1

international events, such as Conferences of Parties for climate change, the CRC has resulted in meaningful changes in the way children are perceived.

Upon ratifying the CRC, states commit to undertaking all measures to respect, protect, and fulfil these rights, and report periodically on their actions to a monitoring body called the Committee on the Rights of the Child (the Committee). The Committee, in turn, provides feedback to states with recommendations on additional measures that are needed to meet their obligations under the CRC (Doek, 2011; Karp, 2000). Nevertheless, despite over three decades of report writing and receiving, challenges to the effectiveness of the process have emerged. Limited resources available to governments undoubtedly contribute to these challenges. However, states are also hampered in monitoring their progress by a severe lack of data and guidance on the evidence required to demonstrate the measures needed or the outcomes that should ensue. Without clearly defined indicators against which to measure progress, states often use the reporting process to list actions they have taken rather than to assess actual changes in the realisation of children's rights. The absence of effective monitoring tools results in diminished accountability to children, as it undermines the ability to measure progress (United Nations Office of the High Commissioner of Human Rights, 2015). There is a pressing need for governments to uphold their accountability under the CRC, which requires both systematic monitoring and comprehensive data collection.

Despite extensive debate on the necessity of child rights-based indicators since the adoption of the CRC, their development has, to date, been piecemeal. The United Nations Office of the High Commission for Human Rights (OHCHR) made a major contribution with the elaboration of the structural, process, and outcome framework for monitoring the realisation of human rights (2012). Numerous indicators have long existed for traditional areas of public policy concerning children, such as health and education, and more recent progress has been made in developing indicators for child protection. This progress is attributable to the Committee's efforts in elaborating and defining the scope and expectations surrounding certain rights, such as protection from violence and harmful practices, and ensuring child-friendly justice. However, there has been less advancement, for example, in civil and political rights. It is insufficient to rely on comparable indicators designed for adults, as children's status and needs differ significantly. Children require higher levels of protection, and their challenges are distinct from those faced by adults.

This publication fills that gap. The comprehensive listing of child rights indicator sets results from the collaborative efforts of the Indicators Development Team (IDT) of the GlobalChild project (2016–2022). These efforts were guided and informed by the input of numerous global experts specialising in children's rights. The IDT consisted of the three editors of this book and two other child rights advocates who are co-authors of the sets of indicators in this book. Adhering to the Structural, Process, and Outcome (SPO) model developed by the OHCHR in 2012, we produced a collection of indicator sets for each right contained in the CRC. This involved building upon the extensive research of many foundational documents and multiple sources of indicators produced over the past 30 years (Vaghri & Erdemli, 2019).

In the companion book of this publication (Vaghri et al., 2022), we presented a compilation of the research put into identifying the attributes of each of the substantive rights of children under the CRC. Attributes are the limited number of characteristics identified for a right that capture the legal standard of that right. Once the attributes were identified, we then built indicator sets for each attribute. In this book, we present the indicators built upon those identified attributes for each CRC right. Identifying the attributes is the first step in developing the indicators for each right, to help make the content of a right concrete. It also links identified indicators of a right with the normative standards of that right in a clearer fashion.

The developed SPO indicator sets were first put online to create the GlobalChild platform, launched in 2022.[2] The online indicators offer a comprehensive monitoring system concerning policy, programming, and outcomes for children aligned with the CRC. Meanwhile, the indicators featured in this book are presented in a table format, enabling readers to access the full sets of indicators corresponding to each attribute of a specified article.

Regardless of their format, the indicator sets assist child rights stakeholders in taking inventory of all capacities, policies and programmes, in support of each right articulated in the CRC, as well as data on child outcomes relevant to that right, to generate a comprehensive and fully contextualised portrait of the status of that right. The review of such data helps understand:

- How or if States Parties are upholding their obligations under the CRC towards rights, by putting in place the necessary laws and policies (structure-related indicators) and sound processes (process-related indicators) to respect and promote each right.
- How or if children, as the rights holders, are enjoying the fulfilment of those rights (outcomes-related indicators).

Examining all indicators highlights the strengths and gaps in the capacities of government in support of each right and the desirable, as well as undesirable, child-level or right-level outcomes, and provides evidence to support data-informed policymaking and programme design. This exercise holds significant potential to drive progress and push forward the agenda of child rights as well as child development.

This book is organised into three parts: Part I consists of, the methodology used in the development of these indicators. It explains the structure of the international team of GlobalChild that had responsibility for the work, along with the various levels of scrutiny, consultation, and accountability integrated into the process. This included a significant global consultation with children through the Global Child Rights Dialog (GCRD) project.[3]

---

[2] This was the 30th anniversary of CRC in Canada. Available at: www.globalchildplatform.com.

[3] The Global Child Rights Dialog (GCRD) was an offshoot of the larger project of GlobalChild and an international consultation undertaken with children, and with close collaboration of the GlobalChild Program of Research in Canada and the Center for Children's Rights in Northern Ireland.

In Part II, we elaborate on the use of indicators and provide a brief history of their application in human and children's rights. The chapter highlights the evolution of the use of indicators, starting from their use in the global governance field as primarily derived from economics and business management, and their recent use in the human rights sector as a process that builds on an earlier, increasingly significant use of indicators in the global governance sector. The chapter acknowledges that the development and use of human rights indicators are one of the tools that can contribute, in combination with other tools, to offering an efficient form of explanation and understanding of the fulfilment of human rights and children's rights in practice. Indicators do not replace all other existing tools, and they are not the only tools for monitoring compliance with international human rights treaties. However they can support the political discussion leading to the implementation of children's rights in practice.

In Part III, Chaps. 4, 5, 6, 7, 8, 9, 10, 11 and 12, we present the indicators grouped into nine clusters, each corresponding to a single chapter. These clusters are structured around common themes of child rights, mirroring the grouping found in the companion book of this publication. Each chapter begins with a brief introduction to the rights within that cluster. Then, the indicator sets for each right are presented along with the core attributes upon which the indicators are built. We have used a table format as it facilitates highlighting how a given indicator question applies to more than one attribute of that right. At the end of each indicator set, guidance is provided with additional information that enables users to perform the necessary calculations to provide the data results.

Finally, glossary for and is a compilation of all the terms used across the book and their definition, with sources.

In the more than 30 years since the adoption of the Convention on the Rights of the Child, the world has witnessed significant change in the perception, understanding and commitment to the human rights of children. The initial enthusiasm for universal ratification, strongly encouraged by UNICEF and other national and international organisations, was followed by a genuine and widespread engagement in the pursuit of legislation, policies, government structures, and resources to give effect to obligations states had undertaken.

Although considerable progress remains to be made in every country across the world, some positive change in children's lives has taken place. For example, there is now enhanced child protection, more girls in education (UNESCO, 2019), greater visibility of children in governments, spaces for children to be heard (Child Rights Connect, 2023), and dedicated youth justice systems (Dünkel, 2016; Hazel, 2008; Tobin, 2019).

In more recent years, there has been a reversal of some of those steps forward, with a push back against human rights, the rule of law, social justice, freedom of speech, and systems of accountability. It is now more important than ever to have accessible tools that not only help governments understand clearly what is expected of them but that can also be used by civil society to help hold governments to account. The indicators elaborated in this publication are an important contribution to that process.

Part I

Part I

Chapter 2
Methodology: A Human Rights-Based Framework for Monitoring Compliance with the CRC

Gerison Lansdown, Ziba Vaghri, and Roberta Ruggiero

The methodology used to develop the GlobalChild indicators, which are presented in this publication, is based on work done by the Office of the High Commissioner for Human Rights (OHCHR) to create human rights-based indicators (2012) and the conceptual framework of the Children's Rights Based Approach (Lundy & McEvoy, 2012).

With reference to the work of the OHCHR, it has conceptualised a framework for the development of human rights-based indicators that involves two stages. First, it is necessary to identify the core attributes of a given right. Each right can be broken down into a limited number of attributes or characteristics that, taken together, provide a comprehensive overview of the issues addressed or raised by that right. A right might comprise three, four, or five attributes. Second, once the attributes are identified, a set of structural, process, and outcome indicators are developed for each of those attributes.

The OHCHR's framework of the development of indicators was blended with the Children's Rights Based Approach, which brought the establishment of a specific theoretical and procedural methodology that is strongly embedded in the principles and provisions of the CRC: ensuring the participation of children and young people in the drafting procedure. The approach involved a reviewing procedure involving

---

G. Lansdown
School of Law, University College Cork, Cork, Ireland

Z. Vaghri
GlobalChild Program of Research, University of New Brunswick, Saint John, NB, Canada

R. Ruggiero (✉)
Centre for Children's Right Studies, Faculty of Law, University of Geneva, Geneva, Switzerland
e-mail: Roberta.ruggiero@unige.ch

Z. Vaghri et al. (eds.), *Children's Rights-Based Indicators*, Children's Well-Being: Indicators and Research 28,
https://doi.org/10.1007/978-3-031-71594-5_2

key experts and stakeholders in the field and with the aim of developing indicators able to assess children's rights implementation.

Blending these two methodologies to create a comprehensive set of child rights-based indicators involved five steps that are elaborated in the following sections.

It is noteworthy that the starting point of this work was a thorough environmental scanning for existing indicators of human rights to identify who has done what on which right. This work compiled a useful summary of the existing indicators for children's rights, such as WHO, UNICEF and Sustainable Development Goals [SDG] indicators.

Establishing the Accountability Framework

The preparatory steps undertaken to develop the indicators involved creating an accountability framework to undertake, oversee, and review the work, as follows:

- A **core team of experts** was recruited to develop the attributes and indicators. The team, known as the Indicator Development Team (IDT), comprised five individuals (three of whom are co-editors and authors of this book), all well-known for their work on children's rights
- A **Steering Committee** was established to oversee the work. This committee comprised several high-profile and well-respected experts in the field of children's rights including former Chairs of the Committee on the Rights of the Child, a UN Special Rapporteur, and academics. The committee met two or three times a year, one of them in person, to review the progress of the work
- A **reference group**, representing a wide range of UN agencies, INGOs, and the Committee on the Rights of the Child, was established with the aim of meeting once a year in Geneva to review and advise on the work. Organisations included UNICEF-Canada, WHO, the EU Fundamental Rights Agency, a member of the UNCRC Committee assigned by the chair at the time, Save the Children, and SOS Children's Villages. Additionally, from time to time, members of other organisations attended these meetings as guest attendees, among them the OHCHR and UNICEF-Geneva.

Elaboration of the Attributes

The IDT looked at each cluster of articles in the Convention as organised in the CRC Reporting Guidelines. The first task was to identify comparable rights in other relevant human rights treaties. Thus, in respect of Article 2, the right to non-discrimination, it was also necessary to consider its wording and application, for example, in the *Universal Declaration*, the two International Covenants, and CEDAW and CERD. The IDT also undertook a comprehensive review of the interpretation of each article, drawing on a broad range of sources:

- Travaux Preparatoires
- Work of the Committee on the Rights of the Child through its Concluding Observations, Optional Protocols, General Comments, and recommendations from Days of General Discussion
- Other relevant international treaties, e.g. International Labour Organization (ILO), Geneva Conventions
- Guidance from international bodies or agencies, e.g. UNHCR, UNICEF, WHO or the UN General Assembly.

This review process identified the core attributes of every article. The aim was to ensure that the attributes of each article fully encapsulated the implications and scope of that article. In addition, the scope of each attribute should not overlap so the attributes would, in effect, be mutually exclusive. For example, the right to privacy was identified as having four core attributes:

- Interference with privacy
- Interference with family, home, or correspondence
- Unlawful attacks on honour and reputation
- Protection of the law against unlawful interference or attacks.

Through this work and the associated review process, short papers were produced for every Article of the CRC (see Appendix 2 for an example of an attributes paper). Each paper highlighted the core attributes and associated jurisprudence, briefly summarising the interpretation of each attribute, in respect of each article, by the CRC Committee. In addition, the paper on each article provided an overview of how the four general principles applied to that right, and listed the other articles which were of direct relevance as well as any other international treaties of significance. This work formed the basis of the companion book to this publication, *Monitoring State Compliance with the UN Convention on the Rights of the Child: An analysis of Attributes*, part of the book series: *Children's Well-Being: Indicators and Research* (Vaghri et al., 2022).

Development of Draft Indicators

The next task was to identify Structural, Process, and Outcome indicators for each attribute of every article.

- **Structural indicators**: to measure the extent to which legislation, regulations and policies have been introduced to give effect to the commitments in respect of a specific right
- **Process indicators**: to measure investment by states to translate the human rights commitments undertaken through laws and policies, into desired results. This might include budgetary allocations, training programmes, or delivery of a particular policy. It measures the level of effort undertaken by a state to fulfil its obligations

- **Outcome indicators**: to measure the actual changes that have arisen in the realisation of children's rights as a consequence of the structural and process measures that have been put in place. They can track evidence of both positive and negative changes at the child level and the scale or incidence of fulfilment or violation of rights at the system level.

Indicators were then elaborated, bearing in mind the following considerations:

1. They had to be directed to monitoring the implementation of that right and be in conformity with those rights. In addition, indicators needed to be developed to ensure that each of the attributes in an article was properly addressed, recognising that some indicators would be transversal and provide data on the implementation of two or more attributes.
2. They should be able to assess children's rights implementation. Therefore, objective and subjective indicators are employed for each article to provide a comprehensive assessment of how rights have been implemented on both a qualitative and quantitative level (Casas, 1997; Ben-Arieh et al., 2014). They could be:

   (a) **Quantitative objective:** articulated in quantitative form and based on information, facts, or events that are observable and verifiable, e.g. infant mortality rate
   (b) **Quantitative subjective:** articulated in quantitative form and based on information that is a perception, opinion, assessment, or judgement, e.g. percentage of children who consider their views are listened to and taken seriously by teachers
   (c) **Qualitative objective**: articulated as a narrative, and based on objects, facts, or events that are, in principle, directly observable and verifiable, e.g. status of ratification of OP3—ratified, signed, neither ratified nor signed
   (d) **Qualitative subjective:** articulated as a narrative, not necessarily in a categorical form, and based on information that is a perception, opinion, assessment, or judgement, e.g. the youth justice system is child friendly.

   The indicator sets in this publication comprise a mixture of all four categories.

3. The indicator selection included a rigorous review of many relevant existing indicator sets. It was recognised that, as far as possible, it was helpful to utilise existing indicators, because these already would have been subjected to scrutiny and testing. In addition, if states were already collecting data that was relevant to the implementation of any of the identified attributes, it would be unhelpful and time-wasting to try and construct additional or alternative indicators. Accordingly, scrutiny was undertaken, for example, of UNICEF and WHO indicators sets, the indicators associated with SDGs, indicators used by INGOs such as Plan International and Save the Children, and indicators linked to other international or regional treaties.

4. The selection of indicators was not restricted by assumptions of there being pre-existing data. It was recognised that for many of the articles, states would have little or no data and would need to undertake additional research or analysis to be able to evaluate compliance. However, one of the aims of the process was to build an aspirational picture for every right as to the measures that would be required to fully achieve its implementation.
5. As far as possible, the indicators needed to have universal application. The idea was to form a comprehensive framework for the necessary measures and desired outcomes for every child, no matter wherethey live. Obviously, a global tool of this nature cannot accommodate all the very different experiences of children in different parts of the world. Thus, individual states may need or want to contextualise the GlobalChild Indicator set by adjusting or complementing them with additional indicators that reflect their realities on the ground. For example, countries with a high incidence of HIV/AIDs might want to include measures to monitor access to treatments or the number of child-headed households. Countries with a significant indigenous population might need to collect data on the availability of targeted services, specific aspects of discrimination or exclusion, or educational drop-out or attainment, and countries with high refugee populations may need to collect additional data to capture how their rights are being adequately met. Conversely, for example, the indicators relating to refugees may not be relevant or applicable in non-recipient countries, and measures to address child labour may be of less relevance in high-income countries.
6. A balance was sought between seeking to capture every dimension of every article of the CRC and trying to limit the numbers to ensure that the task of data collection would be manageable. Efforts were made to restrict the number of indicators for each article. The 41 sets of indicators varied in the number of indicators, from four to forty. The right to health (Article 24), for example, needed more indicators to fully address its scope than the right to illicit transfer and non-return (Article 11), with 39 indicators for health and only 14 for illicit transfer. It is also the case that there were usually fewer indicators of outcomes than of structure and process, as outcomes tend to be the generic result of several different structures and processes.

Once the indicator sets were produced, the members of the IDT reviewed each of the sets developed by other members of the Team. Discussions were held on any proposed amendments and additions, and revisions were made accordingly and prepared ready for the external review process. This involved presenting the structural, process, and outcome indicators around the identified attributes in matrix to both facilitate and demonstrate the identification of indicators that logically flow from each other. Some indicators may relate to one or more of any given attribute.

Consultations with Children

It was imperative to ensure that the final indicators took account of the lived experience of children and the standards or measures that they would identify as critical to the realisation of their rights. Accordingly, a central dimension of the work involved reaching out to children to gain their insights and perspectives. The goal was to explore, in response to the proposed attributes of specific rights, what children would highlight as being appropriate measures to monitor compliance. Through their feedback, it would be possible to compare and contrast their views with the draft indicators already produced and assess any consequent need for revision or, indeed, for additional indicators.

The first stage was a literature review of pre-existing consultations that had been undertaken with children in respect of the realisation of their rights. An analytical overview of the findings was produced. The review focused on exploration of:

- Who has done research/consultations that have involved children?
- What year was the research done (looking back no further than 10 years)?
- What were the research/consultation questions that were addressed?
- How many children were involved?
- Which articles of the Convention were covered?
- What were the outcomes?

Once this data had been collected, the goal was to undertake a major new consultation to build on the evidence already available and to reach out to children from all regions of the globe through focus groups conducted by skilled facilitators from the field. This large-scale global consultation with children was a partnership between the GlobalChild Program of Research (GCh), at the time located at the University of Victoria, Canada, and the Centre for Children's Rights (CCR) at Queen's University, Northern Ireland. The consultation adopted the Children's Rights Based Approach to research developed by the CCR and used in previous global consultations (Lundy & McEvoy, 2012). Save the Children and "Let's Talk About Article 12", an NGO based in Athens, Greece, also joined the collaboration.

The consultations with children represented a significant part of the indicators development process, and followed four stages:

Stage One: Involving Children as Partners in the Consultation Process The CCR established a Children's Advisory Group (CAG) in Northern Ireland comprising 25 young people. The aim of the CAG was to work with the CCR to help design the methodology for the consultation and to pilot the process. The young people were all aged 13–14 years, were students at a Rights Respecting School, and had expressed a strong interest in politics, government, or a related topic. In other words, they were young people who came into the work with a degree of understanding and commitment to the issues being addressed.

Stage Two: Developing the Materials for the Consultation The CCR reviewed a cluster of attributes papers, each of which was around six to eight pages, and redrafted them in a shorter, more child-friendly, and accessible form. These drafts were then shared with CAG to get their input into the language and its accessibility, and to make any suggestions for improvement. Once those versions were finalised, the CCR then produced child-friendly versions of all the other attributes papers.

In addition, a detailed guide for the focus group discussions with children was prepared by the CCR and passed to the GlobalChild team. The guide provided information on how to set and run the groups. It was prepared through a process of collaboration with the CAG, and included material related to:

- Rationale and objectives of the consultation
- Ethical approval and consent
- Recruitment of facilitators
- Child-friendly versions of the attributes of all the rights
- Consultation framework
- Training, capacity building and point of contact for the facilitation partners
- Capacity building and consultation activities
- Reporting requirements.

Stage Three: The Consultation Process Once the consultative methodology and the necessary materials had been prepared, the next stage was to reach out to countries reflecting the broadest possible economic, social, political, and cultural diversity in different regions of the world. The aim was to obtain the perspectives of as comprehensive a representation of respondent children as could be achieved. This consultative process was called the Global Child Rights Dialog (GCRD).

The initial recruitment relied upon the country offices of Save the Children, the international networks of GlobalChild and CCR, and the "Initiative for Article 12 UNCRC" to reach out to their networks and find children that would be interested in participating in the consultation. As the study progressed, there were expressions of interest in participation from other countries, with several universities and other NGOs getting involved. Ultimately, the number of participating countries from each region well exceeded the initial anticipated numbers.

Thirty-five countries, including Northern Ireland, set up focus groups with children using the CCR Child Rights Based Approach methodology and tool kit. Once recruited, CCR and GlobalChild ran a webinar to provide an introductory training session for the facilitators. An online chat room was opened to receive and respond to individual queries during the course of the project. The guidance on the process was disseminated to each country. Furthermore, the GlobalChild team initiated a parallel process of translating the tool kit and guide for non-English countries who joined the study. In some cases, the local facilitators who were trained to conduct the focus groups translated the tools into their local languages. Overall, 52 focus groups, in 35 countries, were held, involving over two thousand children and conducted in 20 different languages. In some countries, such as Canada, China, and India, more than one focus group was set up.

Working with local facilitators is part of CCR's methodology for global consultations, aligned with the belief that local organisations have the best knowledge of rights-related priorities and issues in their regions, and are therefore better positioned to decide which rights to discuss in their focus group. For example, some organisations were able to include street-involved children who shared their concerns about manipulation, fear of being kidnapped, and cases of missing children, while others included incarcerated children speaking about their unfair treatment within juvenile justice systems. In some centres (e.g. The Montreal team in Canada) a pre-focus group event was held with children to decide on which articles the focus group should be set up.

The questions to be discussed within the focus groups were developed by the CCR in collaboration with their pre-existing CAG and included:

- What does this right mean to children in their communities?
- What are the key issues of importance relating to this right?
- Are children able to realise this right?
- What do governments/other duty bearers need to do to make sure this right is realised?
- Is there anything missing from this summary that they think should be included?

It was agreed that the child-friendly versions of each article would be considered in the following clusters of the CRC:

- **Cluster 1**: Measures of implementation—Articles 4, 42, 44
- **Cluster 2:** Definition of the child—Article 1
- **Cluster 3:** General Principles—Articles 2, 3, 6, 12
- **Cluster 4**: Civil rights—Articles 7, 8, 13, 14, 15, 16, 17
- **Cluster 5**: Protection from violence—Articles 19, 37, 39
- **Cluster 6:** Family and alternative care—Articles 5, 9, 10, 11, 18, 20, 21, 25
- **Cluster 7:** Disability and basic health—Articles 23, 24, 26, 27, 33
- **Cluster 8**: Education, leisure, and culture—Articles 28, 29, 30, 31
- **Cluster 9:** Special protection measures—Articles 22, 32, 34, 35, 36, 38, 40.

The articles in most clusters were obviously relevant to all children. However, for some clusters, for example, special protection measures, many of the children involved in the group were unlikely to have had direct or relevant experience in that area of rights. Therefore, during discussions of each cluster of attributes, the group was encouraged to think about other children and the impact of these rights on children's lives.

Stage Four: The Findings The facilitators completed the reporting template provided to them and produced a summary of the key findings from the children in each focus group. These were deposited into a data repository of GlobalChild Program. A coordinator reviewed them and followed up for missing information, when applicable. After the data were cleaned and categorised, first based on articles and then the themes within articles, they were shared with the CCR team, who produced an analysis of the findings. The final report summarising children's views on the attributes of each article was produced by CCR in collaboration with the GlobalChild team.

These draft reports were shared with the Indicators Development Team, who went through each set of findings in relation to the draft indicators that had already been identified for each article in the Convention. An assessment was made as to whether the input from the children indicated a need for an additional indicator or a revision or amendment of any of the existing indicators. Any time a new indicator set was developed, or an existing indicator set was amended because of children's feedback, the indicator was tagged with GCRD to draw the attention of the users of the indicators to the fact that this is children's insight and needed to be given its due weight.

Fundamentally, the methodology of GCRD promoted an inclusive participation model in the development of these children's rights-based indicators. It not only provided safe spaces for the voices of marginalised children, but it also demonstrated a direct influence of children's opinions and insights in shaping the indicators. At the end of the process, a child-friendly analysis of the findings was sent to all the participating centres in order that the children could be provided with feedback on how their contributions had been used. The GlobalChild Program sent a modest honorarium and a certificate of participation to all participating centres except for STC offices. Lastly, the CCR and GCh took all the child-friendly versions of the 41 substantive rights and developed child-friendly child rights educational cards. These tools are available in English, French, and Spanish, and are freely accessible via the websites of GlobalChild Program and CCR.

Review Process for the Draft Indicators

On completion of the GCRD, the draft indicators were reviewed and revised after being submitted to a three-tiered process:

1. Following the analysis of the feedback from the children's consultations, their proposals and observations were applied to the indicators which were amended as appropriate
2. A range of experts in the field of children's rights were approached and asked to provide a critical review of the draft indicators. Each reviewer was selected to respond to the articles that were specifically relevant to their area of expertise. They were asked to share any knowledge of other pre-existing indicators and to amend or add to the draft materials they had received. Once the feedback had been received, the indicator sets were again revised accordingly
3. A week-long face-to-face meeting of the IDT was convened to undertake a rigorous review of every indicator set
4. Each set of indicators was futher subjected to a final review by the editors of this volume to ensure comprehensiveness, accessibility and coherence.

The final outcome of this work is a set of 42 tables, each comprising structural, process, and outcome indicators, drawing on a wide-ranging review and analysis of both existing standards and the jurisprudence of the Committee on the Rights of the Child. The goal is to provide as comprehensive an overview as possible of the measures and actions required by states to meet their obligations in respect of each of the rights embodied in the Convention on the Rights of the Child.

Part II

Chapter 3
Measuring Progress: Evaluating the Use and Added Value of Indicators for Children's Rights Compliance

Roberta Ruggiero, Gerison Lansdown, and Ziba Vaghri

During the last decades, the use of indicators as tools for assessing states' compliance with children's human rights legal provisions included in the related international treaties has rapidly multiplied, both at national and international levels, intended mainly to support policy and strategy reforms to increase social justice, well-being and the implementation of some specific rights.[1] These indicators in the

[1] See: Ennew, J., & Miljeteig, P. (1996). Indicators for children's rights: progress report on project. International Journal of Children's Rights, 4(3), 213–236. Casas, F. (1997). Children's Rights and Children's Quality of Life: Conceptual and Practical Issues. *Social Indicators Research* 42, 283–298. Ben-Arieh, A. (2008). The child indicators movement: Past, present, and future. *Child Indicators Research*, 1, 3–16. European Union Agency for Fundamental Rights (FRA). (2010). *Developing indicators for the protection, respect and promotion of the rights of the child in the European Union*. FRA. Vaghri, Z., Arkadas, A., Kruse, S. and Hertzman, C. (2011). CRC General Comment 7 Indicators Framework: A Tool for Monitoring the Implementation of Child Rights in Early Childhood, *Journal of Human Rights*, 10:2, 178–188. Vaghri, Z., & Erdemli, I. (2019). A

R. Ruggiero (✉)
Centre for Children's Right Studies, Faculty of Law, University of Geneva, Geneva, Switzerland
e-mail: Roberta.ruggiero@unige.ch

G. Lansdown
School of Law, University College Cork, Cork, Ireland

Z. Vaghri
GlobalChild Program of Research, University of New Brunswick, Saint John, NB, Canada

Z. Vaghri et al. (eds.), *Children's Rights-Based Indicators*, Children's Well-Being: Indicators and Research 28,
https://doi.org/10.1007/978-3-031-71594-5_3

human rights sector build on the use of indicators in the global governance sector. As Sally Engle Merry explains in her ethnography of indicators, the use of indicators in global governance today is primarily derived from economics and business management, even though their roots as modes of knowledge and governance date back several centuries to the establishment of modern nation-states in the early nineteenth century and some centuries before that. For example, the gross domestic product is one of the most extensively used and recognised indicators. Development organisations like the World Bank have developed a wide range of indicators, including measures of global governance and the rule of law (Merry, 2011).

Numerous national, regional, and international human rights legal instruments have been adopted since the 1948 Universal Declaration of Human Rights was ratified. The global human rights enterprise has seen both successes and failures throughout this time, and, as described by Landman and Schwarz (2022), there is also growing evidence that human rights law and practice are positively correlated. They explain that:

> This expanding evidence base draws on an emerging consensus on the utility of quantitative indicators for descriptive and inferential statistical analysis. Such analysis captures the spatial and temporal variation in the de jure protection of human rights (i.e. 'rights in principle') and the de facto realization of human rights (i.e. 'rights in practice') worldwide. Standard social scientific approaches to quantitative analysis of human rights include events-based data, standards-based data, survey-based data and socio-economic administrative data. The rise of new forms of data with the advent of the Internet, social media, big data approaches and the application of machine learning and artificial intelligence combined with these more traditional forms of analysis, however, provides exciting and new opportunities for additional systematic analyses of human rights implementation gaps. (Landman & Schwarz, 2022, p. 309)

Landman and Schwarz recognise the potential of this wide-ranging variety of quantitative indicators to measure, visualize, and estimate the gap *between rights-in-principle* and *rights-in-practice* to give policy-makers a solid evidence platform upon which to build national and international interventions to improve the implementation of human rights. However, they also admit that measuring *rights-in-principle* and *rights-in-practice* have both their obstacles and limitations. For

---

desk Top Review of the Existing Indicators on Articles and General Comments of the United Nations Convention on the Rights of the Child. *Zeitschrift für menschenrechte*, 13(1), 94–117. Crowley, A. and Lansdown, G. (2016), *Child participation assessment tool. Implementation Guide*, Council of Europe. Lansdown, G. and Ruggiero, R. (2023). *Measuring impact of the child participation assessment tool. Outcome indicators and guidance for data collections*, European Union and Council of Europe. D'hondt, S. and Péters, C. (2016). *Indicateurs nationaux des droits de l'Enfant. Make them count*, Commission nationale pour les droits de l'Enfant. Belotti, V. and Moretti, E. (2011). *L'Italia "Minore". Mappe di indicatori sulla condizione e le disuguaglianze nel benessere dei bambini e dei ragazzi. Quaderno 51 Condizione dell'infanzia e dell'adolescenza*, Centro Nazionale di Documentazione e Analisi per l'Infanzia e l'Adolescenza. Istituto degli Innocenti. New Brunswick Office of the Child and Youth Advocate. (2013). *Children In Caring Communities: from Knowledge to Responsibility. The 2013 New Brunswick State of the Child Report and The Children's Rights and Well-being Framework for New Brunswick*. Child and Youth Advocate (Office).

example, with reference to coding *rights-in-principle*, the codification of the State Parties' participation in international legal human rights instruments is relatively straightforward. By contrast, the coding and creation of quantitative indicators for legal national legislation "… presents a significant challenge, as the nature, scope, and shape of human rights provisions in domestic law can vary significantly from one country to the next." (Landman & Schwarz, 2022, pp. 314 and 315). However, for the authors, if domestic and international legal instruments and provisions for protecting human rights with their obstacles and limitations remain tractable and visible, the exercise of human rights in practice faces what Landman and Schwarz define as the 'fundamental problem of unobservability'.

During the last decades, a variety of approaches have been developed to produce quantitative indicators that can provide a representation of human rights across their

Table 1 Summary assessment of different modes of measuring human rights in practice

Type of measure	Unit of analysis	Geographical coverage	Advantages for human rights implementation	Disadvantages for human rights implementation
Events	Individual violations	Specific countries over time	Focussed work on specific countries over particular periods	Limited at present to a focus on violations of particular sets of civil and political rights
Standards	Countries	Global	Cross-country and time-series provision of scores for a wide range of human rights	High level of abstraction for general models of human rights performance variation
Surveys	Individuals	Currently between 70 and 80 countries	Cross-country analysis of human rights perceptions and experiences	Limited time-series coverage
Socio-economic	Countries and sub-national units	Global	Representation of fulfilment of human rights	Tendency to focus on economic and social rights
New forms	Mobile phone data Social media text and words relevant to human rights Objects and sites of potential human rights abuse	Global 'big data' Global 'big data' Potentially global, but currently focussed on particular sectors in particular countries	Cross-country and time-series analysis Cross-country and time-series analysis Granular detail on the geographical distribution of sites of abuse	More attuned to measuring mobility than human rights abuse Extensive 'noise' in the data and need to identify human rights abuse Currently limited to particular sectors and particular countries

Source: Landman, T., & Schwarz, K. (2022). "Chapter 16: Human rights indicators and implementation". In Research Handbook on Implementation of Human Rights in Practice. Cheltenham, UK: Edward Elgar Publishing (p. 322)

different categories and societal dimensions. A comparative summary of these approaches identified by Landman and Schwarz is presented in Table 1.

Each one of these modes of measuring has many trade-offs between the levels of resources required to produce systematic and useful data and the regional and temporal coverage of various human rights indicators and their potential utility for assessing human rights implementation (Landman & Schwarz, 2022, p. 322). This leads the two authors to admit that there are no easy methodological 'fixes' but a distinct acknowledgment of the imperfect and fragmentary data that is currently available for the many categories and aspects of human rights. Thus, there is no "magic bullet" when it comes to presenting evidence for human rights using statistics and the use of indicators. (Landman & Schwarz, 2022, p. 326).

Like other scholars, Landman and Schwarz acknowledge that the development and use of human rights indicators are one of the tools that can contribute to combine with others to offer one form of explanation and understanding of human *rights-in-practice*. Along the same lines, but for different reasons, de Beco also emphasises:

> That the expectations placed on human rights indicators are too high. Although they can strengthen human rights monitoring and can give a more concrete picture of a state's human rights situation, they will not replace all other existing tools and be the only tool for monitoring compliance with international human rights treaties. Other ways of monitoring such compliance in conjunction with indicators, like case studies or interviews, should not be neglected because they can provide a good insight into problems encountered by people affected by human rights violations. (de Beco, 2013, p. 383)

In line with this assessment, the sets of children's rights indicators provided in this publication are developed with the idea of offering a tool for monitoring and evaluation. In combination with others, it allows a more prominent use of the information provided for monitoring compliance with international children's human rights treaties, supporting policy development and evaluating progress towards the realisation of children's human rights.

To maximise the use of these children's rights-based indicators, they are built on the following three development pillars:

1. They cover three categories of human rights indicators: structural, process, and outcome indicators, as recommended by the OHCHR (2012). Structure indicators gauge the degree of de jure compliance with international human rights treaties *(rights-in-principle)*, whereas process and result indicators evaluate de facto conformance *(rights-in-practice)*.
2. They combine objective and subjective indicators for each article of the UN Convention on the Rights of the Child to provide a comprehensive assessment of how rights have been implemented and are exercised on both a qualitative and quantitative level. The aim is to complete the quantitative approaches with qualitative ones, to be able to better describe country specific features and why these may matter for children's human rights.
3. They require the collection of data from a very varied range of data collection tools such as, for example, focus groups with children, case studies, and chil-

dren's interviews to provide qualitative and subjective insights into the children's living reality.

In this optic, the children's rights-based indicators provided here are not meant to replace the reporting procedure before the UN Committee on the Rights of the Child but rather to complement it and strengthen national political awareness concerning the children's condition., while also facilitating a focused data collection.

Human rights indicators appeared first in international debates within the Treaty Bodies only in 1993 when the *Vienna Declaration*, in its Programme of Action, emphasised their possible use in evaluating the advancement of human rights implementation.[2] There followed in 1998, the creation of a few indicators related to the right to education by the UN Committee on Economic, Social and Cultural Rights (UN Committee on Economic, Social and Cultural Rights, 1998) and in 2006, a comprehensive set of indicators relating to the right to health (UN Commission on Human Rights, 2006). However, the first attempt to develop a comprehensive framework of human rights indicators appeared in 2006, together with an illustrative list of Structural, Process, and Outcome (SPO) indicators relating to specific human rights (OHCHR, 2006a, 2006b, 2008; de Beco, 2013, pp. 381–382 and de Beco, 2008, pp. 42–43).

Notwithstanding, the UN Treaty Bodies all urge State Parties to create benchmarks, the advancement of which might be gauged by these indicators and invite governments to identify human rights indicators to track their compliance with international human rights treaties (de Beco, 2013, p. 381). Article 4 of the Convention on the Rights of the Child affirms that State Parties are primarily responsible for upholding human rights. They must "undertake all appropriate legislative, administrative, and other measures for the implementation of the rights recognised in the present Convention." (UNCRC, Article 4). Based on this legal provision, the Committee on the Rights of the Child (CRC Committee), since the beginning of its work in 1992 through its Concluding Observations and General Comments, has reiterated this invitation to all the State Parties. In its reporting process, it invites State Parties to develop children's rights qualitative and qualitative indicators to establish:

- A mechanism for its implementation, monitoring and evaluation with clear indicators and benchmarks (for example, CRC/C/AND/CO/3–5 (CRC, 2023) para. 8, CRC/C/STP/CO/5–6 (CRC, 2023), para. 9), CRC/C/AZE/CO/5–6 (CRC, 2023), para. 7)
- A budgeting process that includes a child rights perspective and specifies precise allocations to children in the relevant sectors and agencies, including specific indicators and a tracking system (for example, CRC/C/LIE/CO/3–4 (CRC, 2023), para 10, CRC/C/TGO/CO/5–6 (CRC, 2023), para. 11, CRC/C/DOM/CO/6 (CRC, 2023), para. 9)

[2] Vienna Declaration and Programme of Action, adopted by the World Conference on Human Rights, 25 June 1993, A/Conf.157/23, endorsed by UN General Assembly resolution 48/121, 20 December 1993, Part II, para. 98.

- A process of sharing statistical data and indicators among the ministries and relevant stakeholders concerned to coordinate their actions and endure, monitoring and evaluation of policies, programmes and projects for the effective implementation of the Convention (for example CRC/C/LIE/CO/3–4 (CRC, 2023), para. 11, CRC/C/ALB/CO/5–6 (CRC, 2023), para. 10, CRC/C/BOL/CO/5–6 (CRC, 2023), para 11)

From the *Concluding Observations* of the CRC Committee, a clear call emerges for State Parties to use indicators as a tool to strengthen the reporting process. The push for their use is essentially aimed at better increasing national understanding of the situation of children and giving them better visibility: data collection of quantitative and qualitative indicators will better enable the implementation of children's rights. The same intention emerges clearly from the General Comments. For example, General Comment no. 5 on General Measures of Implementation, adopted in 2003, refers to the collection of sufficient and reliable data on children, disaggregated to enable the identification of discrimination and disparities in the realisation of their rights:

> The Committee reminds States parties that data collection needs … to be coordinated throughout the jurisdiction, ensuring nationally applicable indicators. States should collaborate with appropriate research institutes and aim to build up a complete picture of progress towards implementation with qualitative as well as quantitative studies. … It is essential not merely to establish effective systems for data collection but also to ensure that the data collected are evaluated and used to assess progress in implementation, identify problems, and inform all policy development for children. Evaluation requires the development of indicators related to all rights guaranteed by the Convention. (CRC/GC/2003/5, para. 48. See also CRC/C/GC/2006/7, para. 39)

However, with reference to reporting procedures, they complement the information produced by State Parties through national reports but do not replace the latter. This approach of the CRC Committee well reconnects with the initial idea behind the framework of SPO children's rights-based indicators produced in this publication: indicators are complementary tools of children's human rights evidence production and not the only one.

Following this logic, indicators can also be of great value to the Children's Rights Impact Assessments (CRIAs) process. CRIA is a children's rights-focused variant of the Human Rights Impact Assessments. The CRC Committee has not dedicated a specific General Comment to CRIA. However, several references are related to it in its General Comment No. 14 on the right of the child to have his or her best interests taken as a primary consideration adopted in 2013, including in relation to the business sector, which states that:

> The child-rights impact assessment (CRIA) can predict the impact of any proposed policy, legislation, regulation, budget or other administrative decision which affect children and the enjoyment of their rights and should complement ongoing monitoring and evaluation of the impact of measures on children's rights.[3] CRIA needs to be built into government processes

[3] United Nations Committee on the Rights of the Child General comment No. 16 (2013b) on State obligations regarding the impact of the business sector on children's rights, paras. 78–81.

> at all levels and as early as possible in the development of policy and other general measures in order to ensure good governance for children's rights. (United Nations Committee on the Rights of the Child, 2013a, para. 99)

CRIA is, indeed, a significant metric that State Parties are required to use, and according to scholars such as Lundy, it empowers "decision-makers to put a specific gaze on children and their rights and to identify any disproportionate impact on children." (2020, p. 96). To ensure that children are visible in the policymaking process and that policymakers anticipate and meet their rights and needs, State Parties, as duty-bearers, utilise CRIA to influence decision-making across public, social, and economic domains (European Union-UNICEF, 2014 and Payne, 2019, 2020a and 2020b).

Like all the impact assessment and evaluation processes, it can be used to determine the future consequences of a current or proposed action ex-ante (Children's Rights Impact Assessment (CRIA)) (Foresti et al., 2009), or ex-post facto to assess the actual positive or negative implications of proposed policies, legislation, programmes, and administrative decisions on children and their rights (Children's Rights Impact Evaluation (CRIE))—(Mukherjee et al., 2021; Payne, 2019; and Hoffman, 2020). It is an iterative process, facilitating learning and analysis of the children's living reality observed. However, like the human rights-based indicators, "... it remains an aid to decision-making, not a substitute for political judgment." (European Commission, 2002, p. 3. See also Mukherjee et al., 2021, p. 10).

On how to undertake a CRIA at the national level, the CRC Committee suggests that:

> Different methodologies and practices may be developed when undertaking CRIA. At a minimum, they must use the Convention and its Optional Protocols as a framework, particularly ensuring that the assessments are underpinned by the general principles and have special regard for the differentiated impact of the measure(s) under consideration on children. The impact assessment itself could be based on input from children, civil society and experts, and relevant Government departments, academic research and experiences documented in the country or elsewhere. The analysis should result in recommendations for amendments, alternatives and improvements and be made publicly available. (United Nations Committee on the Rights of the Child, 2014, para. 99)

Based on the comparative review of the practice of CRIA carried out by Payne, the quality and effectiveness of CRIA are also achieved by including children's rights-based measurable indicators. In particular, from this comparative analysis, it emerges that national CRIA assessment practices are too often poor because they fail to include quantifiable indicators that can be used to gauge the effect and enable further assessment. Furthermore, it was underlined that establishing and approving a list of indicators on children's rights results in incredibly challenging and costly procedures (Payne, 2017, pp. 11–12). The children's rights-based indicators provided in this publication aim to be used in support of national CRIA procedures to relieve State Parties from the process of determining these indicators and to focus on selecting those that best suit their national context and to organise the collection of the necessary data for an assessment process that can then be repeated over time.

Finally, it is important to recognise that, integral to the realisation of children's rights, is a child rights-based approach that is both participatory and accountable to children themselves. Human rights can appear very legalistic and remote. It is vital that investment is made to render them more accessible, and to enable citizens, including children, to have greater understanding as to what they entail and what changes might be attained, in their daily lives, through the implementation of their human rights. Indicators are one such mechanism. Framing a core set of indicators that elaborate what states are expected to achieve in terms of structures, processes and outcomes, provides children, parents, NGOs and national human rights institutions, with standards against which to hold them to account. They provide a basis for dialogue, engagement and advocacy (UNICEF, 2016). The rights embodied in the Convention are, necessarily, very broad and general in their framing and have to be understood within their national context, for example, the right to education or to be heard. The indicators translate these rights into ideal conditions and criteria against which child rights advocates can assess progress, and make demands for strengthened action—whether that be in the school, in local health services, within the local community or at the level of national government.

Part III
Children's Rights Indicator Sets

While previous efforts have focused on developing indicators for specific human rights or clusters of rights, this comprehensive set represents a unique attempt to capture the measures required for full compliance with an entire human rights treaty. It serves as a starting point rather than a final or definitive tool. The indicators will need to be adapted to local contexts, expanded, and refined over time. Nonetheless, the authors hope this framework provides a valuable and comprehensive foundation for strengthening the realisation of children's rights, supporting State reporting processes, and guiding advocates in holding States accountable.

The following nine chapters comprise the indicators associated with articles clustered around common themes:

- General principles
- Civil and political rights
- Family environment and alternative care
- Disability, health, and welfare
- Education, leisure, and cultural activities
- Protection measures from violence
- Protection measures from exploitation
- Protection measures for children in vulnerable situations
- General measures of implementation

When using the indicators, please note the following points:

1. The indicators are presented in a table format, with a dedicated table provided for every right in the Convention. The tables enable the user to see:
    - The relationship between the structural, process, and outcome indicators
    - The relationship of the indicators to the relevant attribute
    - Indicators relevant to or capable of monitoring more than one attribute of a right (shown by the indicator transversing multiple attributes).
2. As described in the methodology chapter, a multitude of sources were examined and used to develop the indicators. However, we have only specified the origin

within the tables in relation to two specific sources, namely SDGs: some SDGs are used in their original form. Some have been adapted to focus on children rather than adults. In each case, this is referenced alongside the relevant indicator and GCRD: several indicators were amended or added as a consequence of the Global Child Rights Dialogue. In each case, this is referenced alongside the relevant indicator. All other sources are included in the bibliography at the end of the book.

3. Each table is followed by a set of formulae which provide the framework for evaluating the indicator. These formulae are only provided for indicators where it is necessary to calculate a percentage or rate. They relate, therefore, only to some process indicators and a more significant number of outcome indicators.
4. No guidance is provided on how to assess the degree of compliance with each indicator. This is partly because it would have been impractical to produce detailed scales for degrees of implementation for over 700 indicators. However, more significantly, given that the economic, social and cultural context of States across the globe varies so significantly, it would not be meaningful to seek to construct common baseline standards where the starting points are so different. For example, under Article 2, one indicator relates to the percentage of public buildings that are accessible to children with disabilities. The indicator establishes recognition that this is a goal that should be aspired to and seeks to drive the necessary measures to achieve progress towards accessible buildings. However, countries at different stages of development and with different levels of resources will inevitably chart their progress from different baselines. Thus the indicator has universal relevance but assessment of progress in implementation will vary. With indicators that ask for a percentage or a number, that data can be used as a baseline against which to monitor progress over time in any individual country. By contrast, another indicator under Article 2 addresses the establishment of an independent children's rights institution. Clearly, the quality of such an institution can vary widely depending on its mandate, scope, funding, quality of staff or degree of independence. In any individual country it will be necessary to introduce an assessment of the institution, (using, for example CRC General Comment No.2 CRC/GC/2002/2, 2002) in order to determine the extent to which the legislation, or subsequent measures undertaken, are sufficient to meet the standard of the indicator.
5. The quantitative indicators are formulated either as percentages or as numbers. In general, in contexts where the relevant numbers constitute a very small proportion of a large population of children, numbers will provide a far more relevant and reliable indicator. For example, in seeking to assess the scale of the problem of children unable to be cared for by their parents, a number would be most informative as such children will generally represent a tiny proportion of the whole child population and therefore a percentage would be so small as to be a meaningless figure. However, a number, collected annually, would provide much more informative and useful data. By contrast, in seeking to find out about the type of placements for these children, a percentage would reveal more relevant data. For example, it would be more important to know the percentage of children, from

the whole population of children in care, how many were placed in foster homes than the actual numbers. In this instance, the numbers involved would constitute a sufficiently significant proportion of the relevant population to provide reliably informative percentage data. And where the data is seeking evidence relating to an entire child population, for example in relation to mortality rates or school enrolment, percentages are obviously needed.

6. Rights are indivisible. It is not possible to ensure the realisation of an individual rights without reference to other rights. For example, the four general principles (non-discrimination, best interests, optimum development and the right to be heard) need to be taken into consideration in the realisation of all other rights. The right to heath cannot be realised without recognition of the right to protection from violence, the right to an adequate standard of living and the right to information. Thus, although, the indicators in this publication are organised round individual articles of the Convention, it will often be helpful to have reference to indicators from other articles in order to assess the overall degree of compliance with that right. Some cross referencing has been provided to facilitate with this process, and in some cases, for example, relating to the right to be heard, adapted indicators have been replicated in different articles. However, it is not comprehensive, as so doing would have resulted in a significantly longer and more complex publication.

Following the nine chapters about the indicators, there is a chapter for a glossary of terms used.

Chapter 4
General Principles

Ziba Vaghri, Roberta Ruggiero, Gerison Lansdown, Adem Arkadas-Thibert, and Christian Whalen

This chapter contains the four rights in the Committee that have been identified by the Committee on the Rights of the Child as general principles that must inform the implementation of all other rights.[1]

- Article 2—non-discrimination
- Article 3—the best interests of the child

[1] For further elaboration on the implications and implementation of each of these rights, please read the relevant chapter in the companion publication to this book: *Monitoring State Compliance with the UN Convention on the Rights of the Child: An analysis of attributes*, Vaghri, Zermatten, Lansdown and Ruggiero, Springer, 2022.

Z. Vaghri
GlobalChild Program of Research, University of New Brunswick, Saint John, NB, Canada

R. Ruggiero (✉)
Centre for Children's Right Studies, Faculty of Law, University of Geneva, Geneva, Switzerland
e-mail: Roberta.ruggiero@unige.ch

G. Lansdown
School of Law, University College Cork, Cork, Ireland

A. Arkadas-Thibert
Independent Researcher, Specializing in International Human Rights, Marseille, France

C. Whalen
Faculty of Law, University of New Brunswick, Fredericton, NB, Canada

Z. Vaghri et al. (eds.), *Children's Rights-Based Indicators*, Children's Well-Being: Indicators and Research 28,
https://doi.org/10.1007/978-3-031-71594-5_4

- Article 6—the right to life and optimum development
- Article 12—the right to be heard.

However, they also need to be considered as human rights in their own right, carrying associated obligations for states. Accordingly, this chapter provides a framework of indicators for states to consider in order to fulfil those obligations in respect of non-discrimination, best interests, survival and development and the right to be heard. Throughout the rest of the publication, in the indicators for other rights, specific measures are also included to ensure that these four principles are taken into consideration in the process of implementation. For example, in developing child protection legislation and policies, it is necessary to ensure that children's own perspectives and recommendations are taken into consideration, and that any measures introduced apply to all children without discrimination on any protected grounds.

Article 2—Non-discrimination

1. States Parties shall respect and ensure the rights set forth in the present Convention to each child within their jurisdiction without discrimination of any kind, irrespective of the child's or his or her parent's or legal guardian's race, colour, sex, language, religion, political or other opinion, national, ethnic or social origin, property, disability, birth or other status.
2. States Parties shall take all appropriate measures to ensure that the child is protected against all forms of discrimination or punishment on the basis of the status, activities, expressed opinions, or beliefs of the child's parents, legal guardians, or family members.

Table 1 Article 2 Indicator sets

Core attributes		
Non-discrimination in the realisation of all rights for all children within the jurisdiction	**Non-discrimination on the basis of status, actions, or beliefs, of parents, guardians, or family members**	**Special measures to address discrimination**
Data is collected and disaggregated by prohibited grounds for discrimination including age, sex, ethnicity, disability, when applicable.		
Structural indicators		

(continued)

Table 1 (continued)

1. The state has ratified international human rights treaties relevant to non-discrimination, for example: • *International Covenant on Civil and Political Rights (ICCPR),* 1976 • *International Covenant on Economic, Social and Cultural Rights (ICESCR),* 1966 • *Convention on the Elimination of All Forms of Discrimination Against Woman (CEDAW),* 1979 • *International Convention for the Protection of All Persons from Enforced Disappearance (CED),* 2007 • *Convention on the Rights of Persons with Disabilities (CRPD),* 2007 • *UNESCO Convention Against Discrimination in Education,* 1960. 2. The right to non-discrimination is guaranteed in the constitution. 3. Establishment of independent children's rights institution responsible for promoting and protecting children's rights, including the right to non-discrimination.	
4. Review of existing legislation to ensure compliance with right to non-discrimination. 5. Introduction of legislation defining and guaranteeing the right to non-discrimination: • To every child within the jurisdiction • On all prohibited grounds.	6. Strategy in place to ensure equity for all children through: • Elimination of barriers (e.g. social, economic, cultural, physical, communication, and transportation) • Introduction of positive discrimination measures, as appropriate.
Process indicators	
7. Percentage of received complaints on cases of direct and indirect discrimination addressed by children's commissioner, ombudsperson, or other mechanisms. 8. National public awareness campaign to prevent and address discrimination undertaken since the last CRC report.	
9. Percentage of primary and secondary schools with a comprehensive non-discrimination policy, developed in collaboration with students. 10. Percentage of hospitals with a comprehensive non-discrimination policy, developed in collaboration with children and their families. 11. Percentage of public service buildings with facilities and accessible to children with disabilities.	12. Non-discrimination pre- and/ or in-service training is provided for professionals working with or for children in the following fields: • Education • Health • Police • Social work and child welfare • Alternative care • Early childhood development and childcare • Justice • Immigration, and • Other relevant fields. 13. (GCRD) Support and training is provided to facilitate children to become human rights defenders to address discrimination.[a]

(continued)

Table 1 (continued)

Outcome indicators		
14. Percentage of adjudicated complaints cases of direct and indirect discrimination responded to effectively by the government. 15. (SDG 3.2 adapted) Birth and mortality rates according to population group (e.g. by race, sex, language, religion etc.).		
16. Educational attainments (e.g. numeracy and literacy rates) by targeted population group. 17. Percentage of targeted populations of children below the national poverty line before and after social transfers. 18. Percentage of children held in custody from indigenous or ethnic minority communities in relation to the total youth custodial population. 19. Percentage of children held in custody from indigenous or ethnic minority communities in relation to their representation across the country.	20. Number of immigrant/ asylum seeking children held in custody as a consequence of parental immigration status. 21. Number of immigrant/ asylum seeking children denied access to health care or education as a consequence of parental immigration status. 22. Number of children denied health care or admissions to school or post-secondary education due to parental or caregiver race, ethnicity, social status, etc. 23. Number of hate crimes against children based on status, actions, beliefs of parents or caregivers etc.	24. Percentage of children who feel their aspirations can be achieved by targeted population group. 25. Number of children who have experienced discrimination within the past 12 months by targeted population group. 26. Percentage of professionals working with or for children with an understanding of direct and indirect discrimination. 27. (GCRD) Number of children trained as human rights defenders.

GCRD—an indicator that was influenced by or added through the Global Child Rights Dialogue, the consultation with children informing the indicator development process

Article 2—Guidance

The following provides guidance for the collection of data on specific indicators for Article 2. The number relates to the number of that indicator in the table above. Each indicator is identified as a Process, Structural, or Outcome Indicator, and the formula to calculate the data is described.

Indicator 7—Process

Percentage of received complaints on cases of direct and indirect discrimination addressed by children's commissioner, ombudsperson, or other mechanisms.

Numerator: Number of received complaints on cases of direct and indirect discrimination addressed by children's commissioner, ombudsperson. or other mechanisms.

Denominator: Total number of received complaints by children's commissioner, ombudsperson, or other mechanisms.

Formula: (numerator/denominator) × 100.

Indicator 9—Process

Percentage of primary and secondary schools with a comprehensive non-discrimination policy, developed in collaboration with students.

Numerator: Number of primary and secondary schools with a comprehensive non-discrimination policy, developed in collaboration with students.

Denominator: Total number of primary and secondary schools.

Formula: (numerator/denominator) × 100.

Indicator 10—Process

Percentage of hospitals with a comprehensive non-discrimination policy, developed in collaboration with children and their families.

Numerator: Number of hospitals with a comprehensive non-discrimination policy, developed in collaboration with children and their families.

Denominator: Total number of hospitals.

Formula: (numerator/denominator) × 100.

Indicator 11—Process

Percentage of public service buildings with facilities and accessible to children with disabilities.

Numerator: Number of public service buildings with facilities and accessible to children with disabilities.

Denominator: Total number of public service buildings.

Formula: (numerator/denominator) × 100.

Indicator 14—Outcome

Percentage of adjudicated complaints cases of direct and indirect discrimination responded to effectively by the government.

Numerator: Number of adjudicated complaints cases of direct and indirect discrimination responded to effectively by the government.

Denominator: Total number of adjudicated cases by government.

Formula: (numerator/denominator) × 100.

Indicator 17—Outcome

Percentage of targeted populations of children below the national poverty line before and after social transfers.

Numerator: Number of targeted populations of children below the national poverty line before and after social transfers.

Denominator: Total number of targeted populations of children.

Formula: (numerator/denominator) × 100.

Indicator 18—Outcome

Percentage of children held in custody from indigenous or ethnic minority communities in relation to the total youth custodial population.

Numerator: Number of children held in custody from indigenous or ethnic minority communities.

Denominator: Total number of children held in custody.

Formula: (numerator/denominator) × 100.

Indicator 19—Outcome

Percentage of children held in custody from indigenous or ethnic minority communities in relation to their representation across the country.

Numerator: number of children held in custody from indigenous or ethnic minority communities.

Denominator: Total number of children from ethnic minority or indigenous communities across the age cohort.

Formula: (numerator/denominator) × 100.

Indicator 24—Outcome

Percentage of children who feel their aspirations can be achieved by targeted population group.

Numerator: Number of children who feel their aspirations can be achieved by targeted population group.

Denominator: Total number of children surveyed (by targeted population group).

Formula: (numerator/denominator) × 100.

Indicator 26—Outcome

Percentage of professionals working with or for children with an understanding of direct and indirect discrimination.

Numerator: Number of professionals working with or for children with an understanding of direct and indirect discrimination.

Denominator: Total number of professionals working with or for children.

Formula: (numerator/denominator) × 100.

Article 3—The Best Interests of the Child

1. In all actions concerning children, whether undertaken by public or private social welfare institutions, courts of law, administrative authorities or legislative bodies, the best interests of the child shall be a primary consideration.
2. States Parties undertake to ensure the child such protection and care as is necessary for his or her well-being, taking into account the rights and duties of his or her parents, legal guardians, or other individuals legally responsible for him or her, and, to this end, shall take all appropriate legislative and administrative measures.
3. States Parties shall ensure that the institutions, services and facilities responsible for the care or protection of children shall conform with the standards established by competent authorities, particularly in the areas of safety, health, in the number and suitability of their staff, as well as competent supervision.

Table 2 Article 3 Indicator sets

Core attributes		
The best interests of the child as a primary consideration	**Care and protection: Safety net**	**Adequate standards for institutions, services and facilities dedicated to the care and protection of the child**
Data is collected and disaggregated by prohibited grounds for discrimination including age, sex, ethnicity, disability, when applicable.		
Structural indicators		
1. Ratification of human rights treaties relevant to Article 3, for example: • *Hague Convention on Protection of Children and Co-operation in Respect of Intercountry Adoption*, 1993 2. The best interests of the child as guaranteed in Article 3 is explicitly recognised in legislation as an individual and collective substantive right. 3. Mechanisms and institutions exist to enforce Article 3 including sanctions for violations. 4. Policy measures and protocols for professionals are in place to guarantee the child best interests determination. 5. Child impact assessment in relation to their best interests is required in the legislation, administrative decision-making, and policy and practice at all levels of government concerning: • Budget allocations to the social sector and to children, and between and within departments of government • Social security • Planning and development • Environment • Housing • Transport • Health • Education • Employment • Administration of juvenile and civil justice • The criminal law (e.g. the effects of the sentencing of parents on children, etc.) • Nationality and immigration • Asylum seeking.		
6. State has set a comprehensive system and the required procedural guarantees for the best interests' determination in all actions concerning children whether undertaken by: • Public or private social welfare institutions • Courts of law • Administrative authorities • Legislative bodies.	7. Legislative and administrative provisions require the state to provide care and protection for children unable to be cared for by their families.	8. Appropriate standards are established for state and non-state institutions, services, and facilities responsible for the care or protection of children, in particular, in relation to: • Safety • Health • Protection of children from all forms of violence • The number and suitability of staff • Conformity with all provisions of the convention • Independent inspection and supervision.

(continued)

Table 2 (continued)

<table>
<tr><th colspan="3">Process indicators</th></tr>
<tr><td colspan="3">9. National strategy has been implemented to disseminate information on the child best interests' principle.
10. Pre- and/or in-service training for professionals are in place to guarantee the child best interests determination.
11. Percentage of professionals with training on best interests determination in at least the following fields:
• Education
• Health
• Social work
• Justice and police
• Immigration.
12. Number of child rights impact assessments undertaken within the last 12 months concerning:
• Budget allocations to the social sector and to children, and between and within departments of government
• Social security
• Planning and development
• The environment
• Housing
• Transport
• Health
• Education
• Employment
• Administration of juvenile and civil justice
• The criminal law (e.g. the effects of the sentencing of parents on children, etc.)
• Nationality and immigration
• Asylum seeking.</td></tr>
<tr><td></td><td>13. Number of policies and strategies that had been established and/or revised to ensure children's best interests are taken in due consideration.</td><td></td></tr>
<tr><th colspan="3">Outcome indicators</th></tr>
<tr><td colspan="3">14. Percentage of children knowledgeable about the office of children's commissioner/ ombudsperson/ advocate and its role in ensuring their best interests are protected (where such exists).
15. Percentage of children who feel that their best interests are given due consideration by adults in their lives.
16. Percentage of cases of children in judicial or administrative proceedings where children considered their best interests had been taken into consideration.</td></tr>
<tr><td>17. Percentage of court cases involving children in judicial or administrative proceedings citing the best interests principle.</td><td></td><td>18. Percentage of professionals that are aware of the quality standards in the fields of:
• Education
• Health
• Social work
• Justice and police
• Immigration.</td></tr>
</table>

Article 3—Guidance

The following provides guidance for the collection of data on specific indicators for Article 3. The number relates to the number of that indicator in the table above. Each indicator is identified as a Process, Structural, or Outcome Indicator, and the formula to calculate the data is described.

Indicator 11—Process

Percentage of professionals with training on best interests determination in at least the following fields:

- Education
- Health
- Social work
- Justice and police
- Immigration.

To be undertaken in respect of all the activities listed in the indicator.

Numerator: Number of professionals in the field selected (education, health, social work etc.) with training on best interests determination.

Denominator: Total number of professionals in the field selected.

Formula: (Numerator / Denominator) × 100.

Indicator 14—Outcome

Percentage of children knowledgeable about the office of children's commissioner/ ombudsperson/ advocate and its role in ensuring their best interests are protected (where such exists).

Numerator: number of children knowledgeable about the office of children's commissioner/ombudsperson/ advocate and its role in ensuring their best interests are protected.

Denominator: total number of children.

Formula: (numerator/denominator) × 100.

Indicator 15—Outcome

Percentage of children who feel that their best interests is taken in due consideration by adults in their lives.

Numerator: Number of children who feel that their best interests is taken in due consideration by adults in their lives.

Denominator: Total number of children surveyed.

Formula: (numerator/denominator) × 100.

Indicator 16—Outcome

Percentage of cases of children in judicial or administrative proceedings where children considered their best interests had been taken into consideration.

Numerator: Number of cases of children in judicial or administrative proceedings where children considered their best interests had been taken into consideration.

Denominator: Total number of judicial or administrative cases involving children surveyed.

Formula: (numerator/denominator) × 100.

Indicator 17—Outcome

Percentage of court cases involving children in judicial or administrative proceedings citing the best interests principle.

Numerator: Number of court cases involving children in judicial or administrative proceedings citing the best interests principle.

Denominator: Total number of judicial or administrative cases involving children.

Formula: (numerator/denominator) × 100.

Indicator 18—Outcome

Percentage of professionals that are aware the quality standards in the fields of:

- Education
- Health
- Social work
- Justice and police
- Immigration.

Numerator: Number of professionals in the selected field that are aware of the quality standards.

Denominator: Total number of professionals in the selected field.

Formula: (Numerator/Denominator) × 100.

Article 6—The Right to Life and Optimum Development

1. States Parties recognise that every child has the inherent right to life.
2. States Parties shall ensure to the maximum extent possible the survival and development of the child.

Table 3 Article 6 Indicator sets

Core attributes	
Respect for and protection of inherent right to life of the child	**Ensuring the development and the survival of the child to the maximum extent possible**
Data is collected and disaggregated by prohibited grounds for discrimination including age, sex, ethnicity, disability, when applicable.	
Structural indicators	
1. State's legislation and policies addresses: • Poverty reduction policies that define indicators and benchmarks regarding early childhood development and care to measure progress • Reduction of newborn, infant, and child mortality for all subgroups of population • Criminalising female infanticide and prosecuting violators • Provision of equitable access to preventive and curative healthcare and essential medicine for all children. 2. (SDG 13.1.1 adapted) State has a national and local disaster risk strategy in place. 3. Measures are in place to ensure that deaths of all children and their causes are appropriately recorded, registered, and investigated.	
4. Legislation prohibits capital punishment of children.	
Process indicators	
5. Systems in place to record child suicide. 6. Education on the respect for and protection of the right to life of all children is provided for: • The parent • Health care professionals • Educators, government officials, juvenile justice, and other public sector working for or with children.	7. Percentage of state's gross domestic product (GDP) allocated to early child development. 8. Existence of interventions and services for prevention, early detection, and management of children's developmental difficulties. 9. Provision of targeted financial and other support mechanisms for families of children identified with developmental difficulties. 10. Percentage of education budget allocated to early childhood.

(continued)

Table 3 (continued)

Outcome indicators	
11. Number of reported infanticides, in particular for female infants and infant with disabilities.	12. (SDG 4.2.1) Percentage of children under 5 years of age who are developmentally on track in health, learning and psychosocial well-being. 13. (SDG 3.2.1 adapted) Under-five mortality rate. 14. (SDG 3.2.2 adapted) Neonatal mortality rate. 15. Percentage of children with developmental problems receiving rehabilitation services.
16. Number of violence-related fatalities of children. 17. Number of child deaths in formal care. 18. Number of child deaths occurring in the criminal justice system. 19. Number of children attempting suicide.	

Article 6—Guidance

The following provides guidance for the collection of data on specific indicators for Article 6. The number relates to the number of that indicator in the table above. Each indicator is identified as a Process, Structural, or Outcome Indicator, and the formula to calculate the data is described.

Indicator 7—Process

Percentage of state's GDP earmarked for early child development.

Numerator: Amount earmarked for ECD.

Denominator: GDP of the country.

Formula: (Numerator/denominator) × 100.

Indicator 10—Process

Percentage of education budget devoted for early childhood (Art 28-Ind 20).

Numerator: Amount of education budget devoted for early childhood.

Denominator: Total amount of education budget.

Formula: (numerator/denominator) × 100.

Indicator 12—Outcome

Percentage of children under 5 years of age who are developmentally on track in health, learning and psychosocial well-being.

Numerator: Number of children under 5 years of age who are developmentally on track in health, learning and psychosocial well-being.

Denominator: Total number of children under 5 years of age surveyed.

Formula: (numerator/denominator) × 100.

Indicator 13—Outcome

Under-five mortality rate.

Numerator: Number of deaths between 0 and 4years of age.

Denominator: number of live births within the time period.

Formula: (numerator/denominator) per 1000.

Indicator 14—Outcome

Neonatal mortality rate, disaggregated by sex of the child, ethnicity, and disability.

Numerator: Number of infant deaths (less than 28 days of age).

Denominator: Number of live births within the time period.

Formula: (numerator/denominator) per 1000.

Indicator 15—Outcome

Percentage of children with developmental problems receiving rehabilitation services.

Numerator: Number of children with developmental problems who receive rehabilitation services.

Denominator: Total number of children with developmental problems.

Formula: (numerator/denominator) × 100.

Article 12—The Right to Be Heard

1. States Parties shall assure to the child who is capable of forming his or her own views the right to express those views freely in all matters affecting the child, the views of the child being given due weight in accordance with the age and maturity of the child.
2. For this purpose, the child shall in particular be provided the opportunity to be heard in any judicial and administrative proceedings affecting the child, either directly, or through a representative or an appropriate body, in a manner consistent with the procedural rules of national law.

Table 4 Article 12 Indicator sets

Core attributes			
The right to be heard in all matters affecting the child	**Right to be heard in all judicial and administrative proceedings**	**Access to redress and complaints procedures**	**Education and administrative measures to implement A 12**
Data is collected and disaggregated by prohibited grounds for discrimination including age, sex, ethnicity, disability, when applicable			
Structural indicators			
1. Legal protection for children's right to express views and have them given due weight in matters affecting them is reflected in the national constitution and legislation.			
2. Children's right to express views (individually and collectively) and have them given due weight is explicitly included in cross-sectoral national strategy to implement children's rights.	3. Mechanisms are in place to enable children to be heard in all relevant judicial and administrative proceedings (see also art. 40).	4. Complaints mechanisms for children are mandated by law in all relevant contexts.	
Process indicators			
5. Children's right to express views and have them given due weight is embedded in pre-service (and, as appropriate, in-service) training programmes for all professionals working with and for children.			

(continued)

Table 4 (continued)

6. Policies are implemented and resourced at national and local levels to ensure children's right to be heard: • At all ages • As individuals and collectively • In all matters affecting them. 7. Percentage of the following bodies with mechanisms to enable children to be heard: • Schools with active school councils (art. 28) • Local authorities with an active children/youth council. 8. Percentage of government bodies that have consulted with children on relevant legislation, policies, budgets, and service developments in the last reporting period: • National government ministries • Local authorities or regional entities.	9. All relevant judicial and administrative proceedings are accessible to children and guarantee: • Access to a lawyer • Information about their rights • Opportunity to express views and have them given due weight • Feedback on decisions made and the associated reasoning (see also art. 40). 10. Percentage of judicial and administrative systems with protocols in place to ensure children's right to be heard (see also art. 40).	11. Child-friendly complaints mechanisms are established in at least the following service areas: • Health • Education • Child protection • Immigration • Criminal justice • Family law • Sport. 12. The regulations establishing complaints mechanisms guarantee that complaints can be made by children themselves.	13. National curriculum at primary and secondary education addresses the right of children to express their views and have them taken seriously.
Outcome indicators			
14. Percentage of children expressing self-confidence and a sense of self efficacy. 15. (GCRD) Percentage of children who feel listened to and respected by their parents or carers.			

(continued)

Table 4 (continued)

16. Percentage of children who consider they are able to influence individual decisions affecting their lives, for example: • In the family • In school • In health care • In alternative care settings. 17. Percentage of children who have been engaged in the following activities at school: • Membership of a school or student council • Class representative • Active role in a pupil or student meeting • Peer mediation • Collaboration in the school newspaper • Peer mentorship or counselling. 18. Percentage of children who were engaged in the following social or political activities: • Participation in a child or youth forum or youth council • Participation in a community (local or regional) project • Participation in a collective supporting action (for example collecting signatures) • Involvement in a protest action • Participation in voluntary work.	19. Percentage of cases of children in judicial or administrative proceedings where children considered they had been listened to and their views given due weight (see also art. 40). 20. Percentage of cases of children in judicial or administrative proceedings where children had access to free legal advice and counselling (see also art. 40).	21. Percentage of children who are aware of and confident in complaints mechanisms. 22. Percentage of complaints about services for children resolved satisfactorily. 23. Percentage of children who feel satisfied with the complaint mechanisms.	24. Percentage of children who are aware of their right to be heard in all settings. 25. Percentage of children who feel satisfied about the knowledge/ education they have received on their right to be heard in all settings. 26. (GCRD) Percentage of parents/caregivers expressing positive attitudes towards children's right to be heard. 27. (GCRD) Percentage of children who feel they have a trusted adult they can talk to.

Article 12—Guidance

The following provides guidance for the collection of data on specific indicators for Article 12. The number relates to the number of that indicator in the table above. Each indicator is identified as a Process, Structural, or Outcome Indicator, and the formula to calculate the data is described.

Indicator 7—Process

Percentage of the following bodies with mechanisms to enable children to be heard:

7.1 Schools with active school councils.
Numerator: Number of schools with active school councils with mechanisms to enable children to be heard.
Denominator: Total number of schools.
Formula: (numerator/denominator) × 100.
7.2 Local authorities with an active children/youth council.
Numerator: Number of local authorities with an active children/youth council with mechanisms to enable children to be heard.
Denominator: Total number of local authorities.
Formula: (numerator/denominator) × 100.

Indicator 8—Process

Percentage of government bodies that have consulted with children on relevant legislation, policies, budgets, and service developments in the last reporting period:

8.1 National government ministries.
Numerator: Number of national government ministries that have consulted with children on relevant legislation, policies, budgets, and service developments in the last reporting period.
Denominator: Total number of national government ministries.
Formula: (numerator/denominator) × 100.
8.2 Local authorities or regional entities.
Numerator: Number of local authorities or regional entities that have consulted with children on relevant legislation, policies, budgets, and service developments in the last reporting period.
Denominator: Total number of local authorities or regional entities.
Formula: (numerator/denominator) × 100.

Indicator 10—Process

Percentage of judicial and administrative systems with protocols in place to ensure children's right to be heard.

Numerator: Number of judicial and administrative systems with protocols in place to ensure children's right to be heard.

Denominator: Total number of judicial and administrative systems.

Formula: (numerator/denominator) × 100.

Indicator 14—Outcome

Percentage of children expressing self-confidence and a sense of self efficacy.

Numerator: Number of children expressing self-confidence and a sense of self efficacy.

Denominator: Total number of children surveyed.

Formula: (numerator/denominator) × 100.

Indicator 15—Outcome

Percentage of children who feel listened to and respected by their parents or carers.

Numerator: Number of children who feel listened to and respected by their parents or carers.

Denominator: Total number of children surveyed.

Formula: (numerator/denominator) × 100.

Indicator 16—Outcome

Percentage of children who consider they are able to influence individual decisions affecting their lives:

- In the family
- In school
- In health care
- In alternative care settings.

Numerator: Number of children who consider they are able to influence individual decisions affecting their lives in the family in the selected setting (family, school, health care, alternative care).

Denominator: Total number of children surveyed.

Formula: (numerator/denominator) × 100.

Indicator 17—Outcome

Percentage of children who have been engaged in the following activities at school:

17.1 Membership of a school or student council.

Numerator: Number of children who have been engaged in the membership of a school or student council at school.

Denominator: Total number of both primary and secondary school children surveyed.

Formula: (numerator/denominator) × 100.

17.2 Class representative.

Numerator: Number of children who have been engaged as a class representative at school.

Denominator: Total number of both primary and secondary school children surveyed.

Formula: (numerator/denominator) × 100.

17.3 Active role in a pupil or student meeting.

Numerator: Number of children who have had an active role in a pupil or student meeting.

Denominator: Total number of both primary and secondary school children surveyed.

Formula: (numerator/denominator) × 100.

17.4 Peer mediation.

Numerator: Number of children who have been engaged in peer mediation at school.

Denominator: Total number of both primary and secondary school children surveyed.

Formula: (numerator/denominator) × 100.

17.5 Collaboration in the school newspaper.

Numerator: Number of children who have been engaged in collaboration in the school newspaper.

Denominator: Total number of both primary and secondary school children surveyed.

Formula: (numerator/denominator) × 100.

17.6 Peer mentorship or counselling

Numerator: Number of children who have been engaged in peer mentorship or counselling at school.

Denominator: Total number of both primary and secondary school children surveyed.

Formula: (numerator/denominator) × 100.

Indicator 18—Outcome

Percentage of children who were engaged in the following social or political activities:

18.1 Participation in a child or youth forum or youth council.

Numerator: Number of children engaged in the participation in a child or youth forum or youth council.

Denominator: Total number of children surveyed.

Formula: (numerator/denominator) × 100.

18.2 Participation in a community (local or regional) project.

Numerator: Number of children engaged in the participation of a community (local or regional) project.

Denominator: Total number of children surveyed.

Formula: (numerator/denominator) × 100.

18.3 Participation in a collective supporting action (for example, collecting signatures).

Numerator: Number of children engaged in the participation in a collective supporting action (for example collecting signatures).

Denominator: Total number of children surveyed.

Formula: (numerator/denominator) × 100.

18.4 Involvement in a protest action.

Numerator: Number of children engaged in the involvement in a protest action.

Denominator: total number of children surveyed.

Formula: (numerator/denominator) × 100.

18.5 Participation in voluntary work.

Numerator: Number of children engaged in the participation in voluntary work.

Denominator: Total number of children surveyed.

Formula: (numerator/denominator) × 100.

Indicator 19—Outcome

Percentage of cases of children in judicial or administrative proceedings where children considered they had been listened to and their views given due weight.

Numerator: Number of cases of children in judicial or administrative proceedings where children considered they had been listened to and their views given due weight.

Denominator: Total number of cases of children in judicial or administrative proceedings.

Formula: (numerator/denominator) × 100.

Indicator 20—Outcome

Percentage of cases of children in judicial or administrative proceedings where children had access to free legal advice and counselling.

Numerator: Number of cases of children in judicial or administrative proceedings where children had access to free legal advice and counselling.

Denominator: Total number of cases of children in judicial or administrative proceedings.

Formula: (numerator/denominator) × 100.

Indicator 21—Outcome

Percentage of children who are aware of and confident in complaints mechanisms.

Numerator: Number of children who are aware of and confident in complaints mechanisms.

Denominator: Total number of children surveyed.

Formula: (numerator/denominator) × 100.

Indicator 22—Outcome

Percentage of complaints about services for children resolved satisfactorily.

Numerator: Number of complaints about services for children resolved satisfactorily.

Denominator: Total number of complaints about services for children.

Formula: (numerator/denominator) × 100.

Indicator 23—Outcome

Percentage of children who feel satisfied with the complaint mechanisms.

Numerator: Number of children who feel satisfied with the complaint mechanisms.

Denominator: Total number of children surveyed.

Formula: (numerator/denominator) × 100.

Indicator 24—Outcome

Percentage of children who are aware of their right to be heard in all settings.

Numerator: Number of children who are aware of their right to be heard in all settings.

Denominator: Total number of children surveyed.

Formula: (numerator/denominator) × 100.

Indicator 25—Outcome

Percentage of children who feel satisfied about the knowledge/education they have received on their right to be heard in all settings.

Numerator: Number of children who feel satisfied about the knowledge/education they have received on their right to be heard in all settings.

Denominator: Total number of children surveyed.

Formula: (numerator/denominator) × 100.

Indicator 26—Outcome

Percentage of parents/caregivers expressing positive attitudes towards children's right to be heard.

Numerator: Number of parents/caregivers expressing positive attitudes towards children's right to be heard.

Denominator: Total number of parents/caregivers surveyed.

Formula: (numerator/denominator) × 100.

Indicator 27—Outcome

Percentage of children who feel they have a trusted adult they can talk to.

Numerator: Number of children who feel they have a trusted adult they can talk to.

Denominator: Total number of children surveyed.

Formula: (numerator/denominator) × 100.

Chapter 5
Civil and Political Rights

Ziba Vaghri, Roberta Ruggiero, Gerison Lansdown, Adem Arkadas-Thibert, and Christian Whalen

The Convention on the Rights of the Child gives explicit recognition to the civil and political rights of children.[1] Those rights include:

[1] For further elaboration on the implications and implementation of each of these rights, please read the relevant chapter in the companion publication to this book: *Monitoring State Compliance with the UN Convention on the Rights of the Child: An analysis of attributes*, Vaghri, Zermatten, Lansdown and Ruggiero, Springer, 2022.

Z. Vaghri
GlobalChild Program of Research, University of New Brunswick, Saint John, NB, Canada

R. Ruggiero (✉)
Centre for Children's Right Studies, Faculty of Law, University of Geneva, Geneva, Switzerland
e-mail: Roberta.ruggiero@unige.ch

G. Lansdown
School of Law, University College Cork, Cork, Ireland

A. Arkadas-Thibert
Independent Researcher, Specializing in International Human Rights, Marseille, France

C. Whalen
Faculty of Law, University of New Brunswick, Fredericton, NB, Canada

Z. Vaghri et al. (eds.), *Children's Rights-Based Indicators*, Children's Well-Being: Indicators and Research 28,
https://doi.org/10.1007/978-3-031-71594-5_5

- Article 7—right to birth registration a name, nationality, and to know and be cared for by parent as far as possible
- Article 8—right to preservation of identity
- Article 13—freedom of expression
- Article 14—freedom of thought, conscience, and religion
- Article 15—freedom of association and assembly
- Article 16—right to privacy
- Article 17—right to information.

Although the *International Covenant on Civil and Political Rights* in principle extends to all people by virtue of their humanity, the inclusion of civil and political rights in the *Convention on the Rights of the Child* constitutes the first clear recognition that they apply equally to children. However, there are differences in the formulation of some of these rights, as well as additional rights to take account of children's different legal and developmental status. Thus, for example, Article 7 goes beyond the right to a name and nationality to address children's right to know and be cared for by their parents. Article 8, a new provision, focuses on the preservation of the child's identity in context where a child is removed from their birth parents. Article 17 is another new provision, extending the right to information as elaborated in Article 13, the right to freedom of expression, to assert the right to information from the mass media, recognising its critical role in enabling children to exercise their rights. And in Article 14, the right to freedom of thought and religion, the wording references the rights of parents to provide direction and guidance in accordance with the child's evolving capacities.

If states are to adopt the necessary measures to ensure the realisation of these rights, it is important that they are provided with clear guidance on how to achieve that goal. The indicators in this chapter are derived from the accumulated jurisprudence from the Human Rights Committee in its monitoring the implementation of the *International Covenant*, and developed and adapted for children by the *Committee on the Rights of the Child.* Together they provide an overall picture of what is expected of states and how children can be enabled to exercise these rights.

Article 7—Right to Birth Registration a Name, Nationality, and to Know and Be Cared for by Parent As Far as Possible

1. The child shall be registered immediately after birth and shall have the right from birth to a name, the right to acquire a nationality and. as far as possible, the right to know and be cared for by his or her parents.
2. States Parties shall ensure the implementation of these rights in accordance with their national law and their obligations under the relevant international instruments in this field, in particular where the child would otherwise be stateless.

Table 1 Article 7 Indicator sets

Core attributes		
Free, compulsory, and accessible birth registration immediately after birth of all children	**Acquiring a name, nationality, and prevention of statelessness of a child**	**Knowing and being cared for by their parents**
Data is collected and disaggregated by prohibited grounds for discrimination including age, sex, ethnicity, disability, when applicable.		
Structural indicators		
1. Birth registration (declaration, registration, and issuance of a certificate) is compulsory and continuously accessible throughout the child's life at local and/or national level for all children without discrimination, is accessible and free of charge. 2. Birth registration and certificate include name, date, and place of birth, as well as place of usual residence and nationality of both parents/ legal caregivers.	3. (GCRD) The law provides for the rights to a name and identity of all children. 4. The law ensures that all stateless children living within the jurisdiction have a right to acquire the state's nationality. 5. The law ensures that children have right to acquire nationality from both parents. 6. The law ensures that children are not deprived of their nationality or the right to acquire nationality and be rendered stateless for reasons of the legal or social status of their parents.	7. The law ensures the child's right, as far as possible, to know who their genetic parents are. 8. The law stipulates the child's right, as far as possible, to be cared for by their parents.
Process indicators		
9. Information about the duty of the parents to register a child at birth is available and at no cost. 10. There are child-friendly programmes in place to register older children who were not registered at birth for any reason or lack birth registration/ID. 11. There are procedures in place to facilitate the birth registration at maternity clinics, hospitals as well as by midwives and traditional birth attendants. 12. There are accessible and reliable registration centres in remote areas.	13. Information about acquiring nationality for children is available and at no cost.	14. Information about the right to know one's parents is provided in settings of children separated from their parents.
Outcome indicators		
15. (SDG 16.9.1) Proportion of children under 5 years of age whose births have been registered with a civil authority, by age.	16. Number of stateless children.	17. Percentage of children who sought and successfully received information about their genetic parents.

Article 7—Guidance

The following provides guidance for the collection of data on specific indicators for Article 7. The number relates to the number of that indicator in the table above. Each indicator is identified as a Process, Structural, or Outcome Indicator, and the formula to calculate the data is described.

Indicator 15—Outcome

Proportion of children under 5 years of age whose births have been registered with a civil authority, by age.

Numerator: Number of children under 5 years of age whose births have been registered with a civil authority, by age.

Denominator: All children under 5 years of age within the jurisdiction, by age.

Formula: (numerator/denominator).

Indicator 17—Outcome

Percentage of children who sought and successfully received information about their genetic parents.

Numerator: Number of children below 18 years who sought and successfully received information about their genetic parents.

Denominator: All children below 18 years who are seeking information about their genetic parents.

Formula: (numerator/denominator) × 100.

Article 8—Right to Preservation of Identity

1. States Parties undertake to respect the right of the child to preserve his or her identity, including nationality, name and family relations as recognized by law without unlawful interference.
2. Where a child is illegally deprived of some or all of the elements of his or her identity, States Parties shall provide appropriate assistance and protection, with a view to re-establishing speedily his or her identity.

Table 2 Article 8 Indicator sets

Core attributes	
Establishment of criminal and procedural preventive measures	**Establishment of protective legal and administrative procedures**
Data is collected and disaggregated by prohibited grounds for discrimination including age, sex, ethnicity, disability, when applicable	
Structural indicators	
1. The state has ratified the *International Convention for the Protection of All Persons from Enforced Disappearance*, 2007. 2. National legislation is in place to ensure that indigenous and minority children may receive indigenous names of their parents' choice in accordance with their cultural traditions and the right to preserve their identity.	
3. Laws criminalise falsification, concealment or destruction of documents attesting to the true identity of the child. 4. Laws stipulates unlawful interference with children's rights to preserve their identity is an offence, subject to penalties. 5. There are independent criminal and administrative oversight mechanisms for children affected by loss of identity to seek redress and remedy for their infringed identity rights.	6. There are legal procedures in place to review adoptions and, where appropriate, to annul any adoption or placement of children that originated in an enforced disappearance. 7. Laws and mechanisms are in place to provide for compensation of any damage or loss of rights during time affected with enforced disappearance and/or related cases of irregular adoptions. (Art 39) 8. Laws and mechanisms are in place to protect the child's right to preservation of their identity for children in divorce settings; for stateless children; in situations of conflict for refugee children; for indigenous children; through records of family for children adopted or in care; for children with disabilities
Process indicators	
9. A DNA database is established to re-establish identity for speedy family reunification. (Art 30) 10. Search and family reunification programmes are in place for disappeared children and the return of children to their families of origin. Rehabilitation programmes for affected children until they are 18 years are in place, if needed.	11. (GCRD) Preventive measures are in place such as missing children helplines, public information campaigns for families and children about preservation of identity. 12. Administrative and budgetary resources are provided to trace and unite missing children or missing family members affected with enforced disappearance and/or related cases of irregular adoptions. 13. Government has put in place mechanisms for accessing birth records for children legally adopted or born through assisted reproduction techniques

(continued)

Table 2 (continued)

Outcome indicators	
14. Number of cases of enforced disappearances in which, after the conclusion of the trial: • A conviction was handed down • An acquittal was handed down • A custodial sentence was handed down and enforced • The sentence was time-barred or liability was discharged for failure to enforce it within the established deadline. 15. (SDG 16.101 adapted) Number of verified cases of killing, kidnapping, enforced disappearance of children (and/or adults with children) in the previous 12 months.	16. Number of children or parents affected with enforced disappearance. 17. Percentage of children whose identity was restored after an incidence of enforced disappearance. 18. Percentage of children born through adoption or assisted reproduction techniques able to access information on biological origins in the previous 12 months

Article 8—Guidance

The following provides guidance for the collection of data on specific indicators for Article 8. The number relates to the number of that indicator in the table above. Each indicator is identified as a Process, Structural, or Outcome Indicator, and the formula to calculate the data is described.

Indicator 17—Outcome

Percentage of children whose identity was restored after an incidence of enforced disappearance.

Numerator: Number of children whose identities were restored after an incidence of enforced disappearance.

Denominator: Number of children affected by enforced disappearance.

Formula: (Numerator/denominator) × 100.

Indicator 18—Outcome

Percentage of children born through adoption or assisted reproduction techniques able to access information on biological origins.

Numerator: Number of children born through adoption or assisted reproduction techniques able to access information on biological origins.

Denominator: Total number of children born through adoption or assisted reproduction techniques in the previous 12 months.

Formula: (Numerator/denominator) × 100.

Article 13—Freedom of Expression

1. The child shall have the right to freedom of expression; this right shall include freedom to seek, receive and impart information and ideas of all kinds, regardless of frontiers, either orally, in writing or in print, in the form of art, or through any other media of the child's choice.
2. The exercise of this right may be subject to certain restrictions, but these shall only be such as are provided by law and are necessary:
   (a) For respect of the rights or reputations of others; or.
   (b) For the protection of national security or of public order (*ordre public*), or of public health or morals.

Table 3 Article 13 Indicator sets

Core attributes			
Access to information	**Freedom to impart information**	**Special duties and responsibilities**	**Limitations and restrictions**
Data is collected and disaggregated by prohibited grounds for discrimination including age, sex, ethnicity, disability, when applicable.			
Structural indicators			
1. State has ratified relevant international treaty obligations, in particular: • *International Covenant on Civil and Political Rights*, 1966 • *United Nations Convention on the Rights of Persons with Disabilities*, 2006. 2. Legislation protects Article 13 rights, including children of marginalised groups.			
		3. Legislation is in place to regulate online environments to guarantee children's right to freedom of expression and protect against surveillance, censorship, and arbitrary interference.	4. The only permitted restrictions on the right to freedom of expression are consistent with those set out in paragraph 2 of Article 13.
5. Codes of conduct and ethics in relation to children's right to expression for public and private sector media organisations and person online and offline are in place. 6. An independent monitoring mechanism on access to information and privacy is established with a mandate to address the rights of children.			

(continued)

Table 3 (continued)

Process indicators			
6. Percentage of children who have access to the internet at home, disaggregated by: • Primary school age • Secondary school age			7. Restrictions on the child's right to express views written or verbally, are consistent with paragraph 2 of Article 13 (for the protection of national security, public order, or rights or health of others).
	8. (GCRD) Percentage of primary and secondary schools that educate children about boundaries of freedom of speech to prevent harmful comments.	9. Remedies are in place to protect all children from arbitrary interference with their freedom of expression. (e.g. complaint mechanisms).	
Outcome indicators			
10. Percentage of children who report that their right to freedom of expression (both to access and impart information) is respected at school. 11. Number of complaints filed by children or on behalf of children, to the national authorities for violation of Article 13.			
	12. Number of children who have been prosecuted for exercising their right to freedom of expression (imparting information).		

Article 13—Guidance

The following provides guidance for the collection of data on specific indicators for Article 13. The number relates to the number of that indicator in the table above. Each indicator is identified as a Process, Structural, or Outcome Indicator, and the formula to calculate the data is described.

Indicator 6—Process

Percentage of children who have access to the internet at home, disaggregated by:

6.1 Primary school age

Numerator: Number of primary school-age children who have access to the internet at home.
Denominator: Total number of primary school-age children.
Formula: (numerator / denominator) × 100.

6.2 Secondary school age
Numerator: Number of secondary school-age children who have access to the internet at home.
Denominator: Total number of secondary school-age children.
Formula: (numerator / denominator) × 100.

Indicator 8—Process

Percentage of primary and secondary schools that educate children about boundaries of freedom of speech to prevent harmful comments. For example, racist, sexist, and/or homophobic comments.

Numerator: Number of primary and secondary schools that educate children about boundaries of freedom of speech to prevent harmful comments.
Denominator: Total number of primary and secondary schools in the country.
Formula: (numerator/denominator) × 100.

Indicator 10—Outcome

Percentage of children who report that their right to freedom of expression, both to access and to impart information, is respected at school.

Numerator: Number of children who report that their right to freedom of expression (both to access and impart information) is respected at school.
Denominator: Total number of children going to school, based on the schools surveyed.
Formula: (numerator/denominator) × 100.

Article 14—Freedom of Thought, Conscience, and Religion

1. States Parties shall respect the right of the child to freedom of thought, conscience and religion.
2. States Parties shall respect the rights and duties of the parents and, when applicable, legal guardians, to provide direction to the child in the exercise of his or her right in a manner consistent with the evolving capacities of the child.
3. Freedom to manifest one's religion or beliefs may be subject only to such limitations as are prescribed by law and are necessary to protect public safety, order, health or morals, or the fundamental rights and freedoms of others.

Table 4 Article 14 Indicator sets

Core attributes		
Restrictions on children's freedom of thought, conscience, and religion	**Protection against state indoctrination**	**Protection against religious and moral instruction imposed by parents**
Data is collected and disaggregated by prohibited grounds for discrimination including age, sex, ethnicity, disability, when applicable.		
Structural indicators		
1. State has ratified relevant international treaty obligations, in particular: • *International Covenant on Civil and Political Rights,* 1966 • *United Nations Convention on the Rights of Persons with Disabilities,* 2006. 2. Legislation recognises the child's right to freedom of thought, conscience and religion as guaranteed in Article 14 and provides adequate and effective guarantees to all without exclusion or discrimination. 3. The only permitted restrictions on the right to freedom of thought, conscience and religion are imposed by law and are consistent with Article 14(3).		
Process indicators		
4. Measures are in place to prevent any violations of children's activities in relation to freedom of thought, conscience, and religion.	5. Measures are in place to ensure that religious and moral education (included 'conscientious objection' to military training) in institutions of care and education respect children's own existing and evolving convictions.	6. Measures are in place to ensure that no child, individually or collectively, are compelled to receive religious and moral instruction inconsistent with their convictions, on the basis of parental authority, without considering the age and maturity of the child.

(continued)

Table 4 (continued)

7. Mechanisms and institutions are in place to enforce Article 14 included sanctions for violations. 8. Mechanisms exist for children to make complaints regarding breaches of their right under Article 14. 9. National awareness campaigns have been undertaken to promote religious tolerance, respect for people of different religious commitments and dialogue in society.		
10. Policy measures and protocols are in place to guarantee the children's freedom of thought, conscience, and religion in institutional settings, for example, and not limited to, custodial, formal systems of education and care, and correctional institutions.		
11. Disaggregated data is periodically collected and made public regarding children's religious affiliations	12. Percentage of school and care institutions providing ethical, philosophical and multi religious education.	
Outcome indicators		
13. (SDG 16.10 Adapted target 16.b) Percentage of children aged 12–17 years who aware of their right to freedom of thought, conscience, and religion. 14. Percentage of children aged 12–17 years reporting having felt discriminated against or harassed on the basis of their thought, conscience and/or religion. 15. Number of children aged 12–17 years who have been prosecuted for freedom of thought, conscience, and religion.		

Article 14—Guidance

The following provides guidance for the collection of data on specific indicators for Article 14. The number relates to the number of that indicator in the table above. Each indicator is identified as a Process, Structural, or Outcome Indicator, and the formula to calculate the data is described.

Indicator 12—Process

Percentage of school and care institutions providing ethical, philosophical and multi religious education.

Numerator: Number of school and care institutions providing ethical, philosophical and multi religious education.

Denominator: Total number of school and care institutions.

Formula: (Numerator/denominator) × 100.

Indicator 13—Outcome

Percentage of children aged 12–17 years who are aware of their right to freedom of thought, conscience, and religion.

Numerator: Number of children aged 12–17 years who are aware of their right to freedom of thought, conscience, and religion.

Denominator: Total number of children aged 12–17 years surveyed.

Formula: (numerator/denominator) × 100.

Indicator 14—Outcome

Percentage of children aged 12–17 years reporting having felt discriminated against or harassed on the basis of their thought, conscience and/or religion.

Numerator: Number of children aged 12–17 years reporting having felt discriminated against or harassed on the basis of their thought, conscience and/or religion.

Denominator: Total number of children aged 12–17 years surveyed.

Formula: (numerator/denominator) × 100.

Article 15—Freedom of Association and Assembly

1. States Parties recognize the rights of the child to freedom of association and to freedom of peaceful assembly.
2. No restrictions may be placed on the exercise of these rights other than those imposed in conformity with the law and which are necessary in a democratic society in the interests of national security or public safety, public order (*ordre public*), the protection of public health or morals or the protection of the rights and freedoms of others.

Article 15 Indicator sets		
Core attributes		
Freedom of association	**Freedom of assembly**	**Restrictions limited to compliance with democratic interests**
Data is collected and disaggregated by prohibited grounds for discrimination including age, sex, ethnicity, disability, when applicable.		

<table>
<tr><td colspan="3">Structural indicators</td></tr>
<tr><td colspan="3">1. State has ratified relevant international treaty obligations with no significant exemptions:
• International Covenant on Civil and Political Rights, 1966
• United Nations Convention on the Rights of Persons with Disabilities, 2006
• International Labour Organization (ILO) Conventions No. 87, 1948 and No. 98, 1949
2. Right to freedom of association and assembly, in line with international treaty obligations, and including for children, is enshrined in constitution and legislation.</td></tr>
<tr><td>3. No legislative restrictions exist that impede the establishment of children's organisations.</td><td>4. No legislative age restrictions exist on the right to freedom of assembly.
5. Legislation guarantees relevant and appropriate protection for children exercising the right to peaceful assembly.</td><td>6. Legislation protects against:
• Discrimination in the exercise of freedoms of assembly and association
• Undue restrictions of freedoms of assembly and association beyond those necessary for compliance with democratic interests.</td></tr>
<tr><td colspan="3">7. Safe and accessible mechanisms for complaint or redress for children are in place whose Article 15 rights are denied.</td></tr>
<tr><td colspan="3">Process indicators</td></tr>
<tr><td>8. State provides information and support to facilitate the establishment of children's organisations.
9. Children are able to register their own organisations.
10. Percentage of active, democratically elected school councils in:
• Primary schools
• Secondary schools
11. Percentage of local authorities with active, democratically elected youth councils.
12. Number of trade unions allowing membership of working children.</td><td>13. (GCRD) Percentage of police with appropriate pre- and/or in-service training to support and protect children engaging in peaceful assembly.
14. Effective systems for monitoring and reporting on the use of force have been established by the state.</td><td>15. The criteria for imposition of any restrictions on freedom of association and assembly are publicly available.</td></tr>
<tr><td colspan="3">Outcome indicators</td></tr>
<tr><td colspan="3">16. Percentage of children in primary and secondary school who are aware of their right to freedom of association and assembly, and how to exercise it.</td></tr>
<tr><td>17. Percentage of all working children who are members of a trade union or working children's association.
18. Numbers of children actively and voluntarily participating in child and youth-led organisations.</td><td colspan="2">19. Number of reported formal complaints by or on behalf of children forcibly required to participate in protests, marches, or demonstrations.
20. Number of reported formal complaints by or on behalf of children denied the right to freedom of assembly.
21. Percentage of school-aged children who report feeling safe when meeting friends in public spaces.
22. Percentage of children who report having adequate opportunity to spend time with friends.</td></tr>
</table>

Article 15—Guidance

The following provides guidance for the collection of data on specific indicators for Article 15. The number relates to the number of that indicator in the table above. Each indicator is identified as a Process, Structural, or Outcome Indicator, and the formula to calculate the data is described.

Indicator 10—Process

Percentage of active, democratically elected school councils in:

10.1 Primary schools
Numerator: Number of active democratically elected school councils in primary schools.
Denominator: Total number of primary schools.
Formula: (numerator /denominator) × 100.
10.2 Secondary schools
Numerator: Number of active democratically elected school councils in secondary schools.
Denominator: Total number of schools of secondary schools.
Formula: (numerator /denominator) × 100.

Indicator 11—Process

Percentage of local authorities (for example, city hall or religious organisations) with active, democratically elected youth councils.
Numerator: Number of local authorities with active, democratically elected youth councils.
Denominator: Total number of local authorities.
Formula: (numerator/denominator) × 100.

Indicator 13—Process

Percentage of police with appropriate pre- and/or in-service training to support and protect children engaging in peaceful assembly.
Numerator: Number of police with appropriate pre- and/or in-service training to support and protect children engaging in peaceful assembly.
Denominator: Total number of police.
Formula: (numerator/denominator) × 100.

Indicator 16—Outcome

Percentage of children in primary and secondary school who are aware of their right to freedom of association and assembly, and how to exercise it.

Numerator: Number of children in primary and secondary school who are aware of their right to freedom of association and assembly, and how to exercise it.

Denominator: Total number of children in primary and secondary schools surveyed.

Formula: (numerator/denominator) × 100.

Indicator 17—Outcome

Percentage of all working children who are members of a trade union or working children's association.

Numerator: Number of working children who are members of a trade union or working children's association.

Denominator: Total number of working children.

Formula: (numerator/denominator) × 100.

Indicator 21—Outcome

Percentage of school-aged children who report feeling safe when meeting friends in public spaces.

Numerator: Number of school-aged children who report feeling safe when meeting friends in public spaces.

Denominator: Total number of school-aged children surveyed.

Formula: (numerator/denominator) × 100.

Indicator 22—Outcome

Percentage of children who report having adequate opportunity to spend time with friends.

Numerator: Number of children who report having adequate opportunity to spend time with friends.

Denominator: Total number of children surveyed.

Formula: (numerator/denominator) × 100.

Article 16—Right to Privacy

1. No child shall be subjected to arbitrary or unlawful interference with his or her privacy, family, home or correspondence, nor to unlawful attacks on his or her honour and reputation.
2. The child has the right to the protection of the law against such interference or attacks.

Article 16 Indicator sets			
Core attributes			
Interference with privacy	**Interference with family, home, or correspondence**	**Unlawful attacks upon honour and reputation**	**Protection of the law against unlawful interference or attacks**
Data is collected and disaggregated by prohibited grounds for discrimination including age, sex, ethnicity, disability, when applicable.			
Structural indicators			
1. State has ratified relevant international treaty obligations, in particular: • *International Covenant on Civil and Political Rights*, 1966 • *United Nations Convention on the Rights of Persons with Disabilities*, 2006. 2. Legislation guarantees the right to privacy including data protection. 3. Accessible and enforceable remedies exist to provide recourse to children in cases of privacy violation in relation to cyberbullying, luring, exploitation online, targeted marketing to children, data mining of children's online activities, unauthorised uses of their images, protection of their biological data, informational privacy, their ties to family and intimacy, video surveillance, social media use, and their right to be forgotten. 4. A comprehensive national strategy to protect children's privacy in the digital age is in place.			
Process indicators			
5. Percentage of all reported complaints to specialised human rights institutions in relation to child privacy violations.			
		6. Rate of reporting and removal of online child privacy violations by internet service providers and law enforcement.	7. Percentage of children using the internet who interacted online in the past 12 months with persons they had not met before in person

Outcome indicators		
8. Percentage of children who report having been victims of cyberbullying in the past 2 months (see also art. 19). 9. Percentage of children in primary and secondary school who feel safe reporting an incident of cyberbullying to school officials.	10. Percentage of children living in households where data privacy principles and social media use rules are discussed and respected.	11. Percentage of children who report that their privacy is respected in, for example: • Care • Custody • Schools • Hospitals.

Article 16—Guidance

The following provides guidance for the collection of data on specific indicators for Article 16. The number relates to the number of that indicator in the table above. Each indicator is identified as a Process, Structural, or Outcome Indicator, and the formula to calculate the data is described.

Indicator 5—Process

Percentage of all reported complaints reported to specialised human rights institutions in relation to child privacy violations.

Numerator: Number of reported complaints reported to specialised human rights institutions in relation to child privacy violations.

Denominator: Total number of complaints reported to specialised human rights institutions.

Formula: (numerator/denominator) × 100.

Indicator 6—Process

Rate of reporting and removal of online child privacy violations by Internet Service Providers and law enforcement.

Numerator: Number of online child privacy violations reported and removed (by Internet Service Providers and law enforcement) within the reporting period.

Denominator: Total number of online privacy violation reported and removed (by Internet Service Providers and law enforcement) within the same reporting period.

Formula: (numerator/denominator) Disaggregated by Internet Service Providers and law enforcement, within reporting period.

Indicator 7—Process

Percentage of children using the internet who interacted online in the past 12 months with persons they had not met before in person, by sex and age.

Numerator: Number of children using the internet who interacted online in the past 12 months with person they had not met before in person, by sex and age.

Denominator: Total number of children using the internet surveyed.

Formula: (numerator/denominator) × 100.

Indicator 8—Outcome

Percentage of children who report having been victims of cyberbullying in the past 2 months.

Numerator: Number of children who report having been victims of cyberbullying in the past 2 months.

Denominator: Total number of children surveyed.

Formula: (numerator/denominator) × 100.

Indicator 9—Outcome

Percentage of children in primary and secondary school who feel safe reporting an incident of cyberbullying to school officials.

Numerator: Number of children in primary and secondary school who say they feel safe reporting an incident of cyberbullying to school officials.

Denominator: Total number of children in primary and secondary school surveyed.

Formula: (numerator/denominator) × 100.

Indicator 10—Outcome

Percentage of children living in households where data privacy principles and social media use rules are discussed and respected.

Numerator: Number of children living in households where data privacy principles and social media use rules are discussed and respected.

Denominator: Total number of children living in households surveyed.

Formula: (Numerator/denominator) × 100.

Indicator 11—Outcome

Percentage of children who report that their privacy is respected in, for example:

- Care
- Custody
- Schools
- Hospitals

Numerator: Number of children who report that their privacy is respected in the institutional setting selected.

Denominator: Total number of children surveyed in the selected institutional setting.

Formula: (numerator/denominator) × 100.

Article 17—Right to Information

States Parties recognize the important function performed by the mass media and shall ensure that the child has access to information and material from a diversity of national and international sources, especially those aimed at the promotion of his or her social, spiritual and moral well-being and physical and mental health.

To this end, States Parties shall:

(a) Encourage the mass media to disseminate information and material of social and cultural benefit to the child and in accordance with the spirit of Article 29;
(b) Encourage international co-operation in the production, exchange and dissemination of such information and material from a diversity of cultural, national and international sources;
(c) Encourage the production and dissemination of children's books;
(d) Encourage the mass media to have particular regard to the linguistic needs of the child who belongs to a minority group or who is indigenous;
(e) Encourage the development of appropriate guidelines for the protection of the child from information and material injurious to his or her well-being, bearing in mind the provisions of articles 13 and 18.

Article 17 Indicator sets			
Core attributes			
Diversity of sources and media	**Beneficial information and material**	**Access to mass media**	**Protection from harmful material**
Data is collected and disaggregated by prohibited grounds for discrimination including age, sex, ethnicity, disability, when applicable.			

<table>
<tr><th colspan="4">Structural indicators</th></tr>
<tr><td colspan="4">1. State has ratified relevant international treaty obligations, in particular:
• International Covenant on Civil and Political Rights, 1966
• United Nations Convention on the Rights of Persons with Disabilities, 2006.
2. Relevant international treaty obligations are reflected to the extent possible in domestic rights to access to mass media.
3. (SDG 16.10.2 adapted) Constitutional and/or legislative guarantees for children's access to information are in place.
4. Accessible, safe mechanisms of complaint or redress are in place for children whose Article 17 rights are denied.</td></tr>
<tr><th colspan="4">Process indicators</th></tr>
<tr><td>5. State promotes international cooperation in production, exchange, and dissemination of information from a diversity of sources.
6. Number of media institutions of ethnic, linguistic minority and religious population groups recognised or given public support and are compliant with children's rights.</td><td>7. Children are provided, through as many forums as possible (e.g. social media, TV, radio), with access to socially and culturally beneficial and accurate information promoting, for example:
• Understanding, peace, and tolerance
• Health and healthy lifestyles
• Sexual and reproductive health
• Children's rights
8. (GCRD) School curriculum includes digital literacy education to provide children with the competence and resilience to engage safely and wisely in the digital environment (see also art. 29).</td><td>9. Percentage of children with access to TV and radio broadcasts.
10. Percentage of primary and secondary schools with libraries containing children's literature (see also art. 29).
11. (SDG 9c adapted) Percentage of all children with adequate, affordable, and secure access to the internet in the home.</td><td>12. State has supported the development of guidelines to protect children from material injurious to their well-being.
13. State co-operates with media to develop awareness-raising programmes aimed at protecting children from harmful content.
14. Percentage of school-age children provided with education to promote understanding of keeping safe online and being responsible digital citizens (see also art. 29).</td></tr>
<tr><th colspan="4">Outcome indicators</th></tr>
<tr><td>15. Percentage of children accessing media from multiple sources including TV, radio, digital media, newspapers, magazines, and books.</td><td>16. Percentage of primary and secondary school children citing digital media as a positive source of information (see also art. 29).</td><td>17. Number of school-age children engaged as active participants within mass media.
18. Number of children using public libraries.
19. Percentage of children from different linguistic population groups having access to media broadcasts in their own language (see also art. 30).</td><td>20. Percentage of parents aware of parental controls to mitigate risks for children in the digital environment.
21. Percentage of children citing being exposed to information promoting discrimination, racism, misogyny, violence.</td></tr>
</table>

Article 17—Guidance

The following provides guidance for the collection of data on specific indicators for Article 17. The number relates to the number of that indicator in the table above. Each indicator is identified as a Process, Structural, or Outcome Indicator, and the formula to calculate the data is described.

Indicator 9—Process

Percentage of children with access to TV and radio broadcasts.

Numerator: Number of children with access to TV and radio broadcasts.

Denominator: Total number of children.

Formula: (numerator/denominator) × 100.

Indicator 10—Process

Percentage of primary and secondary schools with libraries containing children's literature.

Numerator: Number of primary and secondary schools with libraries containing children's literature.

Denominator: Total number of primary and secondary schools.

Formula: (numerator/denominator) × 100.

Indicator 11—Process

Percentage of all children with adequate, affordable, and secure access to the internet in the home.

Numerator: Number of children with adequate, affordable, and secure access to the internet in the home.

Denominator: Total number of children.

Formula: (numerator/denominator) × 100.

Indicator 14—Process

Percentage of school-age children provided with education to promote understanding of keeping safe online and being responsible digital citizens.

Numerator: Number of school-age children provided with education to promote understanding of keeping safe online and being responsible digital citizens.

Denominator: Total number of school-age children.

Formula: (numerator/denominator) × 100.

Indicator 15—Outcome

Percentage of children accessing media from multiple sources including TV, radio, digital media, newspapers, magazines, and books.

Numerator: Number of children accessing media from multiple sources including TV, radio, digital media, newspapers, magazines, and books.

Denominator: Total number of children.

Formula: (numerator/denominator) × 100.

Indicator 16—Outcome

Percentage of primary and secondary school children citing digital media as a positive source of information.

Numerator: Number of primary and secondary school children citing digital media as a positive source of information.

Denominator: Total number of school-age children using digital media.

Formula: (numerator/denominator) × 100.

Indicator 19—Outcome

Percentage of children from different linguistic population groups having access to media broadcasts in their own language.

Numerator: Number of children from different linguistic population groups having access to media broadcasts in their own language.

Denominator: Total number of children from different linguistic populations.

Formula: (numerator/denominator) × 100.

Indicator 20—Outcome

Percentage of parents aware of parental controls to mitigate risks for children in the digital environment.

Numerator: Number of parents aware of parental controls to mitigate risks for children in the digital environment.

Denominator: Total number of parents of dependent children.

Formula: (numerator/denominator) × 100.

Indicator 21—Outcome

Percentage of children citing being exposed to information promoting discrimination, racism, misogyny, violence.

Numerator: Number of children citing being exposed to information promoting discrimination, racism, misogyny, violence.

Denominator: Total number of children who are exposed to mass media information.

Formula: (numerator/denominator) × 100.

Chapter 6
Family Environment and Alternative Care Rights

Ziba Vaghri, Roberta Ruggiero, Gerison Lansdown, Adem Arkadas-Thibert, and Christian Whalen

The Convention on the Rights of the Child contains several articles focused on the relationship of the child within the family:[1]

- Article 5—parental guidance and the child's evolving capacities
- Article 9—separation from parents
- Article 10—family reunification

[1] For further elaboration on the implications and implementation of each of these rights, please read the relevant chapter in the companion publication to this book: *Monitoring State Compliance with the UN Convention on the Rights of the Child: An analysis of attributes*, Vaghri, Zermatten, Lansdown and Ruggiero, Springer, 2022.

Z. Vaghri
GlobalChild Program of Research, University of New Brunswick, Saint John, NB, Canada

R. Ruggiero (✉)
Centre for Children's Right Studies, Faculty of Law, University of Geneva, Geneva, Switzerland
e-mail: Roberta.ruggiero@unige.ch

G. Lansdown
School of Law, University College Cork, Cork, Ireland

A. Arkadas-Thibert
Independent Researcher, Specializing in International Human Rights, Marseille, France

C. Whalen
Faculty of Law, University of New Brunswick, Fredericton, NB, Canada

Z. Vaghri et al. (eds.), *Children's Rights-Based Indicators*, Children's Well-Being: Indicators and Research 28,
https://doi.org/10.1007/978-3-031-71594-5_6

- Article 11—illicit transfer and non-return
- Article 18—parental responsibilities
- Article 20—protection of a child without family
- Article 21—adoption
- Article 25—periodic review of placement

Together, these articles provide a comprehensive framework for respecting, protecting, and fulfilling the rights of children in the context of their need for care, whatever their family circumstances. On the one hand, the Convention seeks to affirm the primacy of parents as the main caregivers of their children, and to require the state to meet a range of obligations to support parents in that role. On the other hand, the Convention introduces measures to render the child visible within the context of the family, imposing certain parameters on the autonomy and authority of parents in respect of the nature of direction and guidance they can provide to the child. Additional articles address the measures that are needed to protect the rights of the child when the family is unable to provide appropriate care for a child.

Article 5 introduces the concept of the evolving capacities of the child, recognising the gradual assumption of capacities through the process of childhood, and requiring that parents adapt their direction and guidance in accordance with that transition. It establishes the principle that such guidance must be appropriate and directed to the exercise by the child of their rights. In so doing, Article 5 challenges the traditional assumption that parents 'own' their children. The rights parents have in respect of a child only exist far so long as children cannot exercise their rights for themselves, and their behaviour towards and treatment of the child must always comply with all rights in the Convention.

Articles 9 and 18 focus on the centrality of the family in the lives of children. Article 9 places limitations on the powers of the state to separate children from families unless so doing is in their best interests. Article 18 affirms the importance of both parents in the life of a child, recognises that promoting the child's best interests is parents' primary concern, and places obligations on states to provide assistance and support to families in fulfilling their parenting role.

Articles 10 and 11 address the situations where children might be separated from families. While Article 10 introduces requirements to facilitate family reunification, Article 11 imposes obligations to adopt measures to prevent the illicit transfer and non-return of children abroad.

Finally, Articles 20, 21, and 25 introduce protections and demand appropriate standards of care for children when they are placed in the care of people other than their family. Article 20 requires that forms of alternative care must be provided for children unable to be looked after by their parents. Article 21 addresses the regulatory and protective framework that needs to be in place when children are placed for adoption either within their own country or internationally. Article 25 demands that any child placed away from home for protection, care, or treatment, must have their treatment and circumstances periodically reviewed.

Article 5—The Right to Parental Guidance Consistent with the Evolving Capacities of the Child

1. States Parties recognize that every child has the inherent right to life.
2. States Parties shall ensure to the maximum extent possible the survival and development of the child.

Table 1 Article 5 Indicator sets

Core attributes		
Respect for the primacy of parents and comparable care givers	**Appropriate direction and guidance**	**Evolving capacities of the child**
Data is collected and disaggregated by prohibited grounds for discrimination including age, sex, ethnicity, disability, when applicable.		
Structural indicators		
1. Legislation recognises parental responsibilities, rights and duties as extending to parents or where applicable, members of the extended family or community as provided by local custom, legal guardians, or other persons legally responsible for the child. 2. Legislation recognises different family forms and prohibits discrimination against parents on grounds of marital status, sexual orientation, sexual or gender identity.	3. Legislation provides a detailed definition of parental rights and responsibilities affirming that they: • Must be exercised without discrimination • Must be exercised in accordance with best interests of the child • Must take account of the expressed views of the child • Cannot be exercised in a manner that would serve to violate or neglect any right embodied in the CRC • Must provide guidance and direction for children in exercising their child rights. 4. Legal definition of parental responsibility is embedded in policies related to family support services, early years education, childcare services, child protection, education, and health.	5. Legislation/constitution provides recognition of the child's right to respect for their evolving capacities in the exercise of their rights. 6. Legislation introduces age limits without discrimination to protect children from premature exposure to harm including, for example: • Marriage • Child labour • Use and sale of tobacco • Alcohol • Recruitment into armed forces. 7. Legislation introduces age limits without discrimination recognising children's evolving capacities, for example: • Consent to adoption • Medical consent to treatment • Sexual consent • Access to sexual and reproductive services. 8. Legislation provides that children of any age, and without discrimination, are entitled to access confidential medical counselling (see also art. 24).

(continued)

Table 1 (continued)

Process indicators		
9. Implementation of campaigns to raise awareness of and tolerance towards different family forms.	10. Percentage of parents and other caregivers provided with comprehensive parenting education and support programmes, including on children's rights.	11. Percentage of children provided with information on age limits and their implications in respect of the exercise of rights. 12. Percentage of professionals provided with training on children's rights and respect for their evolving capacities at pre- and/or in-service levels, for example in fields of: • Health • Law • Police • Education • Social work • Social care • Child protection • Early years.
Outcome indicators		
13. Number of cases of children discriminated against on grounds of parental status in the reporting period.	14. Percentage of parents and other caregivers with knowledge about their rights and responsibilities as parents and the rights of the child. 15. Percentage of professionals working with children with knowledge and understanding of legal definition of parental rights and responsibilities. 16. Percentage of all children reporting positive and supportive parental relationships.	17. Percentage of children who consider they are: • Fully aware of relevant age limits in the exercise of rights • Enabled to take responsibility for those decisions/actions they feel competent to take • Supported by relevant adults to take responsibility for those decisions/actions they feel competent to take 18. Percentage of professionals who have knowledge and understanding of children's rights and evolving capacities in the following professional fields, for example: • Health • Law • Police • Education • Social work • Social care • Child protection • Early years 19. Percentage of children aged 14–19 years currently married or in union.

Article 5—Guidance

The following provides guidance for the collection of data on specific indicators for Article 5. The number relates to the number of that indicator in the table above. Each indicator is identified as a Process, Structural, or Outcome Indicator, and the formula to calculate the data is described.

Indicator 10—Process

Percentage of parents and other caregivers provided with comprehensive parenting education and support programmes, including on children's rights.

Numerator: Number of parents and other caregivers provided with comprehensive parenting education and support programmes, including on children's rights.

Denominator: Total number of parents and other caregivers surveyed.

Formula: (numerator/denominator) × 100.

Indicator 11—Process

Percentage of children provided with information on age limits and their implications in respect of the exercise of rights.

Numerator: Number of children provided with information on age limits and their implications in respect of the exercise of rights.

Denominator: Total number of children surveyed.

Formula: (numerator/denominator) × 100.

Indicator 12—Process

Percentage of professionals provided with training on children's rights and respect for their evolving capacities at pre- and/or in-service levels, for example in fields of:

- Health
- Law
- Police
- Education
- Social work
- Social care
- Child protection
- Early years.

Numerator: number of professionals working with children provided with training on children's rights and respect for their evolving capacities at pre- or in-service levels in the selected fields (health, law, police, education, social work, social care, child protection, early years).

Denominator: Total number of professionals working with children.

Formula: (numerator/denominator) × 100.

Indicator 14—Outcome

Percentage of parents and other caregivers with knowledge about their rights and responsibilities as parents and the rights of the child.

Numerator: Number of parents and other caregivers with knowledge about their rights and responsibilities as parents and the rights of the child.

Denominator: Total number of parents and other caregivers surveyed.

Formula: (numerator/denominator) × 100.

Indicator 15—Outcome

Percentage of professionals working with children with knowledge and understanding of legal definition of parental rights and responsibilities.

Numerator: Number of professionals working with children with knowledge and understanding of legal definition of parental rights and responsibilities.

Denominator: Total number of professionals working with children surveyed.

Formula: (numerator/denominator) × 100.

Indicator 16—Outcome

Percentage of all children reporting positive and supportive parental relationships.

Numerator: Number of children reporting positive and supportive parental relationships.

Denominator: Total number of children surveyed.

Formula: (numerator/denominator) × 100.

Indicator 17—Outcome

Percentage of children who consider they are:

17.1 Fully aware of relevant age limits in the exercise of rights.

Numerator: Number of children who consider they are fully aware of relevant age limits in the exercise of rights.

Denominator: Total number of children surveyed.

Formula: (numerator/denominator) × 100.

17.2 Enabled to take responsibility for those decisions/actions they feel competent to take.

Numerator: Number of children who consider they are enabled to take responsibility for those decisions/actions they feel competent to take.

Denominator: Total number of children surveyed.

Formula: (numerator/denominator) × 100.

17.3 Supported by relevant adults to take responsibility for those decisions/actions they feel competent to take.

Numerator: Number of children who consider they are supported by relevant adults to take responsibility for those decisions/actions they feel competent to take.

Denominator: Total number of children surveyed.

Formula: (numerator/denominator) × 100.

Indicator 18—Outcome

Percentage of professionals in the fields of health, law, police, education, social work, social care, child protection, early years, who have knowledge and understanding of children's rights and evolving capacities.

Numerator: Number of professionals in the fields of health, law, police, education, social work, social care, child protection, early years who have knowledge and understanding of children's rights and evolving capacities.

Denominator: Total number of professionals in the fields of health, law, police, education, social work, social care, child protection, early years.

Formula: (numerator/ denominator) × 100.

Indicator 19—Outcome

Percentage of children aged 14–19 years currently married or in union.

Numerator: Number of children aged 14–19 years currently married or in union.

Denominator: Total number of children of children aged 14–19 years.

Formula: (numerator/denominator) × 100.

Article 9—The Right Not to Be Separated from Parents

1. States Parties shall ensure that a child shall not be separated from his or her parents against their will, except when competent authorities subject to judicial review determine, in accordance with applicable law and procedures, that such separation is necessary for the best interests of the child. Such determination may be necessary in a particular case such as one involving abuse or neglect of the child by the parents, or one where the parents are living separately, and a decision must be made as to the child's place of residence.
2. In any proceedings pursuant to paragraph 1 of the present article, all interested parties shall be given an opportunity to participate in the proceedings and make their views known.
3. States Parties shall respect the right of the child who is separated from one or both parents to maintain personal relations and direct contact with both parents on a regular basis, except if it is contrary to the child's best interests.
4. Where such separation results from any action initiated by a State Party, such as the detention, imprisonment, exile, deportation or death (including death arising from any cause while the person is in the custody of the State) of one or both parents or of the child, that State Party shall, upon request, provide the parents, the child or, if appropriate, another member of the family with the essential information concerning the whereabouts of the absent member(s) of the family unless the provision of the information would be detrimental to the well-being of the child. States Parties shall further ensure that the submission of such a request shall of itself entail no adverse consequences for the person(s) concerned.

Table 2 Article 9 Indicator sets

Core attributes			
No separation from parents unless necessary in child's best interests	**No separation from parents without due process before competent authorities**	**Right to maintain contact and relations with parents if separated**	**Right to be informed of whereabouts of parent or child if detained**
Data is collected and disaggregated by prohibited grounds for discrimination including age, sex, ethnicity, disability, when applicable.			
Structural indicators			
1. National legislation explicitly recognises the rights and guarantees embodied in Article 9. 2. Accessible remedies and protections are available to children removed from their parents' care, including: • Child-friendly information and advocacy services • Independent legal representation. 3. The national strategy to protect children's rights includes measures in respect of separation and continued contact with parents.			

(continued)

Table 2 (continued)

Process indicators			
4. Number of cases of children separated from parents by the domestic courts in the past 12 months. 5. Percentage of court cases involving the possible removal of a child that are diverted through alternate dispute resolution processes (collaborative family law practices, family group conferencing, etc.) in the past 12 months. 6. Percentage of independent human rights institution (IHRI) complaints involving children that deal with matters involving the child's separation from their parents. 7. Effective child-friendly justice practices exist in child protection and custody matters (see also art. 12).	8. Percentage of court cases involving placement decisions where the view of the child is given due consideration (see also art. 12).	9. A system for ensuring child/parent contact is in place in different separation contexts, for example: • Child protection • Kinship care or open adoption settings • Child and adult criminal justice • Addictions and psychiatric care • Immigration detention settings.	10. A system is in place to inform children as to the whereabouts of the parent if the parent is detained. 11. A system is in place to inform parents of the whereabouts of the child if the child is detained.
Outcome indicators			
12. Percentage of child-protection matters resolved with a sustainable permanency plan within 24 months.	13. (GCRD) Percentage of children separated from parents who believe that their voices were heard and considered (see also art. 12).		14. Percentage of children of detained parents who report feeling supported and adequately informed through the period of separation.
		15. (GCRD) Percentage of children separated from one or both parents who report being satisfied with the amount of time spent with their family.	

Article 9—Guidance

The following provides guidance for the collection of data on specific indicators for Article 9. The number relates to the number of that indicator in the table above. Each indicator is identified as a Process, Structural, or Outcome Indicator, and the formula to calculate the data is described.

Indicator 5—Process

Percentage of court cases involving the possible removal of a child that are diverted through alternate dispute resolution processes (collaborative family law practices, family group conferencing, etc.) in the past 12 months.

Numerator: Number of court cases involving the possible removal of a child that are diverted through alternate dispute resolution processes.

Denominator: Total number of court cases involving the possible removal of a child.

Formula: (numerator/denominator) × 100.

Indicator 6—Process

Percentage of IHRI complaints involving children that deal with matters involving the child's separation from their parents.

Numerator: Number of IHRI complaints involving children that deal with matters involving the child's separation from their parents.

Denominator: Total number of IHRI complaints involving children.

Formula: (numerator/denominator) × 100.

Indicator 7—Process

Percentage of court cases involving placement decisions where views of the child are given due consideration.

Numerator: Number of court cases involving placement decisions where views of the child are given due consideration.

Denominator: Total number of court decisions involving placement decisions.

Formula: (numerator/denominator) × 100.

Indicator 12—Outcome

Percentage of child-protection matters resolved with a sustainable permanency plan within 24 months.

Numerator: Number of child-protection matters resolved within the year that resulted in a sustainable permanency plan within 24 months of the file being opened.

Denominator: Total number of child-protection matters resolved within the year.

Formula: (numerator/denominator) × 100.

Indicator 13—Outcome

Percentage of children separated from parents who believe that their voices were heard and considered.

Numerator: Number of children separated from parents who believe that their voices were heard and considered.

Denominator: Total number of children separated from parents.

Formula: (numerator/denominator) × 100.

Indicator 14—Outcome

Percentage of children of detained parents who report feeling supported and adequately informed through the period of separation.

Numerator: Number of children of detained parents who report feeling supported and adequately informed through the period of separation.

Denominator: Total number of children of detained parents surveyed.

Formula: (numerator/denominator) × 100.

Indicator 15—Outcome

Percentage of children separated from one or both parents who report being satisfied with the amount of time spent with their family.

Numerator: Number of children separated from one or both parents who report being satisfied with the amount of time spent with their family.

Denominator: Total number of children surveyed.

Formula: (numerator/denominator) × 100.

Article 10—The Right to Family Reunification

1. In accordance with the obligation of States Parties under article 9, paragraph 1, applications by a child or his or her parents to enter or leave a State Party for the purpose of family reunification shall be dealt with by States Parties in a positive, humane and expeditious manner. States Parties shall further ensure that the submission of such a request shall entail no adverse consequences for the applicants and for the members of their family.

2. A child whose parents reside in different States shall have the right to maintain on a regular basis, save in exceptional circumstances personal relations and direct contacts with both parents. Towards that end and in accordance with the obligation of States Parties under article 9, paragraph 1, States Parties shall respect the right of the child and his or her parents to leave any country, including their own, and to enter their own country. The right to leave any country shall be subject only to such restrictions as are prescribed by law and which are necessary to protect the national security, public order (*ordre public*), public health or morals or the rights and freedoms of others and are consistent with the other rights recognized in the present Convention.

Table 3 Article 10 Indicator sets

Core attributes		
Requests to enter or leave a country for family reunification should be dealt with in a positive, humane, and expeditious manner	**Requests to enter or leave a country should entail no adverse consequences for the child, the parent, or their family members**	**Right to maintain relations and regular contact with both parents, if separated and residing in different states**
Data is collected and disaggregated by prohibited grounds for discrimination including age, sex, ethnicity, disability, when applicable.		
Structural indicators		
1. State has ratified relevant international treaties in this area, including: • *UN Convention Relating to the Status of Refugees*, 1951 • *Protocol Relating to the Status of Refugees*, 1967 • *UN International Covenant on Civil and Political Rights*, 1966. 2. State has entered into bilateral agreements in these matters with neighbouring states. 3. Remedies exist for enforcement of family reunification rights for children living in or visiting parents living in the national territory of the state or leaving their national territory for such purposes. 4. National immigration laws and policies ensure compliance with the convention and relevant treaties.		
Process indicators		
5. Systems for addressing all matters relating to family reunification adhere to principles of child-friendly justice. 6. Percentage of immigration, family court, and child-protection officials trained in child rights in relation to family reunification, child migrants, and child-friendly justice principles.		
7. Average length of time (in days) lasting between initial application and the accomplishment of reunification involving children on the move (see also art. 22). 8. Rate of cross-border family reunification involving children achieved in a 1-year period (see also art. 22). 9. Number of registered children pending reunification (see also art. 22).	10. A system is in place to monitor the safety and security of family members making applications for reunification.	11. A system is in place and is monitored to ensure regular contact between family members pending reunification.

(continued)

Table 3 (continued)

Outcome indicators		
12. Percentage of children applying for reunification who report they are satisfied with the level of contact with their family members. 13. Percentage of children applying for family reunification who express satisfaction with their treatment in their country of residence.		
14. Percentage of children who report a high level of satisfaction in relation to their treatment through the family reunification process.	15. Percentage of children or parents who report adverse treatment for their family members because of their decision to request reunification.	

Article 10—Guidance

The following provides guidance for the collection of data on specific indicators for Article 10. The number relates to the number of that indicator in the table above. Each indicator is identified as a Process, Structural, or Outcome Indicator, and the formula to calculate the data is described.

Indicator 6—Process

Percentage of immigration, family court and child-protection officials trained in child rights in relation to family reunification, child migrants and child-friendly justice principles.

Numerator: Number of immigration, family court, and child-protection workers trained in child rights in relation to family reunification, child migrants, and child-friendly justice principles.

Denominator: Total of workers in immigration, family court, and child protection.

Formula: (numerator/denominator) × 100.

Indicator 8—Process

Rate of cross-border family reunification involving children achieved in a 1-year period.

Numerator: Number of cross-border family reunification involving children achieved in 1-year period.

Denominator: Total number of reunification application involving children for the same year.

Formula: (numerator/denominator) within the year, disaggregated by age, gender, nationality, and ethnicity of the child.

Indicator 12—Outcome

Percentage of children applying for reunification report they are satisfied with the level of contact with their family members.

Numerator: Number of children applying for family reunification who report they are satisfied with the level of contact with their family members.

Denominator: Total number of children applying for family reunification.

Formula: (numerator/denominator) × 100.

Indicator 13—Outcome

Percentage of children applying for family reunification who express satisfaction with their treatment in their country of residence.

Numerator: Number of children applying for family reunification who express satisfaction with their treatment in their country of residence.

Denominator: Total number of children who are applying for family reunification.

Formula: (numerator/denominator) × 100.

Indicator 14—Outcome

Percentage of children who report a high level of satisfaction in relation to their treatment through the family reunification process.

Numerator: Number of children who report a high level of satisfaction in relation to their treatment through the family reunification process.

Denominator: Total number of children applying for family reunification.

Formula: (numerator/denominator) × 100.

Indicator 15—Outcome

Percentage of children or parents who report adverse treatment for their family members because of their decision to request reunification.

Numerator: Number of children or parents who report adverse treatment for their family members because of their decision to request reunification.

Denominator: Total number of children or parents who apply for family reunification.

Formula: (numerator/denominator) × 100.

Article 11—The Right to Protection from Illicit Transfer and Non-return of Children Abroad

1. States Parties shall take measures to combat the illicit transfer and non-return of children abroad.
2. To this end, States Parties shall promote the conclusion of bilateral or multilateral agreements or accession to existing agreements.

Table 4 Article 11 Indicator sets

Core attributes	
Measures to combat the illicit transfer and non-return of children abroad	**Measures to promote the conclusion of bilateral or multilateral agreements or accession to existing agreements**
Data is collected and disaggregated by prohibited grounds for discrimination including age, sex, ethnicity, disability, when applicable.	
Structural indicators	
1. State has ratified the *Hague Convention on the Civil Aspects of International Child Abduction, 1980.* 2. Immigration laws of the state allow for entry of a parent or the person, institution, or other body having the legal care of the child who has been separated from a child due to abduction, as well as allowing for the child to leave a country for reunification (see also art. 10). 3. A Central Authority, which Contracting states must establish, exists to facilitate, where appropriate, the return of the child to their home country, pursuant to the *Hague Convention on the Civil Aspects of International Child Abduction,* 1980. 4. The state's border security practices and protocols are in place that specifically address child abduction prevention. 5. The national strategy on children's rights includes measures to combat parental child abduction. 6. Legislation requires establishment of child-friendly procedures across all stages of child abduction and non-return, to facilitate the right of the child to (see also art. 12): • Be heard in any administrative or judicial processes related to child abduction • Have their views be given due weight in accordance with the child's age and maturity.	7. A policy is in place to promote the conclusion of bilateral / multilateral agreements signed to prevent and/or remedy child abduction.

(continued)

Table 4 (continued)

Process indicators	
8. Percentage of cases involving illicit transfer and non-return of children dealt with by specially trained lawyers. 9. Percentage of cases in which legal aid is available to a parent contesting illicit transfer and non-return of children.	10. Bilateral / multilateral agreements have been signed to prevent and/or remedy child abduction.
Outcome indicators	
11. Percentage of all cases filed resulting in: • Voluntary return • Judicial return • Judicial refusal of return applications. 12. Average time taken (in months) from the receipt of the application by the central authority until the final agreement or court decision (including any appeals; voluntary return; judicial return; judicial refusal). 13. Rate of successful access applications under the *Hague Convention on the Civil Aspects of International Child Abduction, 1980, Article 21.*	14. Number of bilateral / multilateral agreements have been signed to prevent and/or remedy child abduction.

Article 11—Guidance

The following provides guidance for the collection of data on specific indicators for Article 11. The number relates to the number of that indicator in the table above. Each indicator is identified as a Process, Structural, or Outcome Indicator, and the formula to calculate the data is described.

Indicator 8—Process

Percentage of cases involving illicit transfer and non-return of children dealt with by specially trained lawyers.

Numerator: Number of cases of illicit transfer and non-return of children dealt by specially trained lawyers.

Denominator: Total cases of illicit transfer and non-return cases filed.

Formula: (numerator/denominator) × 100.

Indicator 9—Process

Percentage of cases in which legal aid is available to a parent contesting illicit transfer and non-return of children.

Numerator: Number of cases in which legal aid is available to a parent contesting illicit transfer and non-return of children.

Denominator: Total number of parents contesting illicit transfer and non-return.
Formula: (numerator/denominator) × 100.

Indicator 11—Outcome

Percentage of all cases filed resulting in:

11.1 Voluntary return.
Numerator: Number of cases filed resulting in voluntary return.
Denominator: Total number of all cases filed.
Formula: (numerator/denominator) × 100.
11.2 Judicial return.
Numerator: Number of cases filed resulting in judicial return.
Denominator: Total number of all cases filed.
Formula: (numerator/denominator) × 100.
11.3 Judicial refusal of return applications
Numerator: Number of cases filed resulting in judicial refusal of return applications.
Denominator: Total number of all cases filed.
Formula: (numerator/denominator) × 100.

Indicator 13—Outcome

Rate of successful access applications under the *Hague Convention on the Civil Aspects of International Child Abduction,* 1980, Article 21.

Numerator: Number of successful access applications within a given time frame.
Denominator: Total number of access applications within the same time frame.
Formula: (numerator/denominator) since the last Committee report (per an appropriate multiplier).

Article 18—Rights Concerning Parental Responsibility

1. States Parties shall use their best efforts to ensure recognition of the principle that both parents have common responsibilities for the upbringing and development of the child. Parents or, as the case may be, legal guardians, have the primary responsibility for the upbringing and development of the child. The best interests of the child will be their basic concern.
2. For the purpose of guaranteeing and promoting the rights set forth in the present Convention, States Parties shall render appropriate assistance to parents and legal guardians in the performance of their child-rearing responsibilities and shall ensure the development of institutions, facilities and services for the care of children.

3. States Parties shall take all appropriate measures to ensure that children of working parents have the right to benefit from childcare services and facilities for which they are eligible.

Table 5 Article 18 Indicator sets

Core attributes			
Common primary responsibilities for the upbringing under the primary consideration of the child best interest	**States appropriate assistance to parents**	**Development of institutions, facilities, and services for the care of children**	**Appropriate measures for the care of children of working parents**
Data is collected and disaggregated by prohibited grounds for discrimination including age, sex, ethnicity, disability, when applicable.			
Structural indicators			
1. Parental primary responsibility is explicitly recognised in legislation and provides adequate and effective guarantees to all without exclusion or discrimination			
2. Ratification of relevant human rights treaties (e.g. *Convention on the Elimination of All Forms of Discrimination Against Women*, 1981). 3. National law recognises the responsibility of both parents to act always with their child's best interests as their primary consideration. 4. The law recognises the common and shared responsibility of both parents in equal measure.	5. Existence of a legal and policy framework that secures assistance to all parents, not exclusively those in need.	6. Legal framework is in place setting out eligibility criteria for institutions, facilities and services provided for the care of the child.	
	7. Existence of standards and related monitoring systems established by the competent authorities, to ensure quality standards of the services provided, in terms of health, safety, and quality of their staff, are in line with Article 3 (3) of the CRC (see also art. 3).		
			8. A legal and policy framework is in place to support working parents in the exercise of their parental responsibilities and entitles them to: • Maternity and paternity leave • To leave if the child is sick.

(continued)

Table 5 (continued)

Process indicators			
9. Training is provided to parents on compliance with the child best interests (see also art. 3). 10. National awareness campaigns (e.g. broadcasting public messages through media) have been undertaken to disseminate the culture of common and shared responsibilities for the upbringing of the children in the family setting.		11. Services are in place to support parents in the exercise of their parental responsibilities.	12. Measures such as daycare and facilities have been provided for the care of children of working parents (see also art. 3).
	13. Measures have been implemented to monitor institutions, facilities, and services for the care for children.		
Outcome indicators			
14. Percentage of parents aware of their common and shared responsibilities for the upbringing of their children. 15. Percentage of parents participating in parental training programmes.		16. Percentage of parents/caregivers benefiting from services created to support them in the exercise their parental responsibility (e.g. maternity and paternity leave).	17. (SDG 5.4.1) Proportion of time spent on unpaid domestic and care work, by sex, age, and location. 18. Percentage of children using daycare facilities • Rate of enrolment in fulltime daycare, age 0–5 (preschool) • Rate of enrolment in part-time daycare, school-age. 19. Percentage of families in receipt of state assistance by age and number of children in family unit.

Article 18—Guidance

The following provides guidance for the collection of data on specific indicators for Article 18. The number relates to the number of that indicator in the table above. Each indicator is identified as a Process, Structural, or Outcome Indicator, and the formula to calculate the data is described.

Indicator 14—Outcome

Percentage of parents aware of their common and shared responsibilities for the upbringing of their children.

Numerator: Number of parents aware of their common and shared responsibilities for the upbringing of their children.

Denominator: Total number of parents surveyed.

Formula: (numerator/denominator) × 100.

Indicator 15—Outcome

Percentage of parents participating in parental training programmes.

Numerator: Number of parents participating in parental training programmes.

Denominator: Total number of parents surveyed.

Formula: (numerator/denominator) × 100.

Indicator 16—Outcome

Percentage of parents/caregivers benefiting from measures created to provide conditions necessary to enable them and other primary caregivers the opportunity to fully exercise their primary responsibility (e.g. maternity and paternity leave).

Numerator: Number of parents/caregivers benefiting of measures created to provide conditions necessary to enable them and other primary caregivers the opportunity to fully exercise their primary responsibility.

Denominator: Total number of parents surveyed.

Formula: (numerator/denominator) × 100.

Indicator 17—Outcome

Proportion of time spent on unpaid domestic and care work, by sex, age, and location.

Numerator: Number of hours spent on unpaid domestic and care work, by sex, age, and location.

Denominator: Total day hours (24).

Formula: (numerator/denominator), × 100 disaggregated by sex, age, and location.

Indicator 18—Outcome

Percentage of children using daycare and facilities in particular:

18.1 Rate of enrolment in fulltime daycare by age 0–5 (preschool).

Numerator: Number of children aged 0–5 (preschool) using daycare and facilities full-time, which had been implemented for the care of children of working parents.

Denominator: Total number of children aged 0–5 (preschool) whose families are seeking programmes for childcare.

Formula: (numerator/denominator) × 100.

18.2 Rate of enrolment in part-time daycare by school age.

Numerator: Number of school-age children using daycare and facilities part-time, which had been implemented for the care of children of working parents.

Denominator: Total number of school-age children whose families are seeking programmes for childcare.

Formula: (numerator/denominator) × 100.

Indicator 19—Outcome

Percentage of families in receipt of state assistance, by age and number of children in family unit.

Numerator: Number of families in receipt of state assistance, by age and number of children in family unit.

Denominator: Total number of families with children who are eligible and require state assistance.

Formula: (numerator/denominator) × 100.

Article 20—The Rights Concerning Children Deprived of their Family Environment

1. A child temporarily or permanently deprived of his or her family environment, or in whose own best interests cannot be allowed to remain in that environment, shall be entitled to special protection and assistance provided by the State.
2. States Parties shall in accordance with their national laws ensure alternative care for such a child.
3. Such care could include, inter alia, foster placement, kafalah of Islamic law, adoption, or, if necessary, placement in suitable institutions for the care of children. When considering solutions, due regard shall be paid to the desirability of continuity in a child's upbringing and to the child's ethnic, religious, cultural, and linguistic background.

Table 6 Article 20 Indicator sets

Core attributes		
Provision of special protection and assistance	**Standards of care**	**Nature of care**
Data is collected and disaggregated by prohibited grounds for discrimination including age, sex, ethnicity, disability, when applicable.		
Structural indicators		
1. Legislation provides for the care and protection of children deprived of their family environment, in line Article 20 and the *UN Guidelines on Alternative Care* (A/RES/64/142) 2. Legislation mandates an obligation to consider and support family reintegration. 3. A system of authorisation, registration, regulation, and monitoring of all formal alternative care provision is in place. 4. Legislation provides that children have the right to be heard at all stages of decision-making relating to alternative care provision (see also art. 12). 5. Legislation provides the right for children to lodge a complaint against placement decisions.		
		6. Legislation explicitly considers non-separation of siblings, while ensuring that the child's best interest remains a paramount consideration. 7. Legislation explicitly considers the child's ethnic, religious, cultural, and linguistic background for care placement decisions, while ensuring that the child's best interest remains a primary consideration (see also art. 30).
Process indicators		
8. Institutional care is used as a last resort and a temporary measure, while ensuring that the child's best interest remains a primary consideration. 9. Programmes supporting and facilitating continuity of care for the child in alternative family settings are in place (e.g. foster care). 10. Programmes are in place to support children transitioning out of care placement that include education, employment, vocational skills trainings, psychosocial counselling, and health care. 11. Government support is provided, for example, care services, financial incentives, to facilitate family reintegration. 12. (GCRD) Government provides and/or supports and supervises training courses for all foster families to ensure they provide quality care.	13. Participatory, multidisciplinary, professional decision-making processes are in place to guarantee the necessity and suitability of any decisions made regarding the care of children. 14. Safe and accessible complaints mechanisms are in place for children placed in alternative care. 15. Reviews are required every 3 months, by a competent designated authority, concerning (see also art. 25): • Quality of the placement • Necessity of the placement. 16. Systems are in place to ensure that the child is heard in decisions and reviews concerning the quality and necessity of the placement (see also art. 12).	

(continued)

Table 6 (continued)

Outcome indicators		
17. Number of children entering formal care during a 12-month period. 18. Percentage of children in foster care placements. 19. Percentage of children in street situations who report having access to a trusted social worker.	20. Educational outcomes of children in care placement: • Percentage of children achieving average numeracy and literacy rates • Percentage of children completing secondary education. 21. Percentage of children in formal care whose placement has been reviewed within the last 3 months. 22. Proportion of all children under 15 years leaving residential care for a family placement, including reunification, in a 12-month period (disaggregated by sex and age, and grounds for care). 23. Number of reported cases of violence and child deaths in formal care during a 12-month period. 24. (GCRD) Rate of reviews per placement in the last 12 months. 25. (GCRD) Percentage of children receiving ongoing support after leaving care e.g. psychosocial or and financial support.	26. The number of children without parental care, disaggregated by cause.

Article 20—Guidance

The following provides guidance for the collection of data on specific indicators for Article 20. The number relates to the number of that indicator in the table above. Each indicator is identified as a Process, Structural, or Outcome Indicator, and the formula to calculate the data is described.

Indicator 18—Outcome

Percentage of children in foster care placements.

Numerator: Number of children in foster care.

Denominator: Total child population in formal care.

Formula: (numerator/denominator) × 100.

Indicator 19—Outcome

Percentage of children in street situations who report having access to a trusted social worker.

Numerator: Number of children in street situations who report having access to a trusted social worker.

Denominator: Total number of children in street situations.

Formula: (numerator/denominator) × 100.

Indicator 20—Outcome

Educational outcomes of children in care placement:

20.1 Percentage of children achieving average numeracy and literacy rates.

Numerator: Number of children in care placement achieving required numeracy and literacy rates.

Denominator: Total child population in care placement.

Formula: (numerator/denominator) × 100.

20.2 Percentage of children completing secondary education.

Numerator: Number of children in care placement completing secondary education.

Denominator: Total child population in care placement.

Formula: (numerator/denominator) × 100.

Indicator 21—Outcome

Percentage of children in formal care whose placement has been reviewed within the last 3 months.

Numerator: Number of children in formal care whose placement was reviewed in the last 3 months.

Denominator: Total number of children in formal care.

Formula: (numerator/denominator) × 100.

Indicator 22—Outcome

Proportion of all children under 15 years leaving residential care for a family placement, including reunification, in a 12-month period.

Numerator: Number of children under 15 years leaving residential care for a family placement (including reunification) in 12-month period.

Denominator: Total number of children under 15 years in residential care within the same 12-month period.

Formula: (numerator/denominator).

Indicator 24—Outcome

Rate of reviews per placement in the last 12 months.

Numerator: Total number of reviews.

Denominator: Total number of children placed in formal care.

Formula: (numerator/denominator).

Indicator 25—Outcome

Percentage of children receiving ongoing support after leaving care, e.g. psychosocial or financial support.

Numerator: Total number of children receiving ongoing support after leaving care.

Denominator: Total number of children leaving care.

Formula: (numerator/denominator) × 100.

Article 21—Adoption

States Parties that recognize and/or permit the system of adoption shall ensure that the best interests of the child shall be the paramount consideration and they shall:

(a) Ensure that the adoption of a child is authorized only by competent authorities who determine, in accordance with applicable law and procedures and on the basis of all pertinent and reliable information, that the adoption is permissible in view of the child's status concerning parents, relatives and legal guardians and that, if required, the persons concerned have given their informed consent to the adoption on the basis of such counselling as may be necessary;

(b) Recognize that inter-country adoption may be considered as an alternative means of child's care, if the child cannot be placed in a foster or an adoptive family or cannot in any suitable manner be cared for in the child's country of origin;
(c) Ensure that the child concerned by inter-country adoption enjoys safeguards and standards equivalent to those existing in the case of national adoption;
(d) Take all appropriate measures to ensure that, in inter-country adoption, the placement does not result in improper financial gain for those involved in it;
(e) Promote, where appropriate, the objectives of the present article by concluding bilateral or multilateral arrangements or agreements, and endeavour, within this framework, to ensure that the placement of the child in another country is carried out by competent authorities or organs.

Table 7 Article 21 Indicator sets

Core attributes		
Authorisation and regulation	**Permissibility of adoption**	**Safeguards for inter-country adoption**
Data is collected and disaggregated by prohibited grounds for discrimination including age, sex, ethnicity, disability, when applicable.		
Structural indicators		
1. State has ratified the *Optional Protocol to the CRC on the Sale of Children, Child Prostitution and Pornography*, 2002.		
2. Where adoption is permitted, it is regulated by legislation which: • Mandates its authorisation by competent authorities • Is underpinned throughout by the principle of the paramountcy of the best interests of the child • Prohibits any discrimination as to which children are eligible for adoption • Prohibits discrimination in relation to particular racial or social groups of potential adoptive parents or children • Requires mechanisms for review, monitoring and follow up • Requires that adoptions can only be carried out by staff with appropriate pre- and in-service training • Provides opportunities for children to trace their origins.	3. Adoption legislation guarantees the following: • Adoptions are only permitted for children whose parents are either unwilling or unable to care for their children • Inter-country adoption can only be considered where appropriate care for the child is not possible within the country • An age limit is in place below the age of 18 years when a child can consent to or refuse an adoption.	4. State has ratified the *Hague Convention on the Protection of Children and Co-operation in Respect of Inter-country Adoption*, 1993. 5. Inter-country adoption legislation provides standards and safeguards in compliance with the principle of subsidiarity as in *UN Guidelines for the Alternative Care of Child and Hague Convention*, 1993. 6. Legislation prohibits and criminalises trafficking in children as an extraditable offence and prohibits improper financial gain or inducement for adoption.

(continued)

Table 7 (continued)

Process indicators		
7. Percentage of senior management and staff/carers working in adoption with minimum qualifications in childcare and development and adoption law. 8. Rate of adoption per 100,000 population.		
9. Existence of mechanisms for formal complaints that allow adopted children to safely report abuse and exploitation. 10. Percentage of adoptions carried out by authorised competent bodies.	11. Existence of mechanisms to ensure appropriate parental consent to adoption. 12. Existence of accessible, safe mechanisms to ensure that children are able to give informed consent to adoption (see also art. 12).	13. Percentage of inter-country adoptions as a proportion of all adoptions disaggregated by sex, age, and disability.
Outcome indicators		
14. Percentage of adoptions that fail or are disrupted, per year.	15. Percentage of adoptive parents expressing satisfaction with the adoption process. 16. Percentage of adopted children expressing satisfaction with the adoption process.	17. Number of prosecutions for trafficking and improper financial inducement in inter-country adoptions (see also art. 19).

Article 21 –Guidance

Indicator 7—Process

Percentage of senior management and staff/carers working in adoption with minimum qualifications in childcare and development and adoption law.

Numerator: Number of senior management and staff/carers working in adoption with minimum qualifications in childcare and development and adoption law.

Denominator: Total number of senior management and staff/carers working in adoption.

Formula: (numerator/denominator) × 100.

Indicator 10—Process

Percentage of adoptions carried out by authorised competent bodies.

Numerator: Number of adoptions carried out by authorised competent bodies in a given year.

Denominator: Total number of adoptions in a given year.

Formula: (numerator/denominator) × 100.

Indicator 13—Process

Percentage of inter-country adoptions as a proportion of all adoptions disaggregated by sex, age, and disability.

Numerator: Number of inter-country adoption, disaggregated by sex, age and disability.

Denominator: Total number of all adoptions.

Formula: (numerator/denominator) × 100.

Indicator 14—Outcome

Percentage of adoptions that fail or are disrupted, per year.

Numerator: Number of adoptions that fail or are disrupted in a given period.

Denominator: total number of adoptions within the same given period.

Formula: (numerator/denominator) × 100.

Indicator 15—Outcome

Percentage of adoptive parents expressing satisfaction with the adoption process.

Numerator: Number of adoptive parents expressing satisfaction with the adoption process in a given period.

Denominator: Total number of adoption parents surveyed within the same given period.

Formula: (numerator/denominator) × 100.

Indicator 16—Outcome

Percentage of adopted children expressing satisfaction with the adoption process.

Numerator: Number of adopted children expressing satisfaction with the adoption process in a given period.

Denominator: total number of adopted children surveyed, within the same given period.

Formula: (numerator/denominator) × 100.

Article 25—The Right to Periodic Review

> States Parties recognize the right of a child who has been placed by the competent authorities for the purposes of care, protection or treatment of his or her physical or mental health, to a periodic review of the treatment provided to the child and all other circumstances relevant to his or her placement.

Table 8 Article 25 Indicator sets

Core attributes		
Scope and authorisation of periodic reviews	**Periodicity and content of reviews of the placement**	**Accountability and transparency**
Data is collected and disaggregated by prohibited grounds for discrimination including age, sex, ethnicity, disability, when applicable.		
Structural indicators		
1. Legislation provides that the review process relating to placement of children in any setting (e.g. foster care, institution, hospital, or detention centre) addresses: • Reason for placement • Assessment of the quality of placement • Frequency of review • Standards for the quality of the review process • Opportunities of reintegration with the family and the community 2. Legislation requires that children are provided with legal and/or non-legal advocacy to assist them through the process of a review or to appeal the outcome of a review.		
Process indicators		
3. Regular reviews of the review process are undertaken by the relevant authorities.	4. Protocols are established to assure the integrity of the review process, knowledge, and skills of the assessors.	5. Independent administrative processes to hear and remedy complaints from children in any placement settings are established (e.g. foster care, institution, hospital, or detention centre). 6. Child-friendly information about the review and complaints procedures is provided to the child before and during any placement (see also art. 12 and art. 17). 7. Independent administrative bodies undertake an annual analysis of the review findings to inform and improve the placement system.
Outcome indicators		
8. Number of complaints from children about quality of the review process. 9. Percentage of reviews made within the timeline articulated within the legislation. 10. Percentage of children who feel that their views were considered during the review process (see also art. 12).		

Article 25—Guidance

The following provides guidance for the collection of data on specific indicators for Article 25. The number relates to the number of that indicator in the table above. Each indicator is identified as a Process, Structural, or Outcome Indicator, and the formula to calculate the data is described.

Indicator 9—Outcome

Percentage of reviews made within the timelines as defined in the legislation.

Numerator: number of reviews made within the timelines as defined in the legislation.

Denominator: total number of children in care and treatment placement.

Formula: (numerator/denominator) × 100.

Indicator 10—Outcome

Percentage of children who feel that their views were considered during the review process.

Numerator: Number of children whose cases were reviewed who felt that their views were considered.

Denominator: All children who cases were reviewed.

Formula: (numerator/denominator) × 100.

Chapter 7
Disability, Health, and Welfare Rights

Ziba Vaghri, Roberta Ruggiero, Gerison Lansdown, Adem Arkadas-Thibert, and Christian Whalen

The Convention on the Rights of the Child includes a broad range of social and economic rights. This section focuses on the social and economic rights that address health and well-being:[1]

- Article 23—the rights of children with disabilities
- Article 24—the right to the best possible health

[1] For further elaboration on the implications and implementation of each of these rights, please read the relevant chapter in the companion publication to this book: *Monitoring State Compliance with the UN Convention on the Rights of the Child: An analysis of attributes*, Vaghri, Zermatten, Lansdown and Ruggiero, Springer, 2022.

Z. Vaghri
GlobalChild Program of Research, University of New Brunswick, Saint John, NB, Canada

R. Ruggiero (✉)
Centre for Children's Right Studies, Faculty of Law, University of Geneva, Geneva, Switzerland
e-mail: Roberta.ruggiero@unige.ch

G. Lansdown
School of Law, University College Cork, Cork, Ireland

A. Arkadas-Thibert
Independent Researcher, Specializing in International Human Rights, Marseille, France

C. Whalen
Faculty of Law, University of New Brunswick, Fredericton, NB, Canada

Z. Vaghri et al. (eds.), *Children's Rights-Based Indicators*, Children's Well-Being: Indicators and Research 28,
https://doi.org/10.1007/978-3-031-71594-5_7

- Article 26—the right to social security
- Article 27—the right to an adequate standard of living
- Article 33—the right to protection from harmful drugs.

Article 23 constitutes the first dedicated provision in a human rights treaty to persons with disabilities, in this case, children, and although included here, its implications go beyond basic health and welfare. Coupled with the explicit recognition of children with disabilities in Article 2 as a group entitled to protection from discrimination, the *Convention on the Rights of the Child* made an important breakthrough in affirming recognition that children with disabilities are holders of rights, and not, as had been traditional in most societies around the world, objects of pity or passive recipients of care. Article 33 is also an innovative provision, addressing children's right to be protected from the illicit use of narcotic drugs.

Articles 24, 26 and 27 build on earlier provisions in the *International Covenant on Economic, Social and Cultural Rights*, and in each case include additional measures in recognition of the implications of children's legal and developmental status. Article 24 sets out an aspirational right to guarantee every child the right to enjoy the highest attainable standard of health, not only through measures targeting disease and malnutrition, and calling for safe drinking water, but also encompassing programmes to address chronic health conditions and the social determinants of health which impact children. Article 26 affirms the right of the child to benefit from social security while also recognising the role of parents in providing for the maintenance of the child. Article 27 also references the role of parents but, importantly, provides a clear benchmark for defining an adequate standard of living. It must be sufficient to support the child's physical, mental, spiritual, moral, and social development.

Article 23—The Rights of Children with Disabilities

1. States Parties recognize that a mentally or physically disabled child should enjoy a full and decent life, in conditions which ensure dignity, promote self-reliance and facilitate the child's active participation in the community.

2. States Parties recognize the right of the disabled child to special care and shall encourage and ensure the extension, subject to available resources, to the eligible child and those responsible for his or her care, of assistance for which application is made and which is appropriate to the child's condition and to the circumstances of the parents or others caring for the child.

3. Recognizing the special needs of a disabled child, assistance extended in accordance with paragraph 2 of the present article shall be provided free of charge, whenever possible, taking into account the financial resources of the parents or others caring for the child, and shall be designed to ensure that the disabled child has effective access to and receives education, training, health care services, rehabilitation services, preparation for employment and recreation opportunities in a manner conducive to the child's achieving the fullest possible social integration and individual development, including his or her cultural and spiritual development.

4. States Parties shall promote, in the spirit of international cooperation, the exchange of appropriate information in the field of preventive health care and of medical, psychological and functional treatment of disabled children, including dissemination of and access to information concerning methods of rehabilitation, education and vocational services, with the aim of enabling States Parties to improve their capabilities and skills and to widen their experience in these areas. In this regard, particular account shall be taken of the needs of developing countries.

Table 1 Article 23 Indicator sets

Core attributes		
Inclusive environments to promote dignity, independence, and participation	**Access to targeted assistance and services**	**International cooperation**
Data is collected and disaggregated by prohibited grounds for discrimination including age, sex, ethnicity, disability, when applicable.		

(continued)

Table 1 (continued)

<table>
<tr><th colspan="3">Structural indicators</th></tr>
<tr><td colspan="3">1. State has ratified the UN Convention on the Rights of Persons with Disabilities (CRPD), 2006.
2. State has reviewed all relevant legislation to ensure compliance with the CRC and CRPD.
3. State has introduced legislation establishing the right to non-discrimination against persons with disabilities on all protected grounds.</td></tr>
<tr><td colspan="2">4. A comprehensive strategy is in place to ensure legislation, policies, services, and funding are directed to the fullest possible inclusion of children with disabilities, including:
• A comprehensive and co-ordinated legislative and policy framework for inclusive education with a time frame for implementation
• Deinstitutionalisation with a time frame for implementation and appropriate re-direction of funds allocated to these institutions
• Early assessment, identification, and treatment programmes
• Investment in community-based programmes and support for parents
• Public awareness-raising campaigns on disability and the significance of inclusion and support of children with disabilities.</td><td>5. Bilateral or multilateral cooperation is sought to promote measures to address causes of disability (e.g. preventable disease, poverty, poor nutrition, worst forms of child labour, armed conflict).
6. Bilateral and multilateral knowledge exchange and support is sought for the development of programmes to promote inclusion.</td></tr>
<tr><th colspan="3">Process indicators</th></tr>
<tr><td colspan="3">7. International development programmes are inclusive of and accessible to children with disability.</td></tr>
<tr><td>8. (SDG 4.A adapted) Percentage of schools (primary, lower, and upper secondary) with adapted infrastructure and materials for students with disabilities.
9. Percentage of teachers in service who have received in-service training in the last 12 months to teach students with special educational needs.
10. (SDG 11.7 adapted) Percentage of public green spaces (parks and recreational facilities) meeting the minimum national standards for accessibility by children with disabilities.
11. (GCRD) Awareness raising and information programmes are provided for parents and caregivers of children with disabilities.</td><td>12. Percentage of parents of children with disabilities receiving targeted subsidies (e.g. cash transfers).
13. Number of trained professionals (health, education, social worker, etc.) on appropriate care and treatment of children with disabilities per 12 months.
14. Percentage of children with disabilities with access to specialist health services they require (including early identification and intervention services, and services designed to minimise or prevent further disability).
15. Percentage of parents of children with disabilities receiving community-based support services.</td><td>16. Percentage of annual budget allocated to measures and programmes designed to promote the inclusion of children with disabilities within public institutions and local communities.
17. Per capita national spending on programmes, services, and assistive devices for children with disabilities.</td></tr>
</table>

Table 1 (continued)

Outcome indicators		
18. Percentage children with disabilities in institutional care. 19. (SDG 4.5 adapted) Percentage of children with disabilities in quality inclusive educational environments. 20. Percentage of children with disabilities completing secondary education. 21. Percentage of children with disabilities who experienced discrimination on the basis of their disability in the last 12 months (see also art. 2). 22. Percentage of school-age children with disabilities reporting having friendships with children without disabilities. 23. Number of school children with disabilities who are involved in extracurricular activities (e.g. student council, sports, etc.).	24. Percentage of parents of children with disabilities satisfied with the access, level, and quality of available community-based support services. 25. (SDG 11.2 adapted) Percentage of children with disabilities able to use public transport. 26. (GCRD) Percentage of children with disabilities with access to appropriate and affordable services, devices, and other assistance for disability-related needs. 27. Number of children with disabilities separated from their parents on the basis of the disability of either the child or of one or both parents within the past 12 months (see also art. 9).	28. Percentage of school-age children with disabilities with access to the digital technology they require for full participation in education on an equal basis with others (see also art. 17).

Article 23—Guidance

The following provides guidance for the collection of data on specific indicators for Article 23. The number relates to the number of that indicator in the table above. Each indicator is identified as a Process, Structural, or Outcome Indicator, and the formula to calculate the data is described.

Indicator 8—Process

Percentage of schools (primary, lower, and upper secondary) with adapted infrastructure and materials for students with disabilities.

Numerator: Number of schools (primary, lower, and upper secondary) with adapted infrastructure and materials for students with disabilities.

Denominator: Total number of schools.

Formula: (numerator/denominator) × 100.

Indicator 9—Process

Percentage of teachers in service who have received in-service training in the last 12 months to teach students with special educational needs.

Numerator: Number of teachers in service who have received in-service training in the last 12 months to teach students with special educational needs.

Denominator: Total number of teachers in service.

Formula: (numerator/denominator) × 100.

Indicator 10—Process

Percentage of public green spaces (parks and recreational facilities) meeting the minimum national standards for accessibility by children with disabilities.

Numerator: Number of public green spaces (parks and recreational facilities) meeting the minimum national standards for accessibility by children with disabilities.

Denominator: Total number of public green spaces (parks and recreational facilities).

Formula: (numerator/denominator) × 100.

Indicator 12—Process

Percentage of parents of children with disabilities receiving targeted subsidies (e.g. cash transfers).

Numerator: Number of parents of children with disabilities receiving targeted subsidies.

Denominator: Total number of parents of children with disabilities.

Formula: (numerator/denominator) × 100.

Indicator 14—Process

Percentage of children with disabilities with access to specialist health services they require (including early identification and intervention services, and services designed to minimise or prevent further disability).

Numerator: Number of children with disabilities with access to specialist health services they require.

Denominator: Total number of children with disabilities.

Formula: (numerator/denominator) × 100.

Indicator 15—Process

Percentage of parents of children with disabilities receiving community-based support services.

Numerator: Number of parents of children with disabilities receiving community-based support services.

Denominator: Total number of parents of children with disabilities.

Formula: (numerator/denominator) × 100.

Indicator 16—Process

Percentage of annual budget allocated for children earmarked for measures and programmes designed to promote the inclusion of children with disabilities within public institutions and local communities.

Numerator: Amount of annual budget allocated for children which has been earmarked for measures and programmes designed to promote the inclusion of children with disabilities within public institutions and local communities.

Denominator: Total budget allocated for children.

Formula: (Numerator/denominator) × 100.

Indicator 17—Process

Per capita national spending on programmes, services, and assistive devices for children with disabilities.

Numerator: Total amount of national spending on programmes, services, and assistive devices for children with disabilities.

Denominator: Total number of children with disabilities.

Formula: numerator/ denominator.

Indicator 18—Outcome

Percentage children with disabilities in institutional care.

Numerator: Number of children with disabilities in institutional care.

Denominator: Total number of children with disabilities.

Formula: (numerator/denominator) × 100.

Indicator 19—Outcome

Percentage of children with disabilities in quality inclusive educational environments.

Numerator: Number of children with disabilities in quality inclusive educational environments.

Denominator: Total number of children with disabilities of primary and secondary school age.

Formula: (numerator/denominator) × 100.

Indicator 20—Outcome

Percentage of children with disabilities completing secondary education.

Numerator: Number of children with disabilities completing secondary education in a given year.

Denominator: Total number of children with disabilities of school leaving age in a given year.

Formula: (numerator/denominator) × 100.

Indicator 21—Outcome

Percentage of children with disabilities who experienced discrimination on the basis of their disability in the last 12 months.

Numerator: Number of children with disabilities who experienced discrimination on the basis of their disability in the last 12 months.

Denominator: Total number of children with disabilities surveyed.

Formula: (numerator/denominator) × 100.

Indicator 22—Outcome

Percentage of school-age children with disabilities reporting having friendships with children without disabilities.

Numerator: Number of school age children with disabilities reporting having friendships with children without disabilities.

Denominator: Total number of school-age children with disabilities surveyed.

Formula: (numerator/denominator) × 100.

Indicator 24—Outcome

Percentage of parents of children with disabilities satisfied with the access, level, and quality of available community-based support services.

Numerator: Number of parents of children with disabilities satisfied with the access, level, and quality of available community-based support services.

Denominator: Total number of parents of children with disabilities surveyed.

Formula: (numerator/denominator) × 100.

Indicator 25—Outcome

Percentage of children with disabilities able to use public transport.

Numerator: Number of children with disabilities able to use public transport.

Denominator: Total number of children with disabilities.

Formula: (numerator/denominator) × 100.

Indicator 26—Outcome

Percentage of children with disabilities with access to appropriate and affordable services, devices, and other assistance for disability-related needs.

Numerator: Number of children with disabilities with access to appropriate and affordable services, devices, and other assistance for disability-related needs.

Denominator: Total number of children with disabilities.

Formula: (numerator/denominator) × 100.

Indicator 28—Outcome

Percentage of school-age children with disabilities with access to the digital technology they require for full participation in education on an equal basis with others.

Numerator: Number of school-age children with disabilities with access to the digital technology they require for full participation in education on an equal basis with others.

Denominator: Total number of school-age children with disabilities.

Formula: (numerator/denominator) × 100.

Article 24—The Right to Health

1. States Parties recognize the right of the child to the enjoyment of the highest attainable standard of health and to facilities for the treatment of illness and rehabilitation of health. States Parties shall strive to ensure that no child is deprived of his or her right of access to such health care services.

2. States Parties shall pursue full implementation of this right and, in particular, shall take appropriate measures:

a. To diminish infant and child mortality;

b. To ensure the provision of necessary medical assistance and health care to all children with emphasis on the development of primary health care;

c. To combat disease and malnutrition, including within the framework of primary health care, through, inter alia, the application of readily available technology and through the provision of adequate nutritious foods and clean drinking water, taking into consideration the dangers and risks of environmental pollution;

d. To ensure appropriate pre-natal and post-natal health care for mothers;

e. To ensure that all segments of society, in particular parents and children, are informed, have access to education and are supported in the use of basic knowledge of child health and nutrition, the advantages of breastfeeding, hygiene and environmental sanitation and the prevention of accidents;

f. To develop preventive health care, guidance for parents and family planning education and services.

3. States Parties shall take all effective and appropriate measures with a view to abolishing traditional practices prejudicial to the health of children.

4. States parties undertake to promote and encourage international co-operation with a view to achieving progressively the full realization of the right recognized in the present article. In this regard, particular account shall be taken of the needs of developing countries.

Table 2 Article 24 Indicator sets

<table>
<tr><th colspan="4">Core attributes</th></tr>
<tr><th>A right to the enjoyment of the highest attainable standard of health</th><th>A right to the basic minimum standards of child health</th><th>Child health accountability mechanisms</th><th>International cooperation for child health in developing countries</th></tr>
<tr><td colspan="4">Data is collected and disaggregated by prohibited grounds for discrimination including age, sex, ethnicity, disability, when applicable.</td></tr>
<tr><td colspan="4">Structural indicators</td></tr>
<tr><td colspan="4">1. Constitutional and/or legislative guarantees are in place to guarantee children's right to health without discrimination.
2. A co-ordinated national child health policy involving public and private sectors is in place.
3. Health sciences, nursing and medical faculties are available to train the professionals needed to meet children's health service needs across the national territory.
4. A National Health Plan of Action is in place and that takes into consideration:
• Multidisciplinary service integration
• Clinical and public health
• Physical and mental health domains
• Child participation
• Social determinants of health
• Committing to international standards and cooperation.</td></tr>
<tr><td colspan="2">5. National health law provides for basic minimum standards of child health, in all domains of health, including mental health.</td><td></td><td></td></tr>
<tr><td colspan="3">6. Regulation and quality standards are in place to ensure quality service delivery.
7. Health quality assurance mechanisms monitor delivery of health care for all children in respect of:
• Availability
• Acceptability
• Accessibility
• Quality.</td><td></td></tr>
<tr><td colspan="4">Process indicators</td></tr>
<tr><td colspan="4">8. Hospitals and health clinics are in place throughout the country providing primary, secondary, and tertiary care (family, parental, maternal, pediatric, child and adolescent).</td></tr>
<tr><td colspan="3">9. Percentage of physical health institutions monitored in respect of availability, acceptability, accessibility, and quality (see also art. 25).
10. Percentage of mental health facilities inspected in respect of availability, acceptability, accessibility, quality (see also art. 25).</td><td></td></tr>
</table>

(continued)

Table 2 (continued)

11. Percentage of births attended by skilled health personnel. 12. Percentage of school children educated in: • Reproductive and sexual health • Healthy behaviours and nutrition.	13. Percentage of children living in households with access to a safe supply of drinking water. 14. Percentage of children immunised against vaccine preventable diseases. 15. Percentage of infants exclusively breastfed during first 6 months. 16. Percentage of children who had regular medical check-ups in the reporting period. 17. Percentage of mothers and babies receiving post-natal care within 2 days of birth.	18. Percentage of complaints to children's commissioner or advocate dealing with access to health service. 19. Hospitalisation rates of adolescents on ground of mental health per 10,000 adolescent population. 20. Percentage of health professionals trained to diagnose and manage mental health conditions. 21. Per capita government expenditure on primary health care and medicines. 22. Density of medical and paramedical personnel per 10,000 population. 23. Percentage of children covered by health insurance and/or government sponsored public health (national or local) plans. 24. Percentage of health professionals who have received pre- and/or in-service training in child rights-based approaches.	25. Number of development aid agreements in place.

(continued)

Table 2 (continued)

Outcome indicators			
26. Percentage of mothers receiving at least four antenatal care visits from skilled health personnel. 27. Rate of pregnant women who experience a live birth with a low birth weight (<5.5 pounds or < 2500 grams) per 1000 live births. 28. Rate of pregnant women who experience a stillbirth per 1000 births. 29. Suicide rates of children by year per 10,000 children 30. Hospitalisation rate for child mental health conditions per 10,000 child population. 31. Life-expectancy at birth or age one.	32. Infant and under-five child mortality rate (per 1000 live births). • Within 1 month of birth • Under 5 years 33. Percentage of underweight children under 5 years of age. 34. Percentage of overweight children. 35. Rate of injury for children aged 12–18 years resulting in limitations in daily living per 100,000 relevant child population.	36. Percentage of children able to access primary care health services. 37. Percentage of children reporting that they have confidence in using health care services. 38. Percentage of children who report their mental health as being very good.	39. Proportion of expenditure on health received from development assistance.

Article 24—Guidance

The following provides guidance for the collection of data on specific indicators for Article 24. The number relates to the number of that indicator in the table above. Each indicator is identified as a Process, Structural, or Outcome Indicator, and the formula to calculate the data is described.

Indicator 9—Process

Percentage of physical health facilities monitored in respect of availability, acceptability, accessibility, quality.

Numerator: Number of physical health facilities monitored.

Denominator: Total number of health facilities.

Formula: (Numerator / Denominator) × 100.

Indicator 10—Process

Percentage of mental health facilities inspected in respect of availability, acceptability, accessibility, and quality.

Numerator: Number of mental health facilities monitored.

Denominator: Total number of mental health facilities.
Formula: (Numerator / Denominator) × 100.

Indicator 11—Process

Percentage of births attended by skilled health personnel.

Numerator: Number of births attended by skilled health personnel (doctors, nurses, midwives), within the reporting period.

Denominator: Total number of births (within the reporting period).

Formula: (numerator /denominator) × 100.

Indicator 12—Process

Percentage of school children educated in:

12.1 Reproductive and sexual health
Numerator: Number of school children educated in reproductive and sexual health.
Denominator: Total number of school children.
Formula: (numerator/denominator) × 100
12.2 Healthy behaviours and nutrition.
Numerator: Number of school children educated in healthy behaviours and nutrition
Denominator: total number of school children
Formula: (numerator/denominator) × 100

Indicator 13—Process

Percentage of children living in households with access to a safe supply of drinking water.

Numerator: Number of households with at least one child that have access to a safe supply of drinking water.

Denominator: All households surveyed.

Formula: (numerator/denominator) × 100.

Indicator 14—Process

Percentage of children immunised against vaccine preventable diseases.

Numerator: Number of children immunised against vaccine preventable diseases, by type of disease.

Denominator: Total number of children.
Formula: (numerator /denominator) × 100.

Indicator 15—Process

Percentage of infants exclusively breastfed during first 6 months.
Numerator: Number of infants exclusively breastfed during first 6 months.
Denominator: Total number of infants.
Formula: (numerator/denominator) × 100.

Indicator 16—Process

Percentage of children who had regular medical check-ups in the reporting period.
Numerator: Number of children who had regular medical check-ups in the reporting period.
Denominator: Total number of children within the same reporting period.
Formula: (numerator/denominator) × 100.

Indicator 17—Process

Percentage of mothers and babies receiving post-natal care within 2 days of birth.
Numerator: Number of mothers and babies receiving post-natal care within 2 days of birth.
Denominator: Total number of mothers and babies within the same reporting period.
Formula: (numerator/denominator) × 100.

Indicator 18—Process

Percentage of complaints to children's commissioner or advocate dealing with access to health services.
Numerator: Number of complaints to children's commissioner or advocate dealing with access to health services.
Denominator: Total number of complaints to children's commissioner or advocate.
Formula: (numerator/denominator) × 100.

Indicator 19—Process

Hospitalisation rates of adolescents on grounds of mental health per 10,000 adolescent population.

Numerator: Total number of adolescents hospitalised on grounds of mental health.

Denominator: Total number of adolescents surveyed.

Formula: (numerator/denominator) per 10,000 adolescent population.

Indicator 20—Process

Percentage of health professionals trained to diagnose and manage mental health conditions.

Numerator: Number of health professionals trained to diagnose and manage mental health conditions/.

Denominator: Number of health professionals.

Formula: (numerator/denominator) × 100.

Indicator 21—Process

Per capita government expenditure on primary health care and medicine.

Numerator: Total government expenditure pf primary health care.

Denominator: Total population.

Formula: (numerator/denominator).

Indicator 22—Process

Density of medical and paramedical personnel per 10,000 population.

Numerator: Total number of medical and paramedical personnel.

Denominator: Total population.

Formula: (numerator/denominator) per 10,000 population.

Indicator 23—Process

Percentage of children covered by health insurance and/or government sponsored public health (national or local) plans.

Numerator: Number of children covered by health insurance and/or government sponsored public health (national or local) plans.

Denominator: Total number of children within the population.

Formula: (numerator/denominator) × 100.

Indicator 24—Process

Percentage of health professionals who have received pre- and/or in-service training in child rights-based approaches.

Numerator: Number of health professionals who have received pre- and/or in-service training in child rights-based approach.

Denominator: Total number of health professionals.

Formula: (numerator/denominator) × 100.

Indicator 26—Outcome

Percentage of mothers receiving at least four antenatal care visits from skilled health personnel.

Numerator: Number of mothers receiving at least four antenatal care visits by skilled health personnel for the last pregnancy.

Denominator: Total number of last pregnancies reported.

Formula: (Numerator / Denominator) × 100.

Indicator 27—Outcome

Rate of pregnant women who experience a live birth with a low birth weight (< 5.5 pounds or < 2500 grams) per 1000 live births.

Numerator: Total number of pregnant women who experience a live birth with a low birth weight (< 5.5 pounds or < 2500 grams).

Denominator: Total number of live births.

Formula: (numerator/denominator) per 1000 births.

Indicator 28—Outcome

Rate of pregnant women who experience a stillbirth, per 1000 births.

Numerator: Total number of pregnant women who experience a stillbirth.

Denominator: Total number of births.

Formula: (numerator/denominator) per 1000 births.

Indicator 29—Outcome

Suicide rates of children by year per 10,000 children.

Numerator: Number of suicides of children.

Denominator: Total number of children.

Formula: (numerator/denominator) per 10,000 children.

Indicator 30—Outcome

Hospitalisation rate for child mental health conditions, per 10,000 child population.

Numerator: Number of hospitalisations for child mental health conditions (within the last reporting period).

Denominator: Total child population (within the same reporting period).

Formula: (numerator/denominator) per 10,000 child population.

Indicator 32—Outcome

Infant and under-five child mortality rate (per 1000 live births).

32.1 Within 1 month of birth

Numerator: Total all-cause child deaths that happened in with 1 month of birth (neonatal period).

Denominator: Total number of all-cause child deaths

Formula: Numerator/Denominator

32.2 Under 5 years.

Numerator: Total number of all-cause deaths in children under age 5 years (in the defined reporting period).

Denominator: Total live births (in the same reporting period).

Formula: Numerator/Denominator per 1000 live births.

Indicator 33—Outcome

Percentage of underweight children under 5 years of age.

Numerator: Number of underweight children under 5 years of age.

Denominator: Total number of children under 5 years of age.

Formula: (numerator/denominator) × 100.

Indicator 34—Outcome

Percentage of overweight children.

Numerator: Number of overweight children.

Denominator: Total number of children.

Formula: (numerator/denominator) × 100.

Indicator 35—Outcome

Rate of injury for children aged 12–18 years resulting in limitations in daily living, per 100,000 relevant child population.

Numerator: Number of injuries for children aged 12–18 years resulting in limitations in daily living within the last reporting period.

Denominator: total number of children aged 12–18 years, in the same reporting period.

Formula: (numerator/denominator) per 100,000 relevant child population.

Indicator 36—Outcome

Percentage of children able to access to primary care health services.

Numerator: Number of children able to access to primary care health services.

Denominator: Total number of children.

Formula: (numerator/denominator) × 100.

Indicator 37—Outcome

Percentage of children reporting that they have confidence in using health care services.

Numerator: Number of children reporting that they have confidence in using health care services.

Denominator: total number of children surveyed.

Formula: (numerator/ denominator) × 100.

Indicator 38—Outcome

Percentage of children who report their mental health as being very good.

Numerator: Number of children who report their mental health as being very good.
Denominator: Total number of children surveyed.
Formula: (numerator/ denominator) × 100.

Indicator 39—Outcome

Proportion of expenditure on health received from development assistance.
Numerator: Expenditure on health received from development assistance.
Denominator: Total expenditure on health.
Formula: (numerator/ denominator) × 100.

Indicator 39—Outcome

Proportion of development assistance expenditure directed towards health provision.
Numerator: Expenditure directed towards health development assistance.
Denominator: Total development assistance budget.
Formula: (numerator/ denominator) × 100.

Article 26—The Right to Benefit from Social Security

1. States Parties shall recognize for every child the right to benefit from social security, including social insurance, and shall take the necessary measures to achieve the full realization of this right in accordance with their national law.
2. The benefits should, where appropriate, be granted, taking into account the resources and the circumstances of the child and persons having responsibility for the maintenance of the child, as well as any other consideration relevant to an application for benefits made by or on behalf of the child.

Table 3 Article 26 Indicator sets

<table>
<tr><th colspan="3">Core attributes</th></tr>
<tr><th>States parties' obligations to undertake all the necessary measures</th><th>Focus on the personal resources and circumstances of the child and caregivers</th><th>Children direct accessibility to the application process to secure social security benefits</th></tr>
<tr><td colspan="3">Data is collected and disaggregated by prohibited grounds for discrimination including age, sex, ethnicity, disability, when applicable.</td></tr>
<tr><td colspan="3">Structural indicators</td></tr>
<tr><td colspan="3">1. Ratification of other international human rights treaties relevant to Article 26, for example:
• Convention on the Elimination of All Forms of Discrimination Against Women, 1979
• International Convention on the Protection of the Rights of All Migrant Workers and Members of Their Families (ICRMW), 1990
• International Labour Organization (ILO) Conventions No. 102, Social Security (Minimum Standards), 1952.
2. The child's right to benefit from social security is explicitly recognised in legislation and ensuring resources to the children most in need.
3. Reservations under the CRC relevant to Article 26 are withdrawn.
4. State has introduced or strengthened a comprehensive system of social security to:
• Cover all the nine traditional branches of social security: Medical care, cash sickness benefits, maternity benefits, old-age benefits, survivors' benefits, employment injury benefits, unemployment benefits and family benefits
• Provide an appropriate system of monitoring
• Ensure access to social security benefits by the most disadvantaged groups.</td></tr>
<tr><td>5. The national social security system complies with the following criteria:
• Availability (social security should be set up or maintained)
• Progressive improvement in terms of quality and quantity of benefits
• Provision is made for all children including directly to children in child-headed households (in particular, but not exclusively in relation to medical care, medical insurance, disability payments and family benefits).</td><td>6. The national social security system considers the resources and the circumstances of the child and of the persons having responsibility for their maintenance.</td><td>7. The national social security system ensures that children are directly eligible where necessary.</td></tr>
<tr><td colspan="3">Process indicators</td></tr>
<tr><td colspan="3">8. Mechanisms and institutions exist to enforce Article 26 and obtain redress where necessary.
9. Policy measures, protocol, and training for professionals are in place to guarantee the children's access to social security benefits.
10. National public awareness-raising campaigns have been undertaken to disseminate information in order to facilitate access to benefits provided by the social security system.</td></tr>
</table>

(continued)

Table 3 (continued)

	11. Strategies have been implemented to ensure that financial support to all children is provided regardless of their parents' circumstances and nationality.	12. Child-friendly processes for applications are in place, where necessary, ensuring the following: • Available staff to support the child • Provision to the child of all the necessary information • Timely processing of applications.
Outcome indicators		
13. (SDG 1.2.1) Proportion of population living below the national poverty line, by sex and age, employment status, and geographical location (urban/rural). 14. (SDG 1.3.1) Proportion of population covered by social protection floors/systems, by sex, distinguishing children, unemployed persons, older persons, persons with disabilities, pregnant women, newborns, work-injury victims and the poor and those under vulnerable circumstances. 15. (SDG 1.3.1 adapted) Proportion of children and households receiving child and family cash benefits, by region. 16. Percentage of children covered by child and family cash benefit schemes. 17. Percentage of GDP allocated to public social protection expenditure, excluding health, for the latest available year. 18. Number of primary and secondary school children who feel they do not have the financial means to purchase food, healthcare or other commodities required for day-to-day life (see also art. 27).		

Article 26—Guidance

The following provides guidance for the collection of data on specific indicators for Article 26. The number relates to the number of that indicator in the table above. Each indicator is identified as a Process, Structural, or Outcome Indicator, and the formula to calculate the data is described.

Indicator 13—Outcome

Proportion of population living below the national poverty line, by sex and age, employment status, and geographical location (urban/rural).

Numerator: Number of people (population) below the national poverty line, by sex, age, employment status, and geographical location (urban/rural).

Denominator: Total number of the population (same disaggregation).

Formula: (numerator/denominator).

Indicator 14—Outcome

Proportion of population covered by social protection floors/systems, by sex, distinguishing children, unemployed persons, older persons, persons with disabilities, pregnant women, newborns, work-injury victims and the poor and those under vulnerable circumstances.

Numerator: Number of people (population) covered by social protection floors/systems, by sex, distinguishing children, unemployed persons, older persons, persons with disabilities, pregnant women, newborns, work-injury victims and the poor and those under vulnerable circumstances.

Denominator: Total population (same disaggregated).

Formula: (numerator/denominator).

Indicator 15—Outcome

Proportion of children and households receiving child and family cash benefits, by region.

Numerator: Number of children and households receiving child or family cash benefits, by region.

Denominator: Total number of children and households.

Formula: (numerator/denominator) by region.

Indicator 16—Outcome

Percentage children covered by child and family cash benefit schemes.

Numerator: Number of children covered by child and family cash benefit schemes.

Denominator: Total number of children.

Formula: (numerator/denominator) × 100.

Indicator 17—Outcome

Percentage of GDP allocated to public social protection expenditure, excluding health, for the latest available year.

Numerator: Total amount of GDP allocated to public social protection expenditure, excluding health, for the latest available year.

Denominator: Total amount of GDP, excluding health, for same latest available year.

Formula: (numerator/denominator) × 100.

Article 27—The Right to a Standard of Living Adequate for Physical, Mental, Spiritual, Moral and Social Development

1. States Parties recognize the right of every child to a standard of living adequate for the child's physical, mental, spiritual, moral and social development.
2. The parent(s) or others responsible for the child have the primary responsibility to secure, within their abilities and financial capacities, the conditions of living necessary for the child's development.
3. States Parties, in accordance with national conditions and within their means, shall take appropriate measures to assist parents and others responsible for the child to implement this right and shall in case of need provide material assistance and support programmes, particularly with regard to nutrition, clothing and housing.
4. States Parties shall take all appropriate measures to secure the recovery of maintenance for the child from the parents or other persons having financial responsibility for the child, both within the State Party and from abroad. In particular, where the person having financial responsibility for the child lives in a State different from that of the child, States Parties shall promote the accession to international agreements or the conclusion of such agreements, as well as the making of other appropriate arrangements.

Table 4 Article 27 Indicator sets

Core attributes		
Securing adequate standard of living for each Child's holistic development	**Obligation to take measures to assist parents and other caretakers**	**Recovery of maintenance for the child**
Data is collected and disaggregated by prohibited grounds for discrimination including age, sex, ethnicity, disability, when applicable.		

Table 4 (continued)

Structural indicators		
1. (GCRD) There is explicit recognition of the right to a standard of living adequate for the child's physical, mental, spiritual, moral, and social development in constitution and subsequent legislation. 2. The legislation provides for: • Families with children to have timely access to social protection • Security of tenure, equal inheritance, and protection against forced eviction • Employment conditions for working parents and caregivers in fulfilling their responsibilities to children. 3. National strategy and plan of action in place with a time frame and budget covering physical, mental, spiritual, moral, and social development of children particularly with regard to nutrition, clothing, and housing.		
		4. The state party enters into bilateral and international agreements that secure recovery of maintenance for the child guided by the best interest principle. 5. The legislation provides for clear definitions and duties of structures for accessible and timely maintenance systems.
Process indicators		
6. Percentage of national budget allocated to poverty reduction measures for children, particularly with regard to nutrition, clothing, and housing.		
7. Number of complaints by children and families lodged to competent institutions (e.g. Independent Human Rights Institutions and Children's Commissioners) within the past 12 months: • On the right to adequate food, food safety and consumer protection law • On the right to housing.		8. Mechanisms in place to enable a parent to recover maintenance in respect of a child.
Outcome indicators		
9. (SDG 1.2.2 adapted) Proportion of children living in poverty according to national definitions. 10. (SDG 1.3.1) Percentage of children covered by social protection floors/systems, by sex, age groups, disability, poverty, vulnerability.		

(continued)

Table 4 (continued)

11. Percentage of children below national poverty line after social transfers. 12. (SDG 11.1.1) Proportion of children in urban settings living in slums, informal settlements, or inadequate housing. 13. (SDG 2.2.1) Prevalence of stunting among children under 5 years of age. 14. (SDG 2.2.2) Prevalence of malnutrition among children under 5 years of age, by type (wasting and overweight). 15. (SDG 4.2.1) Proportion of children under 5 years of age who are developmentally on track in health, learning and psychosocial well-being, by sex. 16. Percentage of children aged 15–19 years not in education, employment, or training as a proportion of the population of the same age group.	17. Percentage of families with sustained access to water resource, sanitation, electricity, waste disposal, and internet access. 18. Number of homeless children. 19. Percentage of children with one or both parents unemployed.	20. Percentage of maintenance orders that are successfully enforced (international and national).

Article 27—Guidance

The following provides guidance for the collection of data on specific indicators for Article 27. The number relates to the number of that indicator in the table above. Each indicator is identified as a Process, Structural, or Outcome Indicator, and the formula to calculate the data is described.

Indicator 9—Outcome

Proportion of children living in poverty according to national definitions.

Numerator: Number of children living in poverty.

Denominator: All children.

Formula: (numerator/denominator) × 100.

Indicator 10—Outcome

Percentage of children covered by social protection floors/systems, by sex, age groups, disability, poverty, and vulnerability.

Numerator: Number of children covered by social protection floors/systems (disaggregated by sex, age groups, disability, poverty, and vulnerability).

Denominator: All children.

Formula: (numerator/denominator) × 100 (disaggregated by sex, age groups, disability, poverty, and vulnerability).

Indicator 11—Outcome

Percentage of children below national poverty line after social transfers.

Numerator: Number of children below national poverty line after social transfers.

Denominator: Total number of children.

Formula: (numerator/denominator) × 100.

Indicator 12—Outcome

Proportion of children in urban settings living in slums, informal settlements, or inadequate housing.

Numerator: Number of children in urban settings living in slums, informal settlements, or inadequate housing.

Denominator: All children in urban settings.

Formula: (numerator/denominator).

Indicator 13—Outcome

Prevalence of stunting among children under 5 years of age.

Numerator: Number of children under 5 years of age who are stunted.

Denominator: All children under 5 years of age.

Formula: (numerator/denominator) × 100.

Indicator 14—Outcome

Prevalence of malnutrition among children under 5 years of age, by type (wasting and overweight).

Numerator: Number of malnutrition cases of children under 5 years of age.

Denominator: All children under the age of 5 years.

Formula: (numerator/denominator) × 100.

Indicator 15—Outcome

Proportion of children under 5 years of age who are developmentally on track in health, learning and psychosocial well-being, by sex.

Numerator: Number of children under 5 years of age who are developmentally on track in health, learning and psychosocial well-being.

Denominator: All children under the age of 5 years.

Formula: (numerator/denominator) × 100.

Indicator 16—Outcome

Percentage of children aged 15–19 years not in education, employment, or training, as a proportion of the population of the same age group.

Numerator: Number of children aged 15–19 years who are not in employment, education, or training.

Denominator: The total number of children aged 15–19.

Formula: (numerator/denominator) × 100.

Indicator 17—Outcome

Percentage of families with sustained access to water resource, sanitation, electricity, waste disposal, and internet access.

Numerator: Number of families with sustained access to water resource, sanitation, electricity, waste disposal, and internet access.

Denominator: Number of all families.

Formula: (numerator/denominator) × 100.

Indicator 19—Outcome

Percentage of children with one or both parents unemployed.

Numerator: Number of children with one or both parents unemployed.
Denominator: Total number of children.
Formula: (numerator/denominator) × 100.

Indicator 20—Outcome

Percentage of maintenance orders that are successfully enforced (international and national).

Numerator: Number of maintenance orders that are successfully enforced.
Denominator: All maintenance orders.
Formula: (numerator/denominator) × 100.

Article 33—The Right to Protection from Illicit Use of Narcotic Drugs and Psychotropic Substances

States Parties shall take all appropriate measures, including legislative, administrative, social and educational measures, to protect children from the illicit use of narcotic drugs and psychotropic substances as defined in the relevant international treaties, and to prevent the use of children in the illicit production and trafficking of such substances.

Table 5 Article 33 Indicator sets

Core attributes		
Protection from the illicit use of narcotic drugs and psychotropic substances	**Prevention of the use of children in illicit production and trafficking**	**'Appropriate measures'—'Rights compliance and effectiveness' as a normative test**
Data is collected and disaggregated by prohibited grounds for discrimination including age, sex, ethnicity, disability, when applicable.		

(continued)

Table 5 (continued)

Structural indicators		
1. Legislation is in place to protect children from the illicit use of narcotic drugs and psychotropic substances and prevent the use of children in illicit drug use, production, and trafficking. 2. National Plan of Action outlines the state's approach to: • Protection of children from drug use and drug related harm, including assistance to families experiencing drug dependency • Children's involvement in the illicit drug trade, including diversion from the criminal justice system, poverty reduction and, where relevant, alternative development strategies • Stigma reduction strategies relating to drug use • Appropriate and effective sanctions and methods of enforcement for adults involving children in drug use, production, and trafficking.		
		3. Legislation prohibits: • Children being subjected to criminal sanction for their drug use/ possession for personal use • Age restrictions excluding legal minors from drug treatment or harm reduction services • Removal from the care of the parent on the basis of parental drug use or drug dependence without evidence of actual neglect or abuse (see also art. 3). 4. Legislation includes: • A definition of child exploitation in the context of involvement in the illicit drug trade • Attention to proportionality sentencing of children for drug offences • Age controls, taxation, and other regulatory controls in legally regulated markets (e.g. new cannabis markets).

(continued)

Table 5 (continued)

Process indicators		
5. Budget allocated for demand reduction initiatives (prevention, drug dependence treatment and harm reduction). 6. (GCRD) Percentage of primary and secondary schools offering evidence-based education about: • The harms of drugs • Safe environments • Illicit use of pharmaceuticals (control of illicit trade in pharmaceuticals and controlled drugs). 7. Evidence-based and recommended drug use prevention measures are in place.	8. Proportion of spending on poverty reduction strategies within drug policy budget.	9. Invasive investigatory practices for children (including random drug testing, strip searches, and sniffer dogs) are avoided at all costs. 10. Voluntary consent from the child is a precondition of drug dependence treatment.
Outcome indicators		
11. Percentage of children using drugs who have access to drug dependence treatment and harm reduction services. 12. Percentage of children using drugs who are also living in households affected by drug dependence.	13. Percentage of children in contact with the criminal justice system because of trafficking and/or production of drugs.	14. Percentage of children excluded from school due to drug use. 15. Percentage of children in drug treatment who are placed on a compulsory basis.

Article 33—Guidance

The following provides guidance for the collection of data on specific indicators for Article 33. The number relates to the number of that indicator in the table above. Each indicator is identified as a Process, Structural, or Outcome Indicator, and the formula to calculate the data is described.

Indicator 6—Process

Percentage of primary and secondary schools offering evidence-based education about:

6.1 The harms of drugs.

Numerator: Number of schools offering evidence-based education about the harms of drugs.

Denominator: Total number of schools.

Formula: (numerator/denominator) × 100.

6.2 Safe environments.

Numerator: Number of schools offering evidence-based education about safe environments.

Denominator: Total number of schools.

Formula: (numerator/denominator) × 100.

6.3 Illicit Use of pharmaceuticals (control of illicit trade in pharmaceuticals and controlled drugs).

Numerator: Number of schools offering evidence-based education about illicit use of pharmaceuticals (control of illicit trade in pharmaceuticals and controlled drugs).

Denominator: Total number of schools.

Formula: (numerator/denominator) × 100.

Indicator 8—Process

Proportion of spending on poverty reduction strategies within total drug policy budget.

Numerator: Total amount spent on drug focused poverty reduction strategies.

Denominator: total drug policy budget.

Formula: (numerator/denominator) × 100.

Indicator 11—Outcome

Percentage of children using drugs who have access to drug dependence treatment and harm reduction services.

Numerator: Number of children using drugs who have access to drug dependence treatment and harm reduction services.

Denominator: Total number of children using drugs.

Formula: (numerator/denominator) × 100.

Indicator 12—Outcome

Percentage of children using drugs who are also living in households affected by drug dependence.

Numerator: Number of children using drugs who are also living in households affected by drug dependence.

Denominator: Total number of children using drugs.

Formula: (numerator/denominator) × 100.

Indicator 13—Outcome

Percentage of children in contact with the criminal justice system because of trafficking and/or production of drugs.

Numerator: Number of children in contact with the criminal justice system because of trafficking and/or production of drugs.

Denominator: Total number of children surveyed.

Formula: (numerator/denominator) × 100.

Indicator 14—Outcome

Percentage of children excluded from school due to drug use.

Numerator: Number of children excluded from school due to drug use.

Denominator: Total number of children surveyed.

Formula: (numerator/denominator) × 100.

Indicator 15—Outcome

Percentage of children in drug treatment who are placed on a compulsory basis.

Numerator: Number of children in drug treatment who are placed on a compulsory basis.

Denominator: Total number of children on drug treatment.

Formula: (numerator/denominator) × 100.

Chapter 8
Education, Leisure, and Cultural Activities Rights

Ziba Vaghri, Roberta Ruggiero, Gerison Lansdown, Adem Arkadas-Thibert, and Christian Whalen

This cluster of articles, relating to education, leisure, and culture, affirm not only the right of every child to learn and play in a safe and stimulating environment, respectful of their own culture and language, but also insist on the importance of respecting the child's agency and contribution to their own development.[1]

- Article 28—the right to education

[1] For further elaboration on the implications and implementation of each of these rights, please read the relevant chapter in the companion publication to this book: *Monitoring State Compliance with the UN Convention on the Rights of the Child: An analysis of attributes.* Vaghri, Zermatten, Lansdown and Ruggiero, Springer, 2022.

Z. Vaghri
GlobalChild Program of Research, University of New Brunswick, Saint John, NB, Canada

R. Ruggiero (✉)
Centre for Children's Right Studies, Faculty of Law, University of Geneva, Geneva, Switzerland
e-mail: Roberta.ruggiero@unige.ch

G. Lansdown
School of Law, University College Cork, Cork, Ireland

A. Arkadas-Thibert
Independent Researcher, Specializing in International Human Rights, Marseille, France

C. Whalen
Faculty of Law, University of New Brunswick, Fredericton, NB, Canada

Z. Vaghri et al. (eds.), *Children's Rights-Based Indicators*, Children's Well-Being: Indicators and Research 28,
https://doi.org/10.1007/978-3-031-71594-5_8

- Article 29—the aims of education
- Article 30—respect for the child's own culture, language, and religion
- Article 31—the right to play, recreation leisure and the arts.

Article 28, the right to education, builds on earlier provisions in the *International Covenant on Economic, Social and Cultural Rights*, and sets out in detail the right to access education. It emphasises that primary education should be both free and compulsory for every child, that secondary education made available to every child, and that higher education should be available according to capacity. Education must be provided on the basis of equality of opportunity at all levels, all forms of school discipline must be administered in a manner consistent with the child's dignity, be provided with equality, and states must make efforts to address school drop-out.

Article 29 elaborates the aims of education, focusing on the development of the child's fullest potential, and insisting that education addresses the promotion of respect for human rights, recognition and respect for the child's own cultural identity, preparation for life in a free society, and respect for the natural environment. The Committee has further emphasised the importance of a participatory pedagogy in schools and for the school environment to be one where children experience respect for their human rights through their lived experience in school.

Articles 30 and 31 reiterate provisions in the *International Covenant on Civil and Political Rights* and include additional references. Article 30, on the right of the child to enjoy their culture and practice their own religion and language, adds recognition of indigenous rights. Article 31 provides an important recognition of childhood by including the right to play, alongside rights to rest and leisure, and to cultural life and the arts.

Article 28—The Right to Education

1. States Parties recognize the right of the child to education, and with a view to achieving this right progressively and on the basis of equal opportunity, they shall, in particular:

   (a) Make primary education compulsory and available free to all;
   (b) Encourage the development of different forms of secondary education, including general and vocational education, make them available and accessible to every child, and take appropriate measures such as the introduction of free education and offering financial assistance in case of need;
   (c) Make higher education accessible to all on the basis of capacity by every appropriate means;
   (d) Make educational and vocational information and guidance available and accessible to all children;
   (e) Take measures to encourage regular attendance at schools and the reduction of drop-out rates.

2. States Parties shall take all appropriate measures to ensure that school discipline is administered in a manner consistent with the child's human dignity and in conformity with the present Convention.
3. States Parties shall promote and encourage international cooperation in matters relating to education, in particular with a view to contributing to the elimination of ignorance and illiteracy throughout the world and facilitating access to scientific and technical knowledge and modern teaching methods. In this regard, particular account shall be taken of the needs of developing countries.

Table 1 Article 28 Indicator sets

Core attributes			
Access to universal primary & secondary education	**Ensuring de jure and de facto equality of and opportunity in education**	**Educational standards and resources**	**Freedom in education**
Data is collected and disaggregated by prohibited grounds for discrimination including age, sex, ethnicity, disability, when applicable.			
Structural indicators			
1. Legislation is in place, including: • Free and compulsory primary for all children everywhere in the country's jurisdiction • Accessible and progressively free education at all other levels and types of education • Accessible and affordable Early Childhood education (ECE) • Corporal punishment in schools is banned • Non-discrimination is guaranteed in relation to all forms of education. 2. The state has adopted national educational policies and a plan of action which assures: • Quality education at all levels is accessible, available, and adaptable to all children • Regular and disaggregated data is collected on different aspects of education • A general inspection system and a body responsible for monitoring education is provided • Conditions for safety and security of the school environment. 3. The state has adopted a national education policy on inclusion, which encompasses: • A definition of inclusive education • Cross-sectoral collaboration • Guarantees for inclusive learning opportunities for all children with the necessary support services • A time-bound commitment to accessible school environments • A commitment to the provision of reasonable accommodations for children • Mechanisms for early identification of, and assessment and support for, children with disabilities • Appropriate provision of learning environments. 4. The state has adopted a national education policy for early childhood education which includes: • Efforts to improve access and retain enrolment to early education programmes for all children including marginalised populations. • Efforts to improve the quality of early education programmes. • Subsidies for early childcare and education are available for low-income groups.			

(continued)

Table 1 (continued)

<table>
<tr><td colspan="3">5. Independent accessible child-friendly complaints mechanisms are established for all children within the education system.</td><td></td></tr>
<tr><td></td><td colspan="3">6. Minimum educational standards are established and are applicable to all schools.</td></tr>
<tr><td>7. The legal minimum age of military recruitment, marriage, criminal responsibility, and employment is the same as, or higher than, the legal maximum age of completion of compulsory education.</td><td></td><td></td><td>8. Laws protect the freedom to establish:
• Private schools (including homeschools)
• Schools that teach according to religious or moral convictions
• Schools for minority groups.</td></tr>
<tr><td colspan="4">Process indicators</td></tr>
<tr><td colspan="4">9. The body responsible for the monitoring process:
• Monitors the minimum education standards to assure that they conform with human rights standards
• Conducts inspections periodically and in a transparent manner
• Produces data and reports periodically which are used for process and quality improvement.</td></tr>
<tr><td colspan="2">10. Processes and strategies are in place to reduce high-school drop-out.</td><td colspan="2">11. Ratio of student to teacher in:
• Primary education
• Secondary education
12. Ratio of qualified to unqualified staff in preschool groups in licensed childcare centres.</td></tr>
<tr><td></td><td colspan="2">13. Measures are in place to provide:
• Accommodations for the schedules of working children
• Encouragement for the continuation of education for child brides and pregnant girls
• Education to reintegrate demobilised child soldiers in the education system
• Educational and vocational information and guidance to demobilised child soldiers and children with disabilities.</td><td></td></tr>
</table>

(continued)

Table 1 (continued)

14. (SDG 4.3.1 adapted) Participation rate of children in formal and non-formal education and training in the previous 12 months. 15. Percentage of schools that have policies and procedures to take action on reported cases of sexual abuse, hate crimes, discrimination, bullying and cyber bullying. 16. Percentage of education budget allocated: • Primary education • Secondary education	17. (GCRD) School-based food programmes are established, ensuring adequate nutrition, especially for children from low-income families.	18. Percentage of Gross National Product (GNP) allocated to education for: • Public schools • Private schools 19. Availability of subsidies to lower income families to support education. 20. (SDG 4.a.1 adapted) Proportion of schools with access to: • Electricity • Internet for pedagogical purposes • Computers for pedagogical purposes • Adapted infrastructure and materials for students with disabilities • Basic drinking water • Single-sex basic sanitation facilities • Basic handwashing facilities • Safe environments for children (e.g. safe play areas, fence, canteen). 21. Effective and sustainable measures are in place to increase the percentage of well-trained teachers in areas where educational outcomes are traditionally lower. 22. (SDG 4.c.1) Proportion of teachers who have received at least the minimum teacher training required at pre-service or in-service for: • Pre-primary • Primary • Lower secondary • Upper secondary education	23. Percentage of teachers belonging to minority groups (see art. 30). 24. Percentage of teachers (not belonging to minority groups) trained in minority culture or languages (see also art. 30 and art. 31).

(continued)

Table 1 (continued)

25. Percentage of children enrolled in school: • Completing primary education • Completing secondary education • Moving to secondary school after completion of primary education. 26. Percentage of primary and secondary school-aged children who are out-of-school, disaggregated by, but not limited to, rurality, gender, disability, LGBTQ+ and refugees. 27. Percentage of children with a disability who receive a funded individualised education plan, when required. 28. Percentage of children completing secondary education who: • Have a disability (see also art. 23) • Are female • Are engaged in seasonal work • Belong to religious and cultural minorities (see also art. 30).	32. (SDG 4.1.1) Proportion of children achieving at least a minimum proficiency level in reading and mathematics, in: • Grades 2 or 3 • End of primary • End of lower secondary. 33. (SDG 4.4.1 adapted) Proportion of children with information and communications technology skills, by type of skills (see also art. 17). 34. (SDG 4.2.1) Proportion of children under 5 years of age who are developmentally on track in health, learning and psychosocial well-being (see also art. 24). 35. Percentage of children receiving individual support for school access and attendance (e.g. free tutoring, food subsidies, school transport).	36. (SDG 4.2.2.) Participation rate in organised learning (1 year before the official primary entry age), by sex. 37. Percentage of students who identify as a minority and who completed secondary education (see also art. 30).
29. Percentage of children who experienced bullying at school during the past 12 months. 30. Percentage of adolescent girls who report receiving support to stay in school rather than getting married. 31. Percentage of girls who are pregnant, who are allowed to stay at school and receive special programmes to help continue their education.		

Article 28—Guidance

The following provides guidance for the collection of data on specific indicators for Article 28. The number relates to the number of that indicator in the table above. Each indicator is identified as a Process, Structural, or Outcome Indicator, and the formula to calculate the data is described.

Indicator 11—Process

Ratios of student to teacher in education:

11.1 Primary education

Outcome indicators

Numerator: Total number of students at the primary education level:

Denominator: Total number of teachers at the primary education level.
Formula: (numerator/denominator)
11.2 Secondary education
Numerator: Total number of students at the secondary education level.
Denominator: Total number of teachers at the secondary education level.
Formula: (numerator/denominator)

Indicator 14—Process

Participation rate of children in formal and non-formal education and training in the previous 12 months, by sex. (SDG 4.3.1 adapted).

Numerator: Number of children in formal and non-formal education and training in the previous 12 months (by sex).

Denominator: Total number of children in the same year.

Formula: (numerator/denominator) × 100 in that year.

Indicator 15—Process

Percentage of schools that have policies and procedures to act on reported cases of sexual abuse, hate crimes, discrimination, bullying and cyber bullying.

Numerator: Number of schools that have policies and procedures to act on reported cases of sexual abuse, hate crimes, discrimination, bullying and cyber bullying.

Denominator: Total number of schools.

Formula: (numerator/denominator) × 100.

Indicator 16—Process

Percentage of education budget allocated to:

16.1 Primary education
Numerator: Amount of education budget allocated to primary education.
Denominator: Total education budget.
Formula: (numerator/denominator) × 100
16.2 Secondary education
Numerator: amount of education budget allocated to secondary education.
Denominator: Total education budget.
Formula: (numerator/denominator) × 100

Indicator 18—Process

Percentage of Gross National Product (GNP) allocated to education for:

18.1 Public schools
Numerator: Amount of GNP allocated to education for public schools.
Denominator: Total GNP.
Formula: (numerator/denominator) × 100
18.2 Private schools
Numerator: Amount of GNP allocated to education for private schools.
Denominator: Total GNP.
Formula: (numerator/denominator) × 100

Indicator 20—Process

Proportion of schools with access to:

20.1 Electricity
Numerator: Number of schools with access to electricity.
Denominator: Total number of schools.
Formula: (numerator/denominator)
20.2 Internet for pedagogical purposes.
Numerator: Number of schools with access to internet for pedagogical purposes.
Denominator: Total number of schools.
Formula: (numerator/denominator)
20.3 Computers for pedagogical purposes.
Numerator: Number of schools with access to computers for pedagogical purposes.
Denominator: Total number of schools.
Formula: (numerator/denominator)
20.4 Adapted infrastructure and materials for students with disabilities.
Numerator: Number of schools with access to adapted infrastructure and materials for students with disabilities.
Denominator: Total number of schools.
Formula: (numerator/denominator)
20.5 Basic drinking water
Numerator: Number of schools with access to basic drinking water.
Denominator: Total number of schools.
Formula: (numerator/**d**enominator)
20.6 Single-sex basic sanitation facilities.
Numerator: Number of schools with access to single-sex basic sanitation facilities.
Denominator: Total number of schools.
Formula: (numerator/**d**enominator)
20.7 Basic handwashing facilities (as per the WASH indicator definitions).
Numerator: Number of schools with access to basic handwashing facilities (as per the WASH indicator definitions).
Denominator: Total number of schools.
Formula: (numerator/denominator)
20.8 Safe environments for children (e.g. safe play areas, fence, canteen).

Numerator: Number of schools with access to safe environments for children (e.g. safe play areas, fence, canteen).
Denominator: Total number of schools.
Formula: (numerator/denominator)

Indicator 22—Process

Proportion of teachers who have received at least the minimum teacher training required at pre-service or in-service for:

22.1 Pre-primary
Numerator: Number of teachers who have received at least the minimum teacher training required at pre-service or in-service for pre-primary.
Denominator: Total number of teachers in pre-primary
Formula: (numerator/denominator)
22.2 Primary
Numerator: Number of teachers who have received at least the minimum teacher training required at pre-service or in-service for primary.
Denominator: Total number of teachers in primary.
Formula: (numerator/denominator)
22.3 Lower secondary
Numerator: Number of teachers who have received at least the minimum teacher training required at pre-service or in-service for lower secondary.
Denominator: Total number of teachers in lower secondary.
Formula: (numerator/denominator)
22.4 Upper secondary education
Numerator: Number of teachers who have received at least the minimum teacher training required at pre-service or in-service for upper secondary.
Denominator: Total number of teachers in upper secondary.
Formula: (numerator/denominator)

Indicator 23—Process

Percentage of teachers belonging to minority groups.
Numerator: Total number of teachers belonging to minority groups.
Denominator: Total number of teachers.
Formula: (numerator/denominator) × 100.

Indicator 24—Process

Percentage of teachers (not belonging to minority groups) trained in minority culture or languages.

Numerator: Number of teachers (not belonging to minority groups) trained in minority culture or languages.

Denominator: Total number of teachers not belonging to minority groups.

Formula: (numerator/denominator) × 100.

Indicator 25—Outcome

Percentage of children enrolled in school:

25.1 Completing primary education

Numerator: Number of children completing primary education in the past 12 months.

Denominator: Total number of children who are enrolled in primary education in the past 12 months.

Formula: (numerator/denominator) × 100

25.2 Completing secondary education.

Numerator: Number of children completing secondary education in the past 12 months.

Denominator: Total number of children who are enrolled in secondary education in the past 12 months.

Formula: (numerator/denominator) × 100

25.3 Moving to secondary school after completion of primary education.

Numerator: Number of children who moved to secondary school after completing primary education in the past 12 months

Denominator: Total number of children who completed primary education in past 12 months

Formula: (numerator/denominator) × 100

Indicator 26—Outcome

Percentage of primary and secondary school-aged children who are out-of-school, disaggregated by, but not limited to, rurality, gender, disability, LGBTQ+ and refugees.

Numerator: Total number of primary and secondary school-aged children who are out-of-school, disaggregated by, but not limited to, rurality, gender, disability, LGBTQ+ and refugees.

Denominator: Total number of children in the population, disaggregated by, but not limited to, rurality, gender, disability, LGBTQ+ and refugees.

Formula: (numerator/denominator) × 100.

Indicator 27—Outcome

Percentage of children with a disability who receive a funded individualised education plan, when required.

Numerator: Number of children with a disability who receive a funded individualised education plan when required.

Denominator: Total number of children with a disability who require a funded individualised education plan.

Formula: (numerator/denominator) × 100.

Indicator 28—Outcome

Percentage of children completing secondary education who:

28.1 Have a disability

Numerator: Number of children completing secondary education with a disability.

Denominator: Total number of children with a disability.

Formula*:* (numerator/denominator) × 100

28.2 Are female.

Numerator: Number of children completing secondary education who are female.

Denominator: Total number of children who are female.

Formula*:* (numerator/denominator) × 100

28.3 Are engaged in seasonal work.

Numerator: Number of children completing secondary education who are engaged in seasonal work.

Denominator: Total number of children who are engaged in seasonal work.

Formula*:* (numerator/denominator) × 100

28.4 Belong to religious and cultural minorities.

Numerator: Number of children completing secondary education who belong to religious and cultural minorities.

Denominator: Total number of children who belong to religious and cultural minorities.

Formula*:* (numerator/denominator) × 100

Indicator 29—Outcome

Percentage of children who experience bullying at school during the past 12 months.

Numerator: Number of children who experience bullying during the past 12 months.

Denominator: Total number of children.

Formula: (numerator/denominator) × 100.

Indicator 30—Outcome

Percentage of adolescent girls who report receiving support to stay in school rather than getting married.

Numerator: Number of adolescent girls who report receiving support to stay in school rather than getting married.

Denominator: Total number of adolescent girls at school surveyed.

Formula: (numerator/denominator) × 100.

Indicator 31—Outcome

Percentage of girls who are pregnant, who are allowed to stay at school and receive special programmes to help continue their education.

Numerator: Number of girls who are pregnant, who are allowed to stay at school and receive special programmes to help continue their education.

Denominator: Total number of girls who are pregnant.

Formula: (numerator/denominator) × 100.

Indicator 32—Outcome

Proportion of children achieving at least a minimum proficiency level in reading and mathematics, in:

32.1 Grades 2 or 3

Numerator: Number of children and young people, by sex, achieving at least a minimum proficiency level in reading and mathematics, in grades 2 or 3.

Denominator: Total number of children in grades 2 or 3.

Formula: (numerator/denominator)

32.2 End of primary.

Numerator: Number of children and young people, by sex, achieving at least a minimum proficiency level in reading and mathematics, in end of primary.

Denominator: Total number of children in end of primary.

Formula: (numerator/denominator)

32.3 End of lower secondary.

Numerator: Number of children and young people, by sex, achieving at least a minimum proficiency level in reading and mathematics, in end of lower secondary.

Denominator: total number of children in end of lower secondary

Formula: (numerator/denominator)

Indicator 33—Outcome

Proportion of children with information and communications technology skills, by type of skills.

Numerator: Number of children with information and communications technology skills, by type of skills.

Denominator: Total number of children.

Formula: (numerator/denominator).

Indicator 34—Outcome

Proportion of children under 5 years of age who are developmentally on track in health, learning and psychosocial well-being, by sex.

Numerator: Number of children under 5 years of age who are developmentally on track, by sex.

Denominator: Total number of children under 5 years of age, by sex.

Formula: (numerator/denominator).

Indicator 35—Outcome

Percentage of children receiving individual support for school access and attendance (e.g. free tutoring, food subsidies, school transport).

Numerator: Number of students in primary and secondary schools receiving individual support for school access and attendance.

Denominator: Total number of students (primary and secondary).

Formula: (numerator/denominator) × 100.

Indicator 36—Outcome

Participation rate in organised learning (1 year before the official primary entry age), by sex.

36.1 Girls

Numerator: Number of preschool girls who are about to start school and have attended an early childhood education centre for at least 1 year.

Denominator: Total number of preschool girls who will start or have started school this year (age of school entry may differ from one country to another).

Formula: (numerator/denominator) at the entry point to elementary school.

36.2 Boys

Numerator: Number of preschool boys who are about to start school and have attended an early childhood education centre for at least 1 year.

Denominator: Total number of preschool boys who will start or have started school this year (age of school entry may differ from one country to another).

Formula: (numerator/denominator) at the entry point to elementary school.

Indicator 37—Outcome

Percentage of students who identify as a minority and who completed secondary education.

Numerator: Number of students who identify as a minority who completed secondary education.

Denominator: Total number of students who identify as a minority.
Formula: (numerator/denominator) × 100.

Article 29—The Aims of Education

1. States Parties agree that the education of the child shall be directed to:
   (a) The development of the child's personality, talents and mental and physical abilities to their fullest potential;
   (b) The development of respect for human rights and fundamental freedoms, and for the principles enshrined in the Charter of the United Nations;
   (c) The development of respect for the child's parents, his or her own cultural identity, language and values, for the national values of the country in which the child is living, the country from which he or she may originate, and for civilizations different from his or her own;
   (d) The preparation of the child for responsible life in a free society, in the spirit of understanding, peace, tolerance, equality of sexes, and friendship among all peoples, ethnic, national and religious groups and persons of indigenous origin;
   (e) The development of respect for the natural environment.
2. No part of the present article or article 28 shall be construed so as to interfere with the liberty of individuals and bodies to establish and direct educational institutions, subject always to the observance of the principle set forth in paragraph 1 of the present article and to the requirements that the education given in such institutions shall conform to such minimum standards as may be laid down by the State.

Table 2 Article 29 Indicator sets

Core attributes			
Ensuring that aims and objectives of education are in conformity with the CRC	**Rights-consistent curricula**	**Rights-respecting pedagogy**	**Rights-reflecting school environment**
Data is collected and disaggregated by prohibited grounds for discrimination including age, sex, ethnicity, disability, when applicable.			
Structural indicators			
1. Legislation is in place enshrining aims of education in compliance with Article 29.			
2. Time-bound plans of action on the aims of education with sufficient budgets are in place.			
3. There is a national focal point and/or body established to develop and implement a plan for mandatory human rights education.			

Table 2 (continued)

	4. School curricula includes: • Child rights education at all levels • Gender equality and awareness raising for school-based violence against girls • Promotion of respect for child's parents and a culture of peace and non-violence • Global citizenship • (SDG 4.7 adapted) Sustainable development and sustainable lifestyles • Health education and healthy lifestyles conducive to child's maximum development.	5. Teacher training curricula includes tools, knowledge and skills needed to promote: • Child rights education at all levels • Gender equality and awareness raising for school-based violence against girls • Respect for child's parents and a culture of peace and non-violence • Global citizenship • (SDG 4.7 adapted) Sustainable development and sustainable lifestyles • Health education and healthy lifestyles conducive to child's maximum development.	6. (GCRD) Legislation guarantees: • Establishment of school councils for students • Child participation in the development of school policies and curricula at the national level • Evaluations of teacher and school administrations through the inclusion of student bodies, in a meaningful and safe manner.
Process indicators			
7. Teachers are evaluated for both their knowledge and their use of human rights in practice.	8. Students are assessed for human rights education, knowledge, skills, and attitudes. 9. Percentage of schools implementing environment, climate, and SDG related awareness-raising activities.	10. Teachers receive human rights training. 11. Percentage of schools that provide evidence-based reproductive and sexual health education (see also art. 24).	12. Percentage of schools with student councils with membership elected by the students (see also art. 12).
Outcome indicators			
	13. Percentage of children with knowledge of: • The CRC • How to claim their rights.	14. Percentage of teachers with knowledge of the CRC.	15. Rate of violent incidents in schools 16. Percentage of children who feel that their views are considered in schools (see also art. 12). 17. Percentage of children who feel that student councils play a meaningful role in schools.

Article 29—Guidance

The following provides guidance for the collection of data on specific indicators for Article 29. The number relates to the number of that indicator in the table above. Each indicator is identified as a Process, Structural, or Outcome Indicator, and the formula to calculate the data is described.

Indicator 9—Process

Percentage of schools implementing environment, climate, and SDG related awareness-raising activities.

Numerator: Number of schools implementing environment, climate, and SDG related awareness-raising activities.

Denominator: Total number of schools surveyed.

Formula: (numerator/denominator) × 100.

Indicator 11—Process

Percentage of schools that provide evidence-based reproductive and sexual health education.

Numerator: Number of schools that provide evidence-based reproductive and sexual health education.

Denominator: Total number of schools.

Formula: (numerator/denominator) × 100.

Indicator 12—Process

Percentage of schools with student councils with membership elected by the students.

Numerator: Number of schools with student councils with membership elected by the students.

Denominator: Total number of schools surveyed.

Formula: (numerator/denominator) × 100.

Indicator 13—Outcome

Percentage of children with knowledge of:

13.1 The CRC

Numerator: Number of children with knowledge of the CRC.
Denominator: Total number of children surveyed.
Formula: (numerator/denominator) × 100
13.2 How to claim their rights.
Numerator: Number of children with knowledge of how to claim their rights.
Denominator: Total number of children surveyed.
Formula: (numerator/denominator) × 100

Indicator 14—Outcome

Percentage of teachers with knowledge of CRC.

Numerator: Number of teachers with CRC knowledge.

Denominator: Total number of teachers surveyed.

Formula: (numerator/denominator) × 100.

Indicator 15—Outcome

Rate of annual violent incidents in schools.

Numerator: Number of violent incidents in schools in the past year, disaggregated by age and gender.

Denominator: Total number of children in the school in the past year, disaggregated by age and gender.

Formula: (numerator/denominator) × 100 children.

Indicator 16—Outcome

Percentage of children who feel that their views are considered in schools.

Numerator: Number of children who feel their views are considering in schools.

Denominator: Total number of children surveyed.

Formula: (numerator/denominator) × 100.

Indicator 17—Outcome

Percentage of children who feel that student councils play a meaningful role in schools.

Numerator: Number of children who feel that student councils play a meaningful role in schools.

Denominator: Total number of children surveyed.

Formula: (numerator/denominator) × 100.

Article 30—Culture, Religious and Linguistic Rights of Minority or Indigenous Children

> In those States in which ethnic, religious or linguistic minorities or persons of indigenous origin exist, a child belonging to such a minority or who is indigenous shall not be denied the right, in community with other members of his or her group, to enjoy his or her own culture, to profess and practise his or her own religion, or to use his or her own language.

Table 3 Article 30 Indicator sets

Core attributes		
Enjoy their own culture	**Profess and practice their own religion**	**Use their own language**
Data is collected and disaggregated by prohibited grounds for discrimination including age, sex, ethnicity, disability, when applicable.		
Structural indicators		
1. State has ratified the *Convention on the Elimination of All Forms of Racial Discrimination.* 2. State has ratified relevant regional instruments: • *Framework Convention for the Protection of National Minorities* • *European Charter for Regional or Minority Languages* • *Inter-American Convention against Racism, Racial Discrimination and Related Forms of Intolerance* • *Inter-American Convention against All Forms of Discrimination and Intolerance* • *African Charter on Human and Peoples' Rights* 3. The legislation provides for: • Anti-discrimination clauses: – List of prohibited conducts – List of prohibited grounds of discrimination – Definition of vulnerable groups including Minority and Indigenous People (M&IP). • The respect of international standards on data protection with respect to the M&IP • Special support mechanisms allocated to respect the protection and promotion of M&IP • Representation of M&IP within educational and cultural institutions • Criminal and administrative penalties for online and offline hate crimes, including bullying against M&IP 4. National strategy and plan of action in place with a time frame and budget to reduce discrimination and increase integration of M&IP into society. 5. National school curricula include topics related to multicultural environment and appreciation of culture of M&IP and different ethnic groups.		
	6. Legislation provides for the right to hold and practice religion individually and in community with others, both in public and private.	

(continued)

Table 3 (continued)

Process indicators		
7. Amount of national budget spent on campaigns to promote respect for children belonging to M&IP during the reporting period. 8. Number of institutions of ethnic, linguistic minority and religious population groups during last 12 months that are: • Accredited • Provided with financial support. 9. Percentage of relevant administrative personnel trained on anti-discrimination/M&IP related legislation within the last 12 months. 10. Amount of total national budget to support research on culture, language, and traditions of M&IP. 11. Amount of total national budget to support activities conducted by • Children belonging to M&IP • M&IP civil society organisations working with children. 12. Amount of the education budget to scholarships for children belonging to M&IP.		
13. Percentage of media institutions of ethnic, linguistic minority and religious population groups that receive public support.	14. Amount of budget to support M&IP religious schools.	15. Percentage of schools where children are taught in both the official language(s) and minority languages (see also art. 29).
Outcome indicator		
16. Percentage of minority and indigenous children in out-of-home care placed within their own cultural community (see also art. 20).	17. Percentage of schools that recognise the right to be excused school during M&IP religious holidays (see aso art. 14 and art. 31). 18. Percentage of children belonging to M&IP who feel that their culture and religion are respected in school.	19. Percentage of children receiving public education in their own language and majority language of the country.

Article 30—Guidance

The following provides guidance for the collection of data on specific indicators for Article 30. The number relates to the number of that indicator in the table above. Each indicator is identified as a Process, Structural, or Outcome Indicator, and the formula to calculate the data is described.

Indicator 9—Process

Percentage of relevant administrative personnel trained on anti-discrimination/ M&IP related legislation during the last 12 months.

Numerator: Number of relevant administrative personnel trained on anti-discrimination/M&IP related legislation during the last 12 months.

Denominator: Number of relevant administrative personnel during the last 12 months.

Formula: (numerator/denominator) × 100.

Indicator 13—Process

Percentage of media institutions of ethnic, linguistic minority and religious population groups that receive public support.

Numerator: Number of media institutions of ethnic, linguistic minority and religious population groups that receive public support.

Denominator: Total number of media institutions of ethnic, linguistic minority and religious population groups.

Formula: (numerator/denominator) × 100.

Indicator 15—Process

Percentage of schools where children are taught in both the official language(s) and minority languages.

Numerator: Number of schools where children are taught in both the official language(s) and minority languages.

Denominator: Total number of schools.

Formula: (numerator/denominator) × 100.

Indicator 16—Outcome

Percentage of minority and indigenous children in out-of-home care placed with extended family or other minority and indigenous caregivers.

Numerator: Number of minority and indigenous children in out-of-home care placed with extended family or other minority and indigenous caregivers.

Denominator: All children placed in out-of-home care with extended family or other caregivers.

Formula: (numerator/denominator) × 100.

Indicator 17—Outcome

Percentage of children belonging to M&IP who are officially excused from school during M&IP religious holidays.

Numerator: Number of children belonging to M&IP who are officially excused from school during M&IP religious holidays.
Denominator: All children belonging to M&IP in schools.
Formula: (numerator/denominator) × 100.

Indicator 18—Outcome

Percentage of children belonging to M&IP who feel that their culture and religion are respected in school.
Numerator: Number of children belonging to M&IP who feel that their culture and religion are respected in school.
Denominator: Total number of children belonging to M&IP in school who were surveyed.
Formula: (numerator/denominator) × 100.

Indicator 19—Outcome

Percentage of children receiving public education in their own language and majority language of the country (Art 28 & Art 29.)
Numerator: Number of children receiving public education in their own language and majority language of the country.
Denominator: Total number of children receiving public education.
Formula: (numerator/denominator) × 100.

Article 31—The Rights to Rest, Play, Recreation, and Cultural and Artistic Activities

1. States Parties recognize the right of the child to rest and leisure, to engage in play and recreational activities appropriate to the age of the child and to participate freely in cultural life and the arts.
2. States Parties shall respect and promote the right of the child to participate fully in cultural and artistic life and shall encourage the provision of appropriate and equal opportunities for cultural, artistic, recreational and leisure activity.

Table 4 Article 31 Indicator sets

<table>
<tr><th colspan="4">Core attributes</th></tr>
<tr><th>Rest and leisure</th><th>Play and recreation</th><th>Cultural life and the arts</th><th>Creating appropriate and equal opportunities for enjoyment of Article 31 rights</th></tr>
<tr><td colspan="4">Data is collected and disaggregated by prohibited grounds for discrimination including age, sex, ethnicity, disability, when applicable.</td></tr>
<tr><td colspan="4">Structural indicators</td></tr>
<tr><td colspan="4">1. State has introduced legislation, supported by a national play strategy, to guarantee Article 31 rights, including a ‘principle of sufficiency’, whereby all children are provided with sufficient opportunity, time, and space to exercise those rights.
2. State has introduced legislation and regulations requiring buildings, facilities, equipment and services for play, recreation, culture arts and sports to be informed by principles of universal design and children’s specific needs.
3. Regulations are in place to ensure that all schools have areas where children, including children with disabilities, can play and where physical education, sporting and recreation activities can be practised.
4. Regulatory framework is in place ensuring safety with regard to all aspects of Article 31 including:
• Safety and accessibility standards for all toys, games, recreational facilities and play equipment
• Appropriate standards and limitations on advertising
• Codes of professional practice in the fields of play, sports, culture, and the arts
• Protection and classification systems for media broadcasting and film
• Online safety.</td></tr>
<tr><td>5. Legislation is in place guaranteeing protection of the right to rest and leisure, as developmentally appropriate for all ages, and in all circumstances, in both work and educational environments.</td><td>6. Legislation is in place imposing obligations on local authorities to provide safe and accessible play and recreational facilities as appropriate for all children of all ages within their community.</td><td>7. (GCRD) National school curriculum for both primary and secondary schools (if in place) incorporates provision for culture and the arts, reflecting all cultural and minority ethnic groups living in the State Party.</td><td>8. State has reviewed and, where necessary repealed, any legislation impeding the exercise of Article 31 rights, for example, curfews.</td></tr>
<tr><td colspan="4">Process indicators</td></tr>
<tr><td colspan="4">9. Clear guidelines, supported by sufficient budgets, have been developed for different levels of government providing targets to be met to realise responsibilities relating to Article 31.
10. Percentage of schools with appropriate rest, leisure, play, sports, recreational and arts facilities that are age and disability appropriate.
11. Availability of pre- and in-service training on importance of play, recreation, rest, leisure, and participation in cultural and artistic activities in children’s development for all professionals dealing with children.</td></tr>
<tr><td>12. Percentage of schools, including preschool, primary and secondary, that provide age-appropriate time for rest and leisure within the school day.</td><td>13. Number of formal and informal play and recreation centres available for children in communities.</td><td>14. Percentage of national/regional arts and culture budget allocated to children’s artistic and cultural activities.</td><td>15. Percentage of parents provided with guidance on the importance of play and recreation in children’s development.
16. Number of municipalities providing affordable public transport for all children.</td></tr>
</table>

(continued)

Table 4 (continued)

Outcome indicators			
17. Percentage of children reporting that rest and leisure times during the school day are adequate.	18. Percentage of children, including those with disabilities and in institutions, who play outside for at least 4 h each week in an adequate environment. 19. Percentage of children, including children with disabilities, who feel that the range and quality of play facilities and spaces they can access in their neighbourhood is adequate. 20. Percentage of children reporting that it is safe to play in their community.	21. Average number of creative or cultural activities that children have participated in within the past 12 months.	22. Number of complaints received by the relevant authorities relating to children's inadequate access to play, recreation, and the arts, in the past 12 months. 23. Number of complaints received by relevant authorities in the past 12 months relating to unsafe or inappropriate experiences by children in the exercise of their Article 31 rights. 24. Percentage of children able to access affordable transport to participate in play, recreation, culture, and the arts on a weekly basis. 25. (GCRD) Percentage of parents who value self-directed play in the home.

Article 31—Guidance

The following provides guidance for the collection of data on specific indicators for Article 31. The number relates to the number of that indicator in the table above. Each indicator is identified as a Process, Structural, or Outcome Indicator, and the formula to calculate the data is described.

Indicator 10—Process

Percentage of schools with appropriate rest, leisure, play, sports, recreational and arts facilities that are age and disability appropriate.

Numerator: Number of schools with appropriate rest, leisure, play, sport, recreational and arts facilities that are age and disability appropriate.

Denominator: Total number of schools.

Formula: (numerator/denominator) × 100.

Indicator 12—Process

Percentage of schools, including preschool, primary and secondary, that provide age-appropriate time for rest and leisure within the school day.

Numerator: Number of selected setting (pre-, primary, or secondary school) that provide age-appropriate time for rest and leisure within the school day.

Denominator: Total number of selected setting (pre-, primary, or secondary school).

Formula: (numerator/denominator) × 100.

Indicator 14—Process

Percentage of national/regional arts and culture budget allocated to children's artistic and cultural activities.

Numerator: Amount of national/regional arts and culture budget allocated to children's artistic and cultural activities.

Denominator: Total national/regional arts and culture budget.

Formula: (numerator/denominator) × 100.

Indicator 15—Process

Percentage of parents provided with guidance on the importance of play and recreation in children's development.

Numerator: Number of parents provided with guidance on the importance of play and recreation in children's development.

Denominator: Total number of parents surveyed.

Formula: (numerator/denominator) × 100.

Indicator 17—Outcome

Percentage of children reporting that rest and leisure times during the school day are adequate.

Numerator: Number of children reporting that rest and leisure times during the school day are adequate.

Denominator: Total number of school children surveyed.

Formula: (numerator/denominator) × 100.

Indicator 18—Outcome

Percentage of children, including those with disabilities and in institutions, who play outside for at least 4 h each week in an adequate environment.

Numerator: Number of children, including those with disabilities and in institutions, who play outside for at least 4 h each week in an adequate environment.

Denominator: Total number of children.

Formula: (numerator/denominator) × 100.

Indicator 19—Outcome

Percentage of children, including children with disabilities, who feel that the range and quality of play facilities and spaces they can access in their neighbourhood is adequate.

Numerator: Number of children, including children with disabilities, who feel that the range and quality of play facilities and spaces they can access in their neighbourhood is adequate.

Denominator: Total number of children.

Formula: (numerator/denominator) × 100.

Indicator 20—Outcome

Percentage of children reporting that it is safe to play in their community.

Numerator: Number of children reporting that it is safe to play in their community.

Denominator: Total number of children surveyed.

Formula: (numerator/denominator) × 100.

Indicator 24—Outcome

Percentage of children able to access affordable transport to participate in play, recreation, culture, and the arts on a weekly basis.

Numerator: Number of children able to access affordable transport to participate in play, recreation, culture, and the arts on a weekly basis.

Denominator: Total number of children surveyed.

Formula: (numerator/denominator) × 100.

Indicator 25—Outcome

Percentage of parents who value self-directed play in the home.

Numerator: Number of parents who value self-directed play in the home.

Denominator: Total number of parents surveyed.

Formula: (numerator/denominator) × 100.

Chapter 9
Measures to Protect Children from Violence

Ziba Vaghri, Roberta Ruggiero, Gerison Lansdown, Adem Arkadas-Thibert, and Christian Whalen

Articles 19, 37, and 39 provide a cluster of provisions that address the right of children to protection from all forms of violence and abuse, and to rehabilitative help if those rights are violated or neglected.[1]

- Article 19—the right to protection from all forms of violence
- Article 37—the right to protection from cruel, inhuman, or degrading treatment

[1] For further elaboration on the implications and implementation of each of these rights, please read the relevant chapter in the companion publication to this book: *Monitoring State Compliance with the UN Convention on the Rights of the Child: An analysis of attributes*, Vaghri, Zermatten, Lansdown and Ruggiero, Springer, 2022.

Z. Vaghri
GlobalChild Program of Research, University of New Brunswick, Saint John, NB, Canada

R. Ruggiero (✉)
Centre for Children's Right Studies, Faculty of Law, University of Geneva, Geneva, Switzerland
e-mail: Roberta.ruggiero@unige.ch

G. Lansdown
School of Law, University College Cork, Cork, Ireland

A. Arkadas-Thibert
Independent Researcher, Specializing in International Human Rights, Marseille, France

C. Whalen
Faculty of Law, University of New Brunswick, Fredericton, NB, Canada

Z. Vaghri et al. (eds.), *Children's Rights-Based Indicators*, Children's Well-Being: Indicators and Research 28,
https://doi.org/10.1007/978-3-031-71594-5_9

- Article 39—the right to recovery and reintegration for children who have been abused, exploited, or experienced other forms of harm.

Article 19 establishes unequivocally that no form of violence against a child is acceptable, and that children have a fundamental human right to protection and to respect for their dignity and integrity in all settings, whether at home, in school, in institutions, or in detention.[2] The Committee has been clear that this prohibition extends to all forms of corporal punishment.

Article 37 goes beyond comparable provisions in earlier treaties and prohibits capital punishment, or life imprisonment without possibility of parole, and the Committee has argued that life imprisonment under any circumstances is an unacceptable punishment for a child. In addition, imprisonment of children must only be used as a measure of last resort, and for the shortest possible time.

Article 39, an innovative provision in international human rights law, introduces the right of children who have experienced any form of violence, abuse, neglect, exploitation, torture, or armed conflict to receive help with physical and psychological recovery and rehabilitation. While the principle of reparation and compensation for human rights violations is well established, Article 39 goes further, imposing a responsibility on States Parties to promote children's positive recovery even where the State Party itself is not responsible for harm that has been experienced.

Article 19—The Right to Protection from all Forms of Violence

1. States Parties shall take all appropriate legislative, administrative, social and educational measures to protect the child from all forms of physical or mental violence, injury or abuse, neglect or negligent treatment, maltreatment or exploitation, including sexual abuse, while in the care of parent(s), legal guardian(s) or any other person who has the care of the child.
2. Such protective measures should, as appropriate, include effective procedures for the establishment of social programmes to provide necessary support for the child and for those who have the care of the child, as well as for other forms of prevention and for identification, reporting, referral, investigation, treatment and follow-up of instances of child maltreatment described heretofore, and, as appropriate, for judicial involvement.

[2] For the purposes of the indicators in Article 19, references to violence extend to all aspects covered in the Article, e.g. physical and mental violence, injury or abuse, and neglect or negligent treatment or exploitation, including sexual abuse.

Table 1 Article 19 Indicator sets

Core attributes			
Protection from all forms of violence	**Protection while in the care of parents, legal guardians, or any other person**	**All appropriate measures**	**Effective identification, reporting, investigation, and treatment of harm**
Data is collected and disaggregated by prohibited grounds for discrimination including age, sex, ethnicity, disability, when applicable.			
Structural indicators			
1. State has ratified relevant treaties to protect children from all forms of violence including: • *Convention on the Elimination of All Forms of Racial Discrimination*, 1965 • *UN Convention on the Rights of Persons with Disabilities*, 2007 • *ILO Convention No. 138* (concerning the minimum age for admission to employment), 1978 • *Convention Against Torture and other Cruel, Inhuman or Degrading Treatment or Punishment*, 1985 • *ILO Convention No. 182* (concerning the prohibition and immediate action for the elimination of the worst forms of child labour), 1999 • *Protocol to Prevent, Suppress and Punish Trafficking in Persons, Especially Women and Children* (Palermo Protocol), 2000 • *Optional Protocol on the Sale of Children, Child Prostitution, and Child Pornography*, 2000 • *Optional Protocol on the Involvement of Children in Armed Conflict*, 2000. 2. Child protection laws are established: • To prohibit all forms of violence, including physical punishment of children, in all settings • To introduce criminal sanctions for violence against children, child sexual abuse and exploitation • To establish child-friendly reporting mechanisms for children experiencing violence • To require the reporting of all suspected incidents of violence against children to the authorities • To provide for the child's safe removal and placement in conformity with the Convention and the Alternative Care Guidelines, if necessary for their best interests • To provide rehabilitation supports and other measures of redress to children for the harm they have experienced. 3. A national coordinating and monitoring framework on violence against children is in place.			
	4. Child-protection services are mandated to address violence towards children in all settings.	5. National guidelines for the health systems are in place to respond to child maltreatment and sexual violence against children.	

(continued)

Table 1 (continued)

Process indicators			
6. Training programmes to help children prevent and respond to violence are developed for schools. 7. Percentage of children who were taught in their classes in the past academic year how to prevent and respond to violence per school level.	8. Percentage of all child victims of violence, placed in alternative care settings for protection purposes. 9. Percentage of all children in alternative settings who report being a victim of violence (e.g. schools, prisons, hospitals, group homes and alternative care settings.)	10. Percentage of child victims of violence, who gained access to services they need, by type of service: educational, medical, psychosocial, or legal. 11. Codes of conduct for all childcare professionals and state officials, are established and adopted for managing Violence Against Children (VAC) incidences. 12. Level of government funding invested in research on VAC within the past 12 months (e.g. to academic institutes, non-governmental organisations, and other research stakeholders). 13. Rate of social service workers with responsibility for child protection (or child welfare) per 100,000 children, according to type (e.g. governmental or non-governmental). 14. Percentage of medical worker, social workers, or police personnel who have received pre- and/or in-service training in identifying VAC in the past 12 months. 15. Percentage of parents that received parental education on VAC. 16. Number of public educational programmes delivered on child rights and VAC.	17. Percentage of complaints of violence against children lodged with the national child rights institution, children's commissioner, advocate, ombudsman, or other mechanism. 18. Rate of calls to confidential helplines for victims of VAC (per 1000 call) during the past 12 months.

(continued)

Table 1 (continued)

Outcome indicators			
19. (SDG 16.1.3 Adapted) Percentage of child victims identified by region, age and type of harm including injury, physical abuse, emotional harm, neglect, sexual harm, trafficking, or enlistment. 20. (SDG 16.2.1) Percentage of children who experienced any physical punishment and/or psychological aggression by caregivers in the past month, by sex and age. 21. Percentage of children aged 13–17 years who experienced sexual violence in the past 12 months, by sex and age. 22. Percentage of children who report having been victims of cyberbullying in the past 12 months. 23. Percentage of child victims who have used child-protection services and whose needs for emotional, psychosocial, physical, and intellectual well-being have been met.	24. Percentage of children aged 13–17 years who report that their parents or guardians understood their problems and worries most of the time or always.	25. Percentage of children aged 13–17 who stayed away from school during the past 12 months because they felt unsafe at, or on the way to/from school or online. 26. Percentage of children who feel safe reporting a situation of abuse to a trusted adult: • At home • In community • Or at school. 27. Percentage of children aged 13–17 who are aware of legislation banning key forms of VAC, such as physical punishment. 28. Percentage of adults who are aware of legislation banning key forms of VAC, such as physical punishment.	29. Percentage of all reported cases of VAC that are investigated and disposed of by type of intervention (child removal, supervision, parental support, kinship placement etc.) in the past 12 months. 30. Rate of persons arrested, adjudicated, convicted. Or serving sentence for crimes against children (per 100,000 child population), by type of offence, in the past 12 months. 31. Percentage of formal investigations on VAC incidences of state officials (e.g. teachers, school administrations, social workers, law enforcement, and other officials) resulting in disciplinary actions or prosecution in the past 12 months 32. Percentage of children who know where to report and are confident to report complaints about their treatment. 33. Percentage of children aged 13–17 years who sought institutional or professional help for physical violence in childhood in the past 12 months. 34. Average duration of sentence for cyberbullying and luring offences.

Article 19—Guidance

The following provides guidance for the collection of data on specific indicators for Article 19. The number relates to the number of that indicator in the table above. Each indicator is identified as a Process, Structural, or Outcome Indicator, and the formula to calculate the data is described.

Indicator 7—Process

Percentage of children who were taught in their classes in the past academic year how to prevent and respond to violence per school level.

Numerator: Number of children who were taught in their classes in the past academic year how to prevent and respond to violence per school level.

Denominator: total number of children in school.

Formula: (numerator/denominator) × 100.

Indicator 8—Process

Percentage of all child victims of violence, placed in alternative care settings for protection purposes.

Numerator: Number of all child victims of violence, placed in alternative care settings for protection purposes.

Denominator: Total number of child victims of violence.

Formula: (numerator/denominator) × 100.

Indicator 9—Process

Percentage of all children in alternative settings (e.g. schools, prisons, hospitals, group homes and alternative care settings) who report being a victim of violence.

Numerator: Number of all children in alternative settings (e.g. schools, prisons, hospitals, group homes and alternative care settings) who report being a victim of violence.

Denominator: Total number of child victims in alternate settings (e.g. schools, prisons, hospitals, group homes and alternative care settings).

Formula: (numerator/denominator) × 100.

Indicator 10—Process

Percentage of child victims of violence who gained access to services they need, by type of service: educational, medical, psychosocial, or legal.

Numerator: Number of child victims of violence who gained access to services they need, by type of service: educational, medical, psychosocial, or legal.

Denominator: Total number of child victims of violence.

Formula:(numerator/denominator) × 100.

Indicator 13—Process

Rate of social service workers with responsibility for child protection (or child welfare) per 100,000 children, according to type (e.g. governmental or non-governmental).

Numerator: Number of social service workers with responsibility for child protection (or child welfare).

Denominator: Total number of children.

Formula: (numerator/denominator) per 100,000 children.

Indicator 14—Process

Percentage of medical workers, social workers, or police personnel who have received pre- and/or in-service training in identifying VAC during the past 12 months.

Numerator: Number of medical workers, social workers, or police personnel who have received pre- and/or in-service training in identifying VAC during the past 12 months.

Denominator: Total number of medical workers, social workers, or police personnel that worked with children during the past 12 months.

Formula: (numerator/denominator) × 100.

Indicator 15—Process

Percentage of parents that received parental education on VAC.

Numerator: Number of parents that received parental education on VAC.

Denominator: Total number of parents surveyed.

Formula: (numerator/denominator) × 100.

Indicator 17—Process

Percentage of complaints of VAC lodged with the national child rights institution, children's commissioner, advocate, ombudsman, or other mechanism.

Numerator: Number of received complaints of VAC investigated or adjudicated by the national child rights institution, children's Commissioner, advocate, ombudsman, or other mechanism, in the reporting period.

Denominator: Total number of complaints of VAC, within the same reporting period.

Formula: (numerator/denominator) × 100.

Indicator 18—Process

Rate of calls to confidential helplines for victims of VAC during the past 12 months.

Numerator: Number of calls to confidential helplines for victims of VAC during the past 12 months.

Denominator: Total number of calls received in the past 12 months.

Formula: (numerator/denominator) per 1000 reported cases.

Indicator 19—Outcome

Percentage of child victims identified by region, age and type of harm including injury, physical abuse, emotional harm, neglect, sexual harm, trafficking, or enlistment (SDG 16.1.3 adapted).

Numerator: Number of child victims identified by region, age and type of harm including injury, physical abuse, emotional harm, neglect, sexual harm, trafficking, or enlistment.

Denominator: Total number of children.

Formula: (numerator/denominator) × 100.

Indicator 20—Outcome

Percentage of children who experienced any physical punishment and/or psychological aggression by caregivers in the past month, by sex and age (SDG 16.2.1).

Numerator: Number of children who experienced any physical punishment and/or psychological aggression by caregivers in the past month.

Denominator: Total number of children.

Formula: (numerator/denominator) × 100.

Indicator 21—Outcome

Percentage of children aged 13–17 years who experienced sexual violence in the past 12 months, by sex and age.

Numerator: Number of children aged 13–17 years who experienced sexual violence in the past 12 months.

Denominator: Total number of children aged 13–17 years surveyed.

Formula: (numerator/denominator) × 100.

Indicator 22—Outcome

Percentage of children who report having been victims of cyberbullying in the past 12 months.

Numerator: Number of children who report having been victims of cyberbullying in the past 12 months.

Denominator: Total number of children surveyed.

Formula: (numerator/denominator) × 100.

Indicator 23—Outcome

Percentage of child victims who have used child-protection services and whose needs for emotional, psychosocial, physical, and intellectual well-being have been met.

Numerator: Number of child victims who have used child-protection services and whose needs for emotional, psychosocial, physical, and intellectual well-being have been met.

Denominator: Total number of child victims surveyed who have used child-protection services.

Formula: (numerator/denominator) × 100.

Indicator 24—Outcome

Percentage of children aged 13–17 years who report that their parents or guardians understood their problems and worries most of the time or always.

Numerator: Number of children aged 13–17 years who report that their parents or guardians understood their problems and worries most of the time or always.

Denominator: Total number of children aged 13–17 years surveyed.

Formula: (numerator/denominator) × 100.

Indicator 25—Outcome

Percentage of children aged 13–17 who stayed away from school during the past month and past 12 months because they felt unsafe at, or on the way to/from school or online.

Numerator: Number of children aged 13–17 who stayed away from school during the past month and past 12 months because they felt unsafe at, or on the way to/from school or online.

Denominator: Total number of children aged 13–17 who participated in the survey.

Formula: (numerator/denominator) × 100.

Indicator 26—Outcome

Percentage of children who feel safe reporting a situation of violence to a trusted adult:

26.1 At home

Numerator: Number of children who feel safe reporting a situation of violence to a trusted adult at home.

Denominator: Total number of children surveyed.

Formula: (numerator /denominator) × 100.

26.2 In the community

Numerator: Number of children who feel safe reporting a situation of violence to a trusted adult in the community.

Denominator: Total number of children surveyed.

Formula: (numerator /denominator) × 100

26.3 At school.

Numerator: Number of children who feel safe reporting a situation of violence to a trusted adult at school.

Denominator: Total number of children surveyed.

Formula: (numerator /denominator) × 100

Indicator 27—Outcome

Percentage of children aged 13–17 who are aware of legislation banning key forms of VAC, such as physical punishment.

Numerator: Number of children aged 13–17 who are aware of legislation banning key forms of VAC, such as physical punishment.

Denominator: Total number of children aged 13–17 surveyed.

Formula: (numerator/denominator) × 100.

Indicator 28—Outcome

Percentage of adults who are aware of legislation banning key forms of VAC, such as physical punishment.

Numerator: Number of adults who are aware of legislation banning key forms of VAC, such as physical punishment.

Denominator: Total number of adults aged surveyed.

Formula: (numerator/denominator) × 100.

Indicator 29—Outcome

Percentage of all reported cases of VAC that are investigated and disposed of by type of intervention (child removal, supervision, parental support, kinship placement etc.) in the past 12 months.

Numerator: Number of all reported cases of VAC that are investigated and disposed of by type of intervention (child removal, supervision, parental support, kinship placement etc.) in the past 12 months.

Denominator: Total number of reported cases in the past 12 months.

Formula: (numerator/denominator) × 100.

Indicator 30—Outcome

Rate of persons arrested, adjudicated, convicted, or serving sentence for crimes against children by type of offence, in the past 12 months.

Numerator: Number of persons arrested, adjudicated, convicted, or serving sentence for crimes against children, by type of offence, in the reporting period.

Denominator: Total number of children, during the same reporting period.

Formula: (numerator/denominator) per 100,000 child population.

Indicator 31—Outcome

Percentage of formal investigations on VAC incidences of state officials (e.g. teachers, school administrations, social workers, law enforcement, and other officials) resulting in disciplinary actions or prosecution in the past 12 months.

Numerator: Number of formal investigations on VAC incidences of state officials (e.g. teachers, school administrations, social workers, law enforcement, and other officials) resulting in disciplinary actions or prosecution in the past 12 months.

Denominator: Total number of formal investigations on VAC of state officials (e.g. teachers, school administrations, social workers, law enforcement, and other officials).

Formula: (numerator/denominator) × 100.

Indicator 32—Outcome

Percentage of children who know where to report and are confident to report complaints about their treatment.

Numerator: Number of children who know where to report and are confident to report complaints about their treatment.

Denominator: Total number of children surveyed that experienced sexual violence.

Formula: (numerator/denominator) × 100.

Indicator 33—Outcome

Percentage of children aged 13–17 years who sought institutional or professional help for physical violence in childhood in the past 12 months.

Numerator: Number of children aged 13–17 years who sought institutional or professional help for physical violence in childhood in the past 12 months.

Denominator: Total number of children aged 13–17 years surveyed who report have experienced physical violence in the past 12 months.

Formula: (numerator/denominator) × 100.

Article 37—Prohibition of Torture, Capital Punishment and Arbitrary Deprivation of Liberty

> States Parties shall ensure that:
>
> (a) No child shall be subjected to torture or other cruel, inhuman or degrading treatment or punishment. Neither capital punishment nor life imprisonment without possibility of release shall be imposed for offences committed by persons below 18 years of age;

(b) No child shall be deprived of his or her liberty unlawfully or arbitrarily. The arrest, detention or imprisonment of a child shall be in conformity with the law and shall be used only as a measure of last resort and for the shortest appropriate period of time;
(c) Every child deprived of liberty shall be treated with humanity and respect for the inherent dignity of the human person, and in a manner which takes into account the needs of persons of his or her age. In particular, every child deprived of liberty shall be separated from adults unless it is considered in the child's best interest not to do so and shall have the right to maintain contact with his or her family through correspondence and visits, save in exceptional circumstances;
(d) Every child deprived of his or her liberty shall have the right to prompt access to legal and other appropriate assistance, as well as the right to challenge the legality of the deprivation of his or her liberty before a court or other competent, independent and impartial authority, and to a prompt decision on any such action.

Table 2 Article 37 Indicator sets

Core attributes			
Prohibition of capital punishment, life imprisonment, torture, or degrading treatment	**Principle of non-detention of children; if necessary, only as last resort and for the shortest appropriate time**	**Humane treatment and respect for human dignity at all times**	**No deprivation of liberty without due process**
Data is collected and disaggregated by prohibited grounds for discrimination including age, sex, ethnicity, disability, when applicable.			
Structural indicators			
1. The state has ratified the 1985 *Convention against Torture* and its 2002 protocol. 2. Legislative guarantees are in place to protect the child's Article 37 rights. 3. A national prevention mechanism for monitoring deprivations of liberty, with a specialised mandate for children, has been established.			

(continued)

Table 2 (continued)

4. Court remedies are in place to protect and compensate children from violations of Article 37 rights.	5. Legislation guarantees the following: • Detention only as a last resort and for the shortest appropriate time (see also art. 40) • No unlawful or arbitrary deprivation of liberty, including on grounds of disability or mental health (see also art. 23) • No detention of migrant or asylum-seeking children (see also art. 22).	6. National Prevention Mechanism and/or independent child rights institution have unconditional access to detention facilities to conduct audits and reviews of service. 7. Legislation requires that children are provided with separate facilities from adults (see also art. 40).	8. Legislation guarantees children due process rights including (see also art. 40): • Right to independent legal representation • The right to maintain contact with family • The right to judicial review of any deprivation of liberty in accordance with principles of child-friendly justice.

(continued)

Table 2 (continued)

Process indicators			
9. Percentage of incidents resulting in the use of force, restraints, segregation per institution, by type of intervention and by disaggregated class of detainees.	10. Rate of deprivations of liberty of children per 10,000 children by: • Length of sentence • Category of offence • Kind of institution (open or closed custody). 11. Percentage of children who are subject to pre-trial detention.	12. Percentage of all staff in settings where children may be deprived of liberty who are trained in relation to non-violent threat response, trauma informed care and child-rights based approaches. 13. Percentage of complaints about detention: • Investigated within 48 hours. • Addressed within 30 days. 14. Numbers of complaints by children alleging abuse of force involving state officials (e.g. staff in detention centres, health professionals or police). 15. Percentage of places of detention that have had an independent inspection visit in last 12 months. 16. A safe and accessible complaints system for children in detention is in place	

(continued)

Table 2 (continued)

Outcome indicators			
17. Percentage of Article 37 complaints responded to effectively by the government in the past 12 months. 18. Percentage of detained children who feel they are treated fairly and humanely at all times.	19. Rate of recidivism amongst child offenders. 20. Number of children in detention, pre- and post-sentence per 100,000 child population.	21. Percentage of children in detention not wholly separated from adults. 22. Percentage of children deprived of liberty who feel that their views are heard, and opinions considered in decisions affecting them. 23. Percentage of children deprived of liberty who report that decisions about their lives and detention are taken in accordance with their best interests 24. Percentage of places of detention with a safe and accessible complaints system. 25. Percentage of children deprived of liberty who have had contact with family within the last 3 months, by: • Frequency of visit • Status of family member contacted • Direct or indirect contact with family • Place of detention. 26. Rate of child deaths and critical injury reports of children in detention in the past 12 months per 1000 children detained.	27. Percentage of children in conflict with the law who report that they feel safe and that they were treated fairly in their interactions with police and court officials (see also art. 40).

Article 37—Guidance

The following provides guidance for the collection of data on specific indicators for Article 37. The number relates to the number of that indicator in the table above. Each indicator is identified as a Process, Structural, or Outcome Indicator, and the formula to calculate the data is described.

Indicator 9—Process

Percentage of incidents resulting in the use of force, restraints, segregation per institution, by type of intervention and by disaggregated class of detainees.

Numerator: Number of incidents resulting in the use of force, restraints, segregation per institution, by type of intervention and by disaggregated class of detainees.

Denominator: Total number of incidents involving detainees.

Formula: (numerator/denominator) × 100.

Indicator 10—Process

Rate of deprivations of liberty of children per 10,000 children by:

10.1 Length of sentence

Numerator: Number of deprivations of liberty of children by length of sentence or category and seriousness of offence.

Denominator: Total number of children.

Formula: (numerator/denominator) per 10,000 (within the given timeframe)

10.2 Category and seriousness of offence.

Numerator: Number of deprivations of liberty of children by category and seriousness of offence.

Denominator: Total number of children.

Formula: (numerator/denominator) per 10,000 (within the given timeframe)

10.3 Kind of institution (open or closed custody).

Numerator: Number of deprivations of liberty of children by kind of institution (open or closed custody).

Denominator: Total number of children.

Formula: (numerator/denominator) per 10,000 (within the given timeframe)

10.4 Year and disaggregated class of detainee.

Numerator: Number of deprivations of liberty of children by year and disaggregated class of detainee.

Denominator: Total number of children.

Formula: (numerator/denominator) per 10,000 (within the given timeframe)

Indicator 11—Process

Percentage of children who are subject to pre-trial detention.

Numerator: Number of children who are subject to pre-trial detention.

Denominator: Total number of accused children.

Formula: (numerator/Denominator) × 100.

Indicator 12—Process

Percentage of all staff in settings where children may be deprived of liberty who are trained in relation to non-violent threat response, trauma informed care and child-rights based approaches.

Numerator: Number of workers in settings where children may be deprived of liberty who are trained in relation to non-violent threat response, trauma informed care and child-rights based approaches.

Denominator: Total number of workers in settings where children may be deprived of liberty.

Formula: (numerator/denominator) × 100.

Indicator 13—Process

Percentage of complaints about detention:

13.1 Investigated within 48 h

Numerator: Number of complaints about detention that are investigated within 48 h.

Denominator: Total number of complaints about detention.

Formula: (numerator/denominator) × 100

13.2 Addressed within 30 days.

Numerator: Number of complaints about detention that are investigated within 30 days.

Denominator: Total number of complaints about detention.

Formula: (numerator/denominator) × 100

Indicator 15—Process

Percentage of places of detention that have had an independent inspection visit in last 12 months.

Numerator: Number of places of detention that have had an independent inspection visit in last 12 months.

Denominator: Total number of places of detention.

Formula: (numerator/denominator) × 100.

Indicator 17—Outcome

Percentage of Article 37 complaints responded to effectively by the government in the past 12 months.

Numerator: Number of Article 37 complaints responded to effectively by the government in the past 12 months.

Denominator: Total number of Article 37 complaints in the past 12 months.
Formula: (numerator/denominator) × 100.

Indicator 18—Outcome

Percentage of detained children who feel they are treated fairly and humanely at all times.

Numerator: Number of detained children who feel they are treated fairly and humanely at all times.
Denominator: Total number of detained children.
Formula: (numerator/denominator) × 100.

Indicator 19—Outcome

Rate of recidivism amongst child offenders.

Numerator: Number of children released from detention committing another offence within 12 months.
Denominator: Total number of children released from detention.
Formula: (numerator/denominator) × 100.

Indicator 20—Outcome

Number of children in detention, pre- and post-sentence per 100,000 child population (Art 40-Ind 22).

Numerator: Number of children in detention, pre- and post-sentence.
Denominator: Total number of children.
Formula: (numerator/denominator) (per 100,000 child population).

Indicator 21—Outcome

Percentage of children in detention not wholly separated from adults.

Numerator: Number of children in detention not wholly separated from adults.
Denominator: Total number of children in detention.
Formula: (numerator/denominator) × 100.

Indicator 22—Outcome

Percentage of children deprived of liberty who feel that their views are heard, and opinions considered in decisions affecting them.

Numerator: Number of children deprived of liberty who feel that their views are heard, and opinions considered in decisions affecting them.

Denominator: Total number of children deprived of liberty surveyed.

Formula: (numerator/denominator) × 100.

Indicator 23—Outcome

Percentage of children deprived of liberty who report that decisions about their lives and detention are taken in accordance with their best interests.

Numerator: Number of children deprived of liberty who report that decisions about their lives and detention are taken in accordance with their best interests.

Denominator: Total number of children deprived of liberty surveyed.

Formula: (numerator/denominator) × 100.

Indicator 24—Outcome

Percentage of places of detention with a safe and accessible complaints system.

Numerator: Number of places of detention with a safe and accessible complaints system.

Denominator: Total number of places of detention.

Formula: (numerator/denominator) × 100.

Indicator 25—Outcome

Percentage of children deprived of liberty who have had contact with family within the last 3 months, by:

25.1 Frequency of visit

Numerator: Number of children in detention who have had contact with family within the last 3 months by frequency of visit.

Denominator: Total number of children deprived of liberty.

Formula: (numerator/denominator) × 100

25.2 Status of family member contacted.

Numerator: Number of children in detention who have had contact with family within the last 3 months by status of family member contacted.

Denominator: Total number of children deprived of liberty.

Formula: (numerator/denominator) × 100

25.3 Direct or indirect contact with family.

Numerator: Number of children in detention who have had contact with family within the last 3 months by direct or indirect contact with family.

Denominator: Total number of children deprived of liberty.

Formula: (numerator/denominator) × 100

25.4 Place of detention.

Numerator: Number of children in detention who have had contact with family within the last 3 months by place of detention.

Denominator: Total number of children deprived of liberty.

Formula: (numerator/denominator) × 100

Indicator 26—Outcome

Rate of child deaths and critical injury reports of children in detention in the past 12 months per 1000 children detained.

Numerator: Number of child deaths and critical injury reports of children in detention in the past 12 month.

Denominator: total number of children in detention in the past 12 months.

Formula: (numerator/denominator) (per 1000 children detained).

Indicator 27—Outcome

Percentage of children in conflict with the law who report that they feel safe and that they were treated fairly in their interactions with police and court officials.

Numerator: Number of children in conflict with the law who report that they feel safe and that they were treated fairly in their interactions with police and country officials.

Denominator: Total number of children in conflict with the law surveyed.

Formula: (numerator/denominator) × 100.

Article 39—The Right to Physical and Psychological Recovery

> States Parties shall take all appropriate measures to promote physical and psychological recovery and social reintegration of a child victim of: any form of neglect, exploitation, or abuse; torture or any other form of cruel, inhuman or degrading treatment or punishment; or armed conflicts. Such recovery and reintegration shall take place in an environment which fosters the health, self-respect and dignity of the child.

Table 3 Article 39 Indicator sets

<table>
<tr><td colspan="2">Core attributes</td></tr>
<tr><td>Quality, appropriateness, and comprehensiveness of the programmes of recovery and reintegration</td><td>Availability, accessibility, and impartiality of programmes of recovery and reintegration</td></tr>
<tr><td colspan="2">Data is collected and disaggregated by prohibited grounds for discrimination including age, sex, ethnicity, disability, when applicable.</td></tr>
<tr><td colspan="2">Structural indicators</td></tr>
<tr><td colspan="2">1. The state has ratified the relevant international treaties including:
• Optional Protocol to the Convention on the Rights of the Child on Involvement of Children in Armed Conflict, 2000
• Optional Protocol to the Convention on the Rights of the Child on the Sale of Children, Child Prostitution and Child Pornography, 2000
• Palermo Protocol to Prevent, Suppress and Punish Trafficking in Persons, 2000.
2. Legislation explicitly guarantees the child's right to physical and psychological recovery and social reintegration after:
• Any form of physical and psychological neglect, exploitation, or abuse, including:
– Sale of children
– Sexual exploitation and abuse
– Child trafficking
– Exploitation of child labour
– Drug abuse
– Online abuse and exploitation.
• Torture or any other form of cruel, inhuman, or degrading treatment or punishment in all institutional settings such as:
– Schools
– Juvenile justice systems
– Institutions of care
– Institutions of treatment
– Institutions for children with disabilities.
• Armed conflicts, including cases of
– Direct involvement
– Indirect involvement</td></tr>
<tr><td>3. Evidence-based quality benchmarks of recovery and rehabilitation programmes have been established to guarantee the health, development, self-respect and dignity and empowerment of the child.
4. Legislation guarantees inclusion of the views of child victims in planning and implementing programmes for recovery and reintegration, including in individual cases.</td><td>5. Legislation guarantees compensation, where applicable, to child victims as a part of recovery and reintegration efforts, including restorative justice where appropriate.</td></tr>
<tr><td colspan="2">Process indicators</td></tr>
<tr><td colspan="2">6. Child-sensitive specialised recovery and rehabilitation programmes are in place for different groups of child victims as defined in the law.
7. Public education, training, and awareness raising for children on all forms of VAC, remedies, and duty to report is available (see also art. 19).
8. Public education, training, and awareness raising for relevant professionals and service providers on all forms of VAC, remedies, and duty to report is available (see also art. 19).</td></tr>
</table>

(continued)

Table 3 (continued)

9. Tools are in place to ensure implementation of established quality benchmarks of the recovery and reintegration processes.	
Outcome indicators	
10. Percentage of children accessing education while receiving treatment. 11. Percentage of children and families who feel satisfied that services and programmes: • Fostered health • Promoted self-respect and dignity for the child • Recognised their needs • Are easily accessible.	12. Percentage of children within the juvenile justice system that have access to recovery and reintegration services and supports. 13. Percentage of identified child victims who have accessed: • Emergency care • Initial assessment • Appropriate and ongoing treatment, care programmes, and services. 14. Percentage of families of identified child victims who have accessed: • Emergency care • Initial assessment • Appropriate and ongoing treatment, care programmes, and services.

Article 39—Guidance

The following provides guidance for the collection of data on specific indicators for Article 39. The number relates to the number of that indicator in the table above. Each indicator is identified as a Process, Structural, or Outcome Indicator, and the formula to calculate the data is described.

Indicator 10—Outcome

Percentage of children accessing education while receiving treatment.

Numerator: Number of children accessing education while receiving treatment.
Denominator: Total number of school-aged children receiving treatment.
Formula: (numerator/denominator) × 100.

Indicator 11—Outcome

Percentage of children and families who feel satisfied that services and programmes:

11.1 Fostered health

Numerator: Number of children and families who feel satisfied that services and programmes fostered health.

Denominator: Total number of children and families receiving these services who were surveyed.

Formula: (numerator/denominator) × 100

11.2 Promoted self-respect and dignity for the child.

Numerator: Number of children and families who feel satisfied that services and programmes promoted self-respect and dignity for the child.

Denominator: Total number of children and families receiving these services who were surveyed.

Formula: (numerator/denominator) × 100

11.3 Recognised their needs.

Numerator: Number of children and families who feel satisfied that services and programmes recognised their needs.

Denominator: Total number of children and families receiving these services who were surveyed.

Formula: (numerator/denominator) × 100

11.4 Are easily accessible.

Numerator: Number of children and families who feel satisfied that services and programmes are easily accessible.

Denominator: Total number of children and families receiving these services who were surveyed.

Formula: (numerator/denominator) × 100

Indicator 12—Outcome

Percentage of children within the juvenile justice system that have access to recovery and reintegration services and supports.

Numerator: Number of children within juvenile justice that have access to recovery and reintegration services and supports.

Denominator: Total number of children within juvenile justice.

Formula: (numerator/denominator) × 100.

Indicator 13—Outcome

Percentage of identified child victims who have accessed:

13.1 Emergency care

Numerator: Number of identified child victims who have accessed emergency care.

Denominator: Total number of identified child victims.

Formula: (numerator/denominator) × 100

13.2 Initial assessment.

Numerator: Number of identified child victims who have accessed an initial assessment.

Denominator: Total number of identified child victims.

Formula: (numerator/denominator) × 100

13.3 Appropriate and ongoing treatment and care programmes and services.

Numerator: Number of child victims who have accessed appropriate and ongoing treatment and care programmes and services.

Denominator: Total number of families of identified child victims who access healthcare services for initial assessment or those who access emergency care, etc.

Formula: (numerator/denominator) × 100

Indicator 14—Outcome

Percentage of families of identified child victims who have accessed:

14.1 Emergency care

Numerator: Number of families of identified child victims who have accessed emergency care.

Denominator: Total number of families of identified child victims.

Formula: (numerator/denominator) × 100

14.2 Initial assessment.

Numerator: Number of families of identified child victims who have accessed an initial assessment.

Denominator: Total number of families of identified child victims.

Formula: (numerator/denominator) × 100.

14.3 Appropriate and ongoing treatment and care programmes and services.

Numerator: Number of families of identified child victims who have accessed appropriate and ongoing treatment and care programmes and services.

Denominator: Total number of families of identified child victims who access healthcare services for initial assessment or those who access emergency care, etc.

Formula: (Numerator/ Denominator) × 100

Chapter 10
Protection Measures from Exploitation

Ziba Vaghri, Roberta Ruggiero, Gerison Lansdown, Adem Arkadas-Thibert, and Christian Whalen

The three articles in this section address different forms of exploitation of children:[1]

- Article 32—right to protection from economic exploitation
- Article 34—right to protections from sexual exploitation
- Article 36—right to protection from all other forms of exploitation.

[1] For further elaboration on the implications and implementation of each of these rights, please read the relevant chapter in the companion publication to this book: *Monitoring State Compliance with the UN Convention on the Rights of the Child: An analysis of attributes*, Vaghri, Zermatten, Lansdown and Ruggiero, Springer, 2022.

Z. Vaghri
GlobalChild Program of Research, University of New Brunswick, Saint John, NB, Canada

R. Ruggiero (✉)
Centre for Children's Right Studies, Faculty of Law, University of Geneva, Geneva, Switzerland
e-mail: Roberta.ruggiero@unige.ch

G. Lansdown
School of Law, University College Cork, Cork, Ireland

A. Arkadas-Thibert
Independent Researcher, Specializing in International Human Rights, Marseille, France

C. Whalen
Faculty of Law, University of New Brunswick, Fredericton, NB, Canada

Z. Vaghri et al. (eds.), *Children's Rights-Based Indicators*, Children's Well-Being: Indicators and Research 28,
https://doi.org/10.1007/978-3-031-71594-5_10

Article 32 addresses the child's right to protection from economic exploitation and work that causes them harm. It does not prohibit children from all forms of work but seeks to reconcile the right to education with participation in the labour market and to ensure that the child does not engage in any form of work detrimental to their health and physical, mental, spiritual, or moral development.

The Convention does not sit alone in seeking to address the scale and severity of the problem of exploitative child labour. It must be understood in the context of a broad range of international instruments addressing economic exploitation, including conventions of the International Labour Organisation and the Optional Protocols to the Convention on the Rights of the Child on Armed Conflict and Commercial Sexual Exploitation. The Committee on the Rights of the Child has stressed the need for states to take measures to remove the drivers of exploitative child labour, including poverty, poor education, discrimination and social exclusion, and lack of knowledge and awareness.

Article 34 emphasises the child's right to protection from sexual abuse and exploitation, including coercion into unwanted sexual activity, prostitution, use in pornographic materials, and child sex tourism. It explicitly demands that State Parties undertake bilateral and multilateral measures to protect children from sexual abuse and exploitation. Significantly increased levels of risk exist in the contexts of migration and conflict, and in the digital environment. Article 34 is reinforced by other instruments, including the Optional Protocols to the Convention and the outcome documents of the World Congresses against Commercial Sexual Exploitation.

Article 36 is an umbrella provision to protect children from any form of exploitation that might be prejudicial to the child's welfare and that is not explicitly addressed in other articles. It serves to ensure that any new or emerging forms of exploitation can be adequately addressed, and places an obligation on States Parties to take proactive measures to respond to all forms of exploitation.

Article 32—The Right to Protection from Economic Exploitation and Hazardous Activities

1. States Parties recognize the right of the child to be protected from economic exploitation and from performing any work that is likely to be hazardous or to interfere with the child's education, or to be harmful to the child's health or physical, mental, spiritual, moral or social development.
2. States Parties shall take legislative, administrative, social and educational measures to ensure the implementation of the present article. To this end, and having regard to the relevant provisions of other international instruments, States Parties shall in particular:

(a) Provide for a minimum age or minimum ages for admission to employment;
(b) Provide for appropriate regulation of the hours and conditions of employment;
(c) Provide for appropriate penalties or other sanctions to ensure the effective enforcement of the present article.

Table 1 Article 32 Indicator sets

Core attributes			
Protection from economic exploitation and harmful work	**Regulatory framework to provide protection**	**Penalties and enforcement for effective protection**	**Administrative, social, and educational measures for protection**
Data is collected and disaggregated by prohibited grounds for discrimination including age, sex, ethnicity, disability, when applicable.			
Structural indicators			
1. State has ratified: • *Optional Protocol on sale of children*, 2000 • *Optional Protocol on involvement of children in armed conflict*, 2000 • *International Labour Organization (ILO) Conventions* No. 138, 1973 and No. 182, 1999 • *International Covenant on Civil and Political Rights*, 1996 • *International Covenant on Economic, Social and Cultural Rights*, 1966.			
2. Legislation is in place stipulating the following: • A minimum age for full time work, consistent with ILO 138. • Proscriptions on hours and conditions of work and rest times, including full and part-time work. • Consistency between school leaving age and entry into full time employment. • Definition and prohibition of the worst forms of child labour consistent with ILO 182. • Prohibition of hazardous work that jeopardises the physical, mental, or moral well-being of a child. • Prohibition of violence, coercion, and corporal punishment in the workplace.	3. A regulatory framework and labour inspectorate is in place which is guided by the CRC, including the views of the child and the best interests of the child.	4. Appropriate and effective sanctions and methods of enforcement are in place to protect children from child labour.	5. Social and economic measures in place to protect children from child labour: • Universal access to quality inclusive primary and secondary education. • Family support programmes. • Poverty eradication programmes. • Decent work programmes for children above the minimum age. • Access to disability and gender inclusive vocational and skill training. • Opportunities for play and leisure.

(continued)

Table 1 (continued)

Process indicators	
6. State cooperation procedures in place with *ILO/International Programme on the Elimination of Child Labour (IPEC)* to eliminate child labour. 7. State consultation procedures in place with children on regulatory framework governing children and work.	
8. Percentage of enterprises/businesses inspected for compliance with child labour legislation. 9. Rate of enterprises/businesses inspected for compliance with child labour legislation in the last 12 months. 10. Percentage of inspections resulting in administrative action or prosecution. 11. Percentage of working children who understand their rights to be protected from the worst forms of child labour and their legal position.	12. Percentage of families provided with awareness-raising programmes on risks of child labour and economic exploitation. 13. Percentage of families provided with support from the state to prevent child labour. 14. Percentage of working children who are part of working children's groups or associations to support them in defending their rights.
Outcome indicators	
15. Percentage and number of children in employment by age group: • Percentage children aged 5 to 11 years engaged in at least 1 h of economic work or 28 h of unpaid household services per week. • Percentage children aged 12 to 14 years engaged in at least 14 h of economic work or 28 h of unpaid household services per week. • Percentage children aged 15 to 17 years engaged in at least 43 h of economic or unpaid household services per week. 16. Percentage of children in hazardous or worst forms of child labour. 17. (SDG 4.1 adapted) Percentage of children who master a broad range of foundational skills, including in literacy and mathematics by the end of the primary school cycle (based on credibly established national benchmarks). 18. (SDG 4.4 adapted) Percentage children leaving secondary school with relevant skills, including technical and vocational skills, for employment, decent jobs, and entrepreneurship. 19. Percentage working children reporting satisfaction with the hours and nature of employment in which they are engaged.	
20. Reported cases of violation of child labour laws.	

Article 32—Guidance

The following provides guidance for the collection of data on specific indicators for Article 32. The number relates to the number of that indicator in the table above. Each indicator is identified as a Process, Structural, or Outcome Indicator, and the formula to calculate the data is described.

Indicator 8—Process

Percentage of enterprises and businesses inspected for compliance with child labour legislation.

Numerator: Number of businesses inspected for compliance with child labour legislation.

Denominator: Total number of registered enterprises and businesses.

Formula: (numerator/denominator) × 100.

Indicator 9—Process

Rate of enterprises and businesses inspected for compliance with child labour legislation in the last 12 months.

Numerator: Total number of inspections of registered enterprises/businesses for compliance with child labour legislation within the last 12 months.

Denominator: Total number of registered enterprises/businesses.

Formula: (Numerator/denominator) in 12 months.

Indicator 10—Process

Percentage of inspections resulting in administrative action or prosecution.

Numerator: Number of inspections resulting in administrative action or prosecution within the last 12 months.

Denominator: total number of inspections within last 12 months.

Formula: (numerator/denominator) × 100.

Indicator 11—Process

Percentage of working children who understand their rights to be protected from the worst forms of child labour and their legal position.

Numerator: Number of working children who understand their rights to be protected from the worst forms of child labour and their legal position.

Denominator: Total number of working children.

Formula: (numerator/denominator) × 100.

Indicator 12—Process

Percentage of families provided with awareness-raising programmes on risks of child labour and economic exploitation.

Numerator: Number of families provided with awareness-raising programmes on risks of child labour and economic exploitation.

Denominator: Total number of households with children.

Formula: (numerator/denominator) × 100.

Indicator 13—Process

Percentage of families provided with support from the state to prevent child labour.

Numerator: Number of families provided with support from the state to prevent child labour.

Denominator: Total number of families.

Formula: (Numerator/denominator) × 100.

Indicator 14—Process

Percentage of working children who are part of working children's groups or associations to support them in defending their rights.

Numerator: Number of working children who are part of working children's groups or associations to support them in defending their rights.

Denominator: Total number of working children.

Formula: (numerator/denominator) × 100.

Indicator 15—Outcome

Percentage and number of children in employment by age group.

15.1 Percentage children aged 5 to 11 years engaged in at least 1 h of economic work or 28 h of unpaid household services per week

Numerator: Number of children aged 5 to 11 years engaged in at least 1 h of economic work or 28 h of unpaid household services per week.

Denominator: Total number of children aged 5–11.

Formula: (numerator/denominator) × 100

15.2 Percentage children aged 12 to 14 years engaged in at least 14 h of economic work or 28 h of unpaid household services per week.

Numerator: Number of children aged 12 to 14 years engaged in at least 14 h of economic work or 28 h of unpaid household services per week.

Denominator: Total number of children aged 12 to 14 years.

Formula: (numerator/denominator) × 100

15.3 Percentage children aged 15 to 17 years engaged in at least 43 h of economic or unpaid household services per week.

Numerator: Number of children aged 15 to 17 years engaged in at least 43 h of economic or unpaid household services per week.

Denominator: Total number of children aged 15 to 17 years.

Formula: (numerator/denominator) × 100

Indicator 16—Outcome

Percentage of children in hazardous or worst forms of child labour.

Numerator: Number of children in hazardous or worst forms of child labour.

Denominator: Total number of working children.

Formula: (numerator/denominator) × 100.

Indicator 17—Outcome

Percentage of children who master a broad range of foundational skills, including in literacy and mathematics by the end of the primary school cycle, based on credibly established national benchmarks (SDG 4.1 adapted).

Numerator: Number of children who master a broad range of foundational skills, including in literacy and mathematics by the end of the primary school cycle, in a given year, based on credibly established national benchmarks.

Denominator: Total number of children leaving primary school within the same given year.

Formula: (numerator/denominator) × 100.

Indicator 18—Outcome

Percentage children leaving secondary school with relevant skills, including technical and vocational skills, for employment, decent jobs, and entrepreneurship (SDG 4.4 adapted).

Numerator: Number of children leaving secondary school with relevant skills, including technical and vocational skills, for employment, decent jobs, and entrepreneurship, in a given year.

Denominator: Total number of children leaving secondary school within the same year.

Formula: (numerator/denominator) × 100.

Indicator 19—Outcome

Percentage working children reporting satisfaction with the hours and nature of employment in which they are engaged.

Numerator: Number of working children reporting satisfaction with the hours and nature of employment in which they are engaged.

Denominator: Total number of working children.

Formula: (numerator/denominator) × 100.

Article 34—The Right to Protection from all Forms of Sexual Exploitation and Sexual Abuse

States Parties undertake to protect the child from all forms of sexual exploitation and sexual abuse. For these purposes, States Parties shall in particular take all appropriate national, bilateral and multilateral measures to prevent:

(a) The inducement or coercion of a child to engage in any unlawful sexual activity;
(b) The exploitative use of children in prostitution or other unlawful sexual practices;
(c) The exploitative use of children in pornographic performances and materials.

Table 2 Article 34 Indicator sets

Core attributes	
Protection from sexual exploitation and abuse	**All appropriate national, bilateral, and multilateral measures to prevent sexual exploitation of children**
Data is collected and disaggregated by prohibited grounds for discrimination including age, sex, ethnicity, disability, when applicable.	

(continued)

Table 2 (continued)

<table>
<tr><th colspan="2">Structural indicators</th></tr>
<tr><td colspan="2">1. The state has ratified:
• Optional Protocol on the Sale of Children, Child Prostitution and Child Pornography (OPSC), 2000
• International Labour Organization (ILO) No. 182, 1999
• Council of Europe Convention on the Protection of Children against Sexual Exploitation and Sexual Abuse, 2007
• Council of Europe Convention on Cybercrime, 2001
• Council of Europe Convention on preventing and combating violence against women and domestic violence, 2011
2. Legislation against sexual exploitation of children is in place with following components:
• Crimes committed domestically and/or transnationally at all settings as well as online
• Protection of children online is covered (in the media and information communications technologies such as mobile, internet, chat rooms, social media sites, (GCRD) dating apps and self-created images, etc.)
• Specialised judicial procedures for all Sexual and Exploitation of Children (SEC) in line with the United Nations Guidelines on Justice in Matters involving Child Victims and Witnesses of Crime
• Appropriate forms of assistance, rehabilitation, reintegration, redress, and compensation for each SEC survivor/victim
• Criminalisation of all offline and online acts and failure or complicity to act of the perpetrators of SEC in accordance with Article 34 and other relevant international standards
• Definition, prohibition, and criminalisation of all acts of sexual exploitation of children in their jurisdiction, irrespective of any set age of consent or marriage or cultural practice, even when the adult is unaware of the child's age.</td></tr>
<tr><td>3. Specialised protective mechanisms are in place including:
• Special police units and child-friendly legal counselling units to combat sexual exploitation and abuse crimes against children
• Helplines
• Shelters
• Medical services offered to child victims
• Psychosocial counselling services.</td><td>4. A time-bound and budgeted national (and sub-national where necessary) SEC prevention strategy (standalone or integrated) is in place with coordination, monitoring, mechanisms and data collection, analysis, and dissemination systems.
5. SEC prevention (including sexual education and reproductive health and rights) is included in the curricula from pre-primary to high school.
6. SEC prevention is included in training curricula (including tertiary, pre-service and in-service training) for professionals working in health, education, justice, child welfare systems, and any other professions working for and/or with children.</td></tr>
</table>

(continued)

Table 2 (continued)

Process indicators	
7. Percentage of prosecutions and convictions for the SEC offences, disaggregated by offence. 8. Percentage of child victims provided with information of their rights, their role and the scope, timing, and progress of the proceedings and of the disposition of their cases by state-funded legal services. 9. Percentage of child victims provided with supportive services for physical, psychological, or social recovery.	10. Continuous SEC awareness-raising programmes in place targeting families, communities, and community/religious leaders to combat taboos, cultural resistance societal tolerance and to promote child protective norms. 11. Percentage of population reached by targeted SEC prevention programmes including media campaigns, disaggregated by medium used. 12. Percentage of civil servants who received pre- and/or in-service training preventive and protective measures to address SEC, disaggregated by profession (such as teachers, care providers, social workers, public prosecutors, judges, etc.), 13. Targeted programmes against SEC including training, information, ethical codes of conduct for business sector, especially in tourism, travel, and information technologies are established. 14. Percentage of parents and caregivers who understand SEC risks and their rights to protect their children.
Outcome indicators	
15. (SDG 16.2 adapted) Number of child victims of SEC, disaggregated by type of exploitation and location—National/international. 16. (SDG 16.3.1) Proportion of victims of violence in the previous 12 months who reported their victimisation to competent authorities or other officially recognised conflict resolution mechanisms. 17. (SDG 5.2.1 adapted) Proportion of ever-partnered girls aged 18 years and below subjected to physical, sexual, or psychosocial violence by a current or former intimate partner in the previous 12 months, by form of violence and by age. 18. (SDG 5.2.2 adapted) Proportion of girls aged 18 years and below subjected to sexual violence by persons other than an intimate partner in the previous 12 months, by age and place of occurrence. 19. (SDG 16.1.3 adapted) Proportion of children subjected to sexual violence in the previous 12 months. 20. (SDG 16.2.3) Proportion of young women and men aged 18–29 years who experienced sexual violence by age 18 years. 21. (SDG 5.3.1) Proportion of women aged 20–24 years who were married or in a union before age 15 and before age 18	

Article 34—Guidance

The following provides guidance for the collection of data on specific indicators for Article 34. The number relates to the number of that indicator in the table above. Each indicator is identified as a Process, Structural, or Outcome Indicator, and the formula to calculate the data is described.

Indicator 7—Process

Percentage of prosecutions and convictions for SEC offences, disaggregated by offence.

Numerator: Number of prosecutions and convictions for the SEC offences.

Denominator: Total number of reported SEC offences.

Formula: (Numerator / denominator) × 100 (disaggregated by offence).

Indicator 8—Process

Percentage of child victims provided with information of their rights, their role and the scope, timing, and progress of the proceedings and of the disposition of their cases by state-funded legal services.

Numerator: Number of child survivors/victims provided with information of their rights, their role and the scope, timing, and progress of the proceedings and of the disposition of their cases by state-funded legal services.

Denominator: Total number of child survivors/victims.

Formula: (numerator/denominator) × 100.

Indicator 9—Process

Percentage of child victims provided with supportive services for physical, psychological, or social recovery.

Numerator: Number of child survivors/victims provided with support services for physical, psychological, or social recovery.

Denominator: Total number of child survivors/victims.

Formula: (numerator/denominator) × 100.

Indicator 11—Process

Percentage of population reached by targeted SEC prevention programmes including media campaigns, disaggregated by medium used.

Numerator: Population reached by targeted SEC prevention programmes including media campaigns.

Denominator: Total population.

Formula: (numerator/denominator) × 100 (disaggregated by medium used).

Indicator 12—Process

Percentage of civil servants who received pre- and/or in-service training preventive and protective measures to address SEC, disaggregated by profession (such as teachers, care providers, social workers, public prosecutors, judges, etc.).

Numerator: Number of civil servants who received pre- and/or in-service training preventive and protective measures to address SEC.

Denominator: The total number civil servants.

Formula: (numerator/denominator) × 100 (disaggregated by profession).

Indicator 14—Process

Percentage of parents and caregivers who understand SEC risks and their rights to protect their children.

Numerator: Number of parents and caregivers who understand SEC risks and their rights to protect their children.

Denominator: Total number of parents/caregivers surveyed.

Formula: (numerator/denominator) × 100.

Indicator 16—Outcome

Proportion of victims of violence in the previous 12 months who reported their victimisation to competent authorities or other officially recognised conflict resolution mechanisms (SDG 16.3.1).

Numerator: Number of victims of violence in the previous 12 months who reported their victimisation to competent authorities or other recognised conflict resolution mechanisms.

Denominator: Total number of victims of violence in the previous 12 months.

Formula: (numerator/denominator).

Indicator 17—Outcome

Proportion of ever-partnered girls aged 18 years and below subjected to physical, sexual, or psychosocial violence by a current or former intimate partner in the previous 12 months, by form of violence and by age.

Numerator: Number of ever-partnered girls aged 18 years and below subjected to physical, sexual, or psychosocial violence by a current or former intimate partner in the previous 12 months.

Denominator: Total number of ever-partnered girls aged 18 years and below surveyed.

Formula: (numerator/denominator) (disaggregated by form of violence and age).

Indicator 18—Outcome

Proportion of girls aged 18 years and below subjected to sexual violence by persons other than an intimate partner in the previous 12 months, by age and place of occurrence.

Numerator: Number of girls aged 18 years and below subjected to sexual violence by persons other than an intimate partner in the previous 12 months.

Denominator: Total number of girls aged 18 years and below surveyed.

Formula: (numerator/denominator) (disaggregated by age and place of occurrence).

Indicator 19—Outcome

Proportion of children subjected to sexual violence in the previous 12 months.

Numerator: Number of children subjected to sexual violence in the previous 12 months.

Denominator: Total number of children surveyed.

Formula: (numerator/denominator).

Indicator 20—Outcome

Proportion of young women and men aged 18–29 years who experienced sexual violence by age 18 years.

Numerator: Number of young women and men aged 18–29 years who experienced sexual violence by age 18 years.

Denominator: Total number of young women and men aged 18–29 years surveyed.

Formula: (numerator/denominator).

Indicator 21—Outcome

Proportion of women aged 20–24 years who were married or in a union before age 15 and before age 18.

Numerator: Number of women aged 20–24 years who were married or in a union before the age 15 and before age 18.

Denominator: Total number of women aged 20–24 years who are married or in a union surveyed.

Formula: (numerator/denominator) (disaggregated by before the age of 15 years and before the age of 18 years).

Article 36—The Right to Protection from Other Forms of Violence

> States Parties shall protect the child against all other forms of exploitation prejudicial to any aspects of the child's welfare.

Table 3 Article 36 Indicator sets

<table>
<tr><th colspan="2">Core attributes</th></tr>
<tr><th>Monitoring and identification of all other forms of exploitation prejudicial to any aspects of the child's welfare</th><th>Prevention and protection from all other forms of exploitation prejudicial to any aspects of the child's welfare</th></tr>
<tr><td colspan="2">Data is collected and disaggregated by prohibited grounds for discrimination including age, sex, ethnicity, disability, when applicable.</td></tr>
<tr><td colspan="2">Structural indicators</td></tr>
<tr><td colspan="2">1. Legal framework guarantees that children are protected from all forms of exploitation prejudicial to any aspects of the child's rights and welfare in such settings including but not limited to:
• Sports training programmes
• Advertisements
• Commercial use
• In cinema and TV
• Selling of data
• Internet including chatrooms, social networks and dating apps.</td></tr>
<tr><td>2. State code of conduct encourages telecommunications companies to waive costs for incoming calls to child helplines by means of toll-free telephone numbers.</td><td>3. National law requires business enterprises and other stakeholders including online and offline media and entertainment businesses to undertake due diligence in order to identify, prevent and mitigate their impact on the rights of the child.</td></tr>
<tr><td colspan="2">Process indicators</td></tr>
<tr><td colspan="2">4. The child-protection system includes support services, assistance and psychological recovery for children subjected to the following:
• Violation of rights and privacy
• Violence
• Cyberbullying and cyber harassment
• Sexual exploitation or abuse in the digital environment.
5. The child-protection system is gender sensitive at all levels.</td></tr>
</table>

(continued)

Table 3 (continued)

6. A specialised police unit for cyber-crimes is in place to prevent and protect against potential exploitation of children.	7. Online helplines and complaints mechanisms are in place specifically for children.
Outcome indicators	
8. Number of crimes against children identified by the law enforcement agencies in following settings: • Sports training programmes • Advertisements • Commercial use • In cinema and TV • Selling of data • Internet including chatrooms, social networks and dating apps. 9. Number of cases where a conviction with a remedial sentence was handed down and enforced: • Sports training programmes • Advertisements • Commercial use • In cinema and TV • Selling of data • Internet including chatrooms, social networks and dating apps.	10. Number of calls relating to concerns of exploitation to helplines in last 12 months.

Chapter 11
Protection Measures for Children in Vulnerable Situations

Ziba Vaghri, Roberta Ruggiero, Gerison Lansdown, Adem Arkadas-Thibert, and Christian Whalen

Children can encounter a range of challenging situations that expose them to particular risk of rights violations and which, accordingly, demand additional forms of protection. In this section, the rights of four such groups of children are addressed:[1]

- Article 22—rights of refugee children
- Article 35—right to protection from sale, trafficking and abduction

[1] For further elaboration on the implications and implementation of each of these rights, please read the relevant chapter in the companion publication to this book: *Monitoring State Compliance with the UN Convention on the Rights of the Child: An analysis of attributes*, Vaghri, Zermatten, Lansdown and Ruggiero, Springer, 2022.

Z. Vaghri
GlobalChild Program of Research, University of New Brunswick, Saint John, NB, Canada

R. Ruggiero (✉)
Centre for Children's Right Studies, Faculty of Law, University of Geneva, Geneva, Switzerland
e-mail: Roberta.ruggiero@unige.ch

G. Lansdown
School of Law, University College Cork, Cork, Ireland

A. Arkadas-Thibert
Independent Researcher, Specializing in International Human Rights, Marseille, France

C. Whalen
Faculty of Law, University of New Brunswick, Fredericton, NB, Canada

Z. Vaghri et al. (eds.), *Children's Rights-Based Indicators*, Children's Well-Being: Indicators and Research 28,
https://doi.org/10.1007/978-3-031-71594-5_11

- Article 38—right to protection from armed conflict
- Article 40—right to protection in the juvenile justice system

In each case, the Convention builds on already existing international instruments developed to strengthen the commitment to appropriate protection for children caught in these circumstances. And such circumstances must not be used by states to undermine any of the other rights in the Convention. Indeed, the vulnerability of refugee children, or those caught up in trafficking, armed conflict, or the justice system are entitled to additional protections to guarantee their rights.

Article 22 affirms existing recognition in international law that refugee children are entitled to special care and protection, and addresses rights to protection and assistance, respect for rights cooperation, and family reunification.

Article 35 has been strengthened through the *Optional Protocol on Sexual Exploitation* and the 2000 *Trafficking Protocol*. These reflect the significant increase in the scale and nature of abduction, trafficking, and sale of children, aided primarily by the digital environment and rapid globalisation since the Convention was drafted. The article introduces obligations to adopt all possible political, social, economic, and cultural measures to prevent such exploitation, as well as legislative and policy measures to criminalise, investigate, and prosecute all perpetrators of crimes of exploitation against children, nationally, regionally, and internationally.

Children and armed conflict are addressed in Article 38, which integrates human rights and international humanitarian law. The final text reflects a compromise that afforded lower levels of protection than many members of the drafting group on the Convention were seeking. It requires states to ensure compliance with international humanitarian law, protect children under the age of 15 from direct participation in hostilities, refrain from recruiting children under 15 into armed forces, and take measures to protect civilian children affected by armed conflict. The *Optional Protocol on children and armed conflict*, adopted in 2000, strengthens these provisions.

Article 40 introduces a child rights-based approach to youth justice policy. It places obligations on states to ensure consideration of the child's best interests, due process, minimum ages of criminal responsibility, diversion from the criminal justice system, and reintegration. It also demands specialised youth justice systems with a focus on rehabilitation and restorative justice rather than retribution and repression.

Article 22—The Right to Protection for Refugee and Asylum-Seeking Children

1. States Parties shall take appropriate measures to ensure that a child who is seeking refugee status or who is considered a refugee in accordance with applicable international or domestic law and procedures shall, whether unaccompanied or accompanied by his or her parents or by any other person, receive appropriate protection and humanitarian assistance in the enjoyment of applicable rights set forth in the present Convention and in other international human rights or humanitarian instruments to which the said States are Parties.
2. For this purpose, States Parties shall provide, as they consider appropriate, cooperation in any efforts by the United Nations and other competent intergovernmental organisations or non-governmental organisations co-operating with the United Nations to protect and assist such a child and to trace the parents or other members of the family of any refugee child in order to obtain information necessary for reunification with his or her family. In cases where no parents or other members of the family can be found, the child shall be accorded the same protection as any other child permanently or temporarily deprived of his or her family environment for any reason, as set forth in the present Convention.

Table 1 Article 22 Indicator sets

Core attributes			
Appropriate protection and humanitarian assistance	**Preservation of rights**	**Duty to protect and assist through international cooperation**	**Best interests and family reunification principles**
Data is collected and disaggregated by prohibited grounds for discrimination including age, sex, ethnicity, disability, when applicable.			
Structural indicators			
1. The state has ratified relevant international and multilateral treaties in relation to refugee children and their families and incorporated them into domestic law, including the: • *Convention to the Status of Refugees*, 1951, and its 1967 Protocol • *Convention on the Rights of the Child Optional Protocol on the sale of children, child prostitution and child pornography*, 2000 • *Convention on the Rights of the Child Optional Protocol on the Rights of the Child on the involvement of children in armed conflict*, 2000 • *Protocol to Prevent, Suppress and Punish Trafficking in Persons, especially Women and Children*, 2000 • *Protocol against the Smuggling of Migrants by Land Sea Air*. 2000 • *International Convention on the Protection of the Rights of All Migrants and Members of their Families*, 1990 • *Global Compact on Refugees*, 2018 • *International Labour Organization (ILO) No. 138, 1973, and No. 182*, 1999.			
2. Immigration detention of children is prohibited (see also art. 37).			
3. Constitutional and human rights guarantees apply equally to citizens and non-citizens so as to guarantee refugee children equality before the law.			

(continued)

Table 1 (continued)

4. Legislation is in place to ensure appropriate care and assistance is provided to unaccompanied refugee and asylum-seeking children.	5. National Immigration law guarantees the right to all services, including education and health, on an equal basis with other children.	6. National Immigration laws comply with the best interests principle in line with Convention Child General Comment No. 13 on best interests, and: • Guarantee systems for a fair hearing and due process rights • Provide legal aid. 7. Mechanisms are in place for cooperation with UN and international refugee agencies, to trace their families and be reunited with them.	
Process indicators			
8. Data collection mechanisms are in place on refugee and asylum-seeking children.	9. Trauma-based trainings are provided for all professionals working with refugee and asylum-seeking children.	10. Percentage of unaccompanied refugees and asylum-seeking children provided with independent representation. 11. Percentage of unaccompanied refugees and asylum-seeking children who are registered for family reunification services.	
Outcome indicators			
12. Percentage of refugee and asylum-seeking children that within 30 days of arrival access the following services, including: • Basic child • Welfare • Health • Education. 13. Rate of refugee and asylum-seeking children in receipt of social security benefits, through the child, family, or guardian (see also art. 26).	14. Percentage of refugee and asylum-seeking children completing secondary education. 15. Percentage of refugee and asylum-seeking children who drop out of: • Primary education • Secondary education. 16. Percentage of refugee and asylum-seeking children who are registered with a family doctor.	17. Rate of refugee and asylum-seeking children who feel confident in the knowledge of the language of their country of destination within 24 months of arrival.	18. Percentage of unaccompanied refugee and asylum-seeking children who are reunited with their families: • In country of destination • In a third country • In country of origin. 19. Percentage of unaccompanied refugee and asylum-seeking children (unable to be reunited with their families) who are adopted or provided with alternative care.

Article 22—Guidance

The following provides guidance for the collection of data on specific indicators for Article 22. The number relates to the number of that indicator in the table above. Each indicator is identified as a Process, Structural, or Outcome Indicator, and the formula to calculate the data is described.

Indicator 10—Process

Percentage of unaccompanied refugees and asylum-seeking children provided with independent representation.

Numerator: Number of unaccompanied refugee and asylum-seeking children.

Denominator: Total unaccompanied refugee and asylum-seeking children population.

Formula: (numerator/denominator) × 100.

Indicator 11—Process

Percentage of unaccompanied refugees and asylum-seeking children who are registered for family reunification services.

Numerator: Number of unaccompanied refugees and asylum-seeking children who are registered for family reunification services.

Denominator: Total number of unaccompanied refugees and asylum-seeking children needing registration for family reunification services.

Formula: (numerator/denominator) × 100.

Indicator 12—Outcome

Rate of refugee and asylum-seeking children that within 30 days of arrival access core services, including basic child welfare, health, and education).

Numerator: Number of refugee and asylum-seeking children that within 30 days of arrival access core services, including basic child welfare, health, and education.

Denominator: Total number of refugee and asylum-seeking children arriving over 30 days.

Formula: (numerator/denominator) per 30 days.

Indicator 13—Outcome

Percentage of refugee and asylum-seeking children in receipt of social security benefits, through the child, family, or guardian.

Numerator: Number of refugee and asylum-seeking children in receipt of social security benefits, through the child, family, or guardian.

Denominator: Total number of refugee and asylum-seeking children.

Formula: (numerator/denominator) × 100.

Indicator 14—Outcome

Percentage of refugee and asylum-seeking children completing -secondary education.

Numerator: Number of refugee and asylum-seeking children completing -secondary education.

Denominator: Total number of refugee and asylum-seeking children completing -secondary education.

Formula: (numerator/denominator) × 100.

Indicator 15—Outcome

Percentage of refugee and asylum-seeking children who drop out of:

15.1 Primary education

Numerator: Number of refugee and asylum-seeking children who drop out of primary school

Denominator: Total number of refugee and asylum-seeking children in primary school.

Formula: (numerator/denominator) × 100

15.2 Secondary education.

Numerator: Number of refugee and asylum-seeking children who drop out of secondary school.

Denominator: Total number of refugee and asylum-seeking children in secondary school.

Formula: (numerator/denominator) × 100

Indicator 16—Outcome

Percentage of refugee children and asylum-seeking children who are registered with a family doctor.

Numerator: Number of refugee and asylum-seeking children who are registered with a family doctor.

Denominator: Total number of refugee and asylum-seeking children.

Formula: (numerator/denominator) × 100.

Indicator 17—Outcome

Rate of refugee and asylum-seeking children who feel confident in the knowledge of the language of their country of destination within 24 months of arrival.

Numerator: Number of refugee and asylum-seeking children who feel confident in the knowledge of the language of their country of destination within 24 months of arrival.

Denominator: Total number of refugee and asylum-seeking children arriving within 24 months.

Formula: (numerator/denominator) per 24 months.

Indicator 18—Outcome

Percentage of unaccompanied refugee and asylum-seeking children who are reunited with their families, preferably disaggregated according to:

- In country of destination
- In a third country
- In country of origin.

Numerator: Number of unaccompanied refugee and asylum-seeking children who are reunited with their families.

Denominator: Total number of unaccompanied refugee and asylum-seeking children registered for reunification.

Formula: (numerator/denominator) × 100.

Indicator 19—Outcome

Percentage of unaccompanied refugee and asylum-seeking children (unable to be reunited with their families) who are adopted or provided with alternative care.

Numerator: Number of unaccompanied refugee and asylum-seeking children (unable to be reunited with their families) who are adopted or provided with alternative care.

Denominator: Total number of unaccompanied refugee and asylum-seeking children (unable to be reunited with their families) needing alternative care.

Formula: (numerator/denominator) × 100.

Article 35—Prevention of Abduction, Sale and Trafficking

States Parties shall take all appropriate national, bilateral and multilateral measures to prevent the abduction of, the sale of or traffic in children for any purpose or in any form.

Table 2 Article 35 Indicator sets

<table>
<tr><td colspan="3">Core attributes</td></tr>
<tr><td>National, bilateral, and multilateral measures to prevent abduction, sale, and trafficking</td><td>Establishing preventive and protective legal and policy framework</td><td>Protection of survivors/victims of abduction, sale and trafficking</td></tr>
<tr><td colspan="3">Data is collected and disaggregated by prohibited grounds for discrimination including age, sex, ethnicity, disability, when applicable.</td></tr>
<tr><td colspan="3">Structural indicators</td></tr>
<tr><td colspan="3">1. The state has ratified:
• Optional Protocol on the Sale of Children, Child prostitution and Child Pornography, 2000
• UN Protocol to Prevent, Suppress and Punish, Trafficking in Persons, especially Women and Children, 2000
• Hague Convention on Inter-Country Adoption, 1993.
2. The state has harmonised national (and sub-national law where relevant) law in line with all relevant international law.
3. Criminal law provides for separate definitions for abduction, sale, prostitution, pornography and trafficking of children.
4. There is a comprehensive and child rights-centred national strategy and plan of action addressing abduction, sale, prostitution, pornography, and trafficking of children.</td></tr>
<tr><td>5. The state has multilateral and bilateral agreements to identify and prosecute perpetrators.
6. Laws establish clear jurisdictional authority to prosecute extraterritorial crimes against children.</td><td></td><td>7. Legislation recognises the rights of child victims to:
• Confidentiality
• Physical safety
• Right to be heard in relevant hearings
• Care and accommodation
• Legal counselling
• Medical including psychological assistance
• Compensation for damages
• Protection from criminal procedures or sanctions for offences related to their situation.</td></tr>
<tr><td colspan="3">Process indicators</td></tr>
<tr><td>8. Policies are in place to decrease risk factors at national and transnational level.
9. Systems are in place to monitor and exchange information at national and transnational levels to reduce risk of crimes against children under this attribute.</td><td>10. The number of cases of identified crimes against children under this attribute.
11. A monitoring mechanism is in place to identify children at risk of being victims of crime under this attribute.
12. Public awareness campaigns are in place.
13. Specific trained police units exist throughout the country.</td><td>14. States establish, run and/or financially support:
• Accessible child and gender sensitive help and information services
• Sheltered accommodation for child victims
• Psychosocial and, medical rehabilitation services
• Legal advice and representation.</td></tr>
</table>

(continued)

Table 2 (continued)

Outcome indicators		
15. Number of requests for extradition made or received for any crimes under this attribute within the past 12 months. 16. Percentage of extradition requests that have been honoured. 17. Percentage of victims who have been returned or reintegrated successfully.	18. Number of successful prosecutions of crimes under this attribute within the past 12 months.	19. Number of children within the past 12 months accessing the following services: • Help and information services • Sheltered accommodation or care (e.g. foster parents or guardians) • Psychosocial and medical rehabilitation services • Legal services. 20. (SDG 16.2 adapted) Number of victims of human trafficking per 100,000 population by form of exploitation in the past 12 months. 21. Number of victims placed in detention facilities during criminal investigations or proceedings in the past 12 months. 22. Number of cases in which victims received compensation in the past 12 months.

Article 35—Guidance

The following provides guidance for the collection of data on specific indicators for Article 35. The number relates to the number of that indicator in the table above. Each indicator is identified as a Process, Structural, or Outcome Indicator, and the formula to calculate the data is described.

Indicator 16—Outcome

Percentage of extradition requests that have been honoured.

Numerator: Number of extradition requests that have been honoured.

Denominator: Total number of extradition requests.

Formula: (numerator/ denominator) × 100.

Indicator 17—Outcome

Percentage of victims who have been returned or reintegrated successfully.

Numerator: Number of who have been returned or reintegrated successfully.
Denominator: Total number of victims.
Formula: (numerator/ denominator) × 100.

Article 38—The Right to Protection from Armed Conflict

1. States Parties undertake to respect and to ensure respect for rules of international humanitarian law applicable to them in armed conflicts which are relevant to the child.
2. States Parties shall take all feasible measures to ensure that persons who have not attained the age of 15 years do not take a direct part in hostilities.
3. States Parties shall refrain from recruiting any person who has not attained the age of 15 years into their armed forces. In recruiting among those persons who have attained the age of 15 years but who have not attained the age of 15 years, States Parties shall endeavour to give priority to those who are oldest.
4. In accordance with their obligations under international humanitarian law to protect the civilian population in armed conflicts, States Parties shall take all feasible measures to ensure protection and care of children who are affected by an armed conflict.

Table 3 Article 38 Indicator sets

Core attributes			
Respect for international humanitarian law (IHL) applicable to the child	**Age limits on participation on hostilities**	**Age of recruitment**	**All feasible measures of care and protection**
Data is collected and disaggregated by prohibited grounds for discrimination including age, sex, ethnicity, disability, when applicable.			
Structural indicators			
1. State has ratified: • *Optional Protocol to the Convention on the Rights of the Child on the involvement of children in armed conflict*, 2000 • *Optional Protocol on the sale of children, child prostitution and child pornography,* 2000 • *International Labour Organization (ILO) Convention no. 182*, 2000 • *Geneva Conventions and subsequent Optional Protocols*, 1949 • *Rome Statute of the International Criminal Court*, 1998 • *Ottawa Convention on Landmines*, 1997.			
2. State has signed up to the *Paris Principles and Guidelines on Children Associated with Armed Forces or Armed Groups*, 2007.			

(continued)

Table 3 (continued)

	3. Legislation prohibits any participation in hostilities under the age of 18 years. 4. Children accused of crimes committed by children in the context of hostilities are considered primarily as victims rather than perpetrators and treated in accordance with CRC Article 39 and the Paris principles.	5. Legislation prohibits compulsory or forced recruitment into armed forces under the age of 18 years. 6. Legislation prescribes that 18 years is the minimum age for voluntary recruitment into armed forces, together with safeguards to guarantee against coercion.	
Process indicators			
7. State applies IHL, for monitoring compliance with Article 38. 8. The state's armed forces are provided with pre- and/or in-service training on IHL and children's rights.	9. (GCRD) Programmes for all children below the age of 18 years are in place, where appropriate to: • Raise awareness of the risks of participation in hostilities • Raise awareness of rights to protection from participation in hostilities • Provide alternative opportunities to reduce likelihood of participation.	10. Where voluntary recruitment of under 18 years is permitted, children are: • Provided with comprehensive information on implications of enlisting • Prohibited from direct participation in conflict or working with firearms • Entitled to leave armed forces at any stage • Provided with appropriate counselling and psychosocial support. 11. State has taken active measures to demobilise any children already recruited, in a manner consistent with the *Paris Principles.* 12. State has systems in place to facilitate recovery and rehabilitation of demobilised children in a manner consistent with the *Paris Principles.*	13. State guarantees special protection measures for children in accordance with 3rd and 4th *Geneva Conventions* and protocols 1 & 2. 14. Safe access to education for all children, including early years, is provided and protected in situations of armed conflict.

(continued)

Table 3 (continued)

15. Judicial mechanisms are in place to tackle gross violations of IHL and children's rights in situations of armed conflict. 16. State consistently seeks and gives due weight to the views of children in all matters related to demobilisation and rehabilitation.			
Outcome indicators			
17. Percentage of members of armed forces trained and knowledgeable concerning IHL and the CRC.			
	18. (GCRD) Percentage of children aware of their right to protection from participation in hostilities. 19. Number of children participating directly or indirectly in hostilities over a 12-month period.	20. Number of children below the age of 18 years recruited into armed forces within the past 12 months. 21. Number of children below the age of 18 years recruited into militia or armed groups within a 12-month period.	22. Number of children within the past 12 months: • Affected by armed conflict • Affected by sexual exploitation and/or gender-based violence in a situation of armed conflict • Physically or psychologically harmed by armed conflict • Killed by armed conflict • Displaced internally or outside the country. 23. Percentage of children provided with access to education in situations of armed conflict. 24. Percentage of children participating in hostilities demobilised and reintegrated within their families and communities. 25. Percentage of children demobilised and provided with recovery and rehabilitation.

Article 38—Guidance

The following provides guidance for the collection of data on specific indicators for Article 38. The number relates to the number of that indicator in the table above. Each indicator is identified as a Process, Structural, or Outcome Indicator, and the formula to calculate the data is described.

Indicator 17—Outcome

Percentage of members of armed forces trained and knowledgeable concerning IHL and the CRC.

Numerator: Number of members of armed forces trained and knowledgeable concerning IHL and the CRC.

Denominator: Total number of members of armed forces.

Formula: (numerator/denominator) × 100.

Indicator 18—Outcome

Percentage of children aware of their right to protection from participation in hostilities.

Numerator: Number of children aware of their right to protection from participation in hostilities.

Denominator: Total number of children at risk of participation in hostilities.

Formula: (Numerator/denominator) × 100.

Indicator 23—Outcome

Percentage of children provided with access to education in situations of armed conflict.

Numerator: Number of children provided with access to education in situations of armed conflict.

Denominator: Total number of children in situations of armed conflict.

Formula: (Numerator / denominator) × 100.

Indicator 24—Outcome

Percentage of children participating in hostilities demobilised and successfully reintegrated within their families and communities.

Numerator: Number of children participating in hostilities demobilised and successfully reintegrated within their families and communities.

Denominator: Total number of children participating in hostilities.

Formula: (numerator/denominator) × 100.

Indicator 25—Outcome

Percentage of children demobilised and provided with recovery and rehabilitation.

Numerator: Number of children demobilised and provided with recovery and rehabilitation.

Denominator: Total number of children participating in hostilities.

Formula: (numerator/denominator) × 100.

Article 40—The Rights in a Juvenile Justice Setting

1. States Parties recognize the right of every child alleged as, accused of, or recognized as having infringed the penal law to be treated in a manner consistent with the promotion of the child's sense of dignity and worth, which reinforces the child's respect for the human rights and fundamental freedoms of others and which takes into account the child's age and the desirability of promoting the child's reintegration and the child's assuming a constructive role in society.
2. To this end, and having regard to the relevant provisions of international instruments, States Parties shall, in particular, ensure that:

   (a) No child shall be alleged as, be accused of, or recognized as having infringed the penal law by reason of acts or omissions that were not prohibited by national or international law at the time they were committed;

   (b) Every child alleged as or accused of having infringed the penal law has at least the following guarantees:

(i) To be presumed innocent until proven guilty according to law;
(ii) (ii) To be informed promptly and directly of the charges against him or her, and, if appropriate, through his or her parents or legal guardians, and to have legal or other appropriate assistance in the preparation and presentation of his or her defence;
(iii) To have the matter determined without delay by a competent, independent and impartial authority or judicial body in a fair hearing according to law, in the presence of legal or other appropriate assistance and, unless it is considered not to be in the best interest of the child, in particular, taking into account his or her age or situation, his or her parents or legal guardians;
(iv) Not to be compelled to give testimony or to confess guilt; to examine or have examined adverse witnesses and to obtain the participation and examination of witnesses on his or her behalf under conditions of equality;
(v) If considered to have infringed the penal law, to have this decision and any measures imposed in consequence thereof reviewed by a higher competent, independent and impartial authority or judicial body according to law;
(vi) To have the free assistance of an interpreter if the child cannot understand or speak the language used;
(vii) To have his or her privacy fully respected at all stages of the proceedings.

3. States Parties shall seek to promote the establishment of laws, procedures, authorities and institutions specifically applicable to children alleged as, accused of, or recognized as having infringed the penal law, and, in particular:

   (a) The establishment of a minimum age below which children shall be presumed not to have the capacity to infringe the penal law;
   (b) Whenever appropriate and desirable, measures for dealing with such children without resorting to judicial proceedings, providing that human rights and legal safeguards are fully respected.

4. A variety of dispositions, such as care, guidance and supervision orders; counselling; probation; foster care; education and vocational training programmes and other alternatives to institutional care shall be available to ensure that children are dealt with in a manner appropriate to their well-being and proportionate both to their circumstances and the offence.

Table 4 Article 40 Indicator sets

Core attributes			
The specialised juvenile justice system and the related comprehensive policy	**The diversion process and alternatives measures to institutionalisation**	**The establishment of the minimum age of criminal responsibility (MACR)**	**Fair trial principles for children**
Data is collected and disaggregated by prohibited grounds for discrimination including age, sex, ethnicity, disability, when applicable.			
Structural indicators			
1. Ratification of human rights treaties relevant to Article 40 and harmonisation of national legislation dealing with the administration of juvenile justice in compliance with the relevant international instruments. 2. A specialised juvenile justice legislation and policies ensure: • Establishment of dedicated laws • Setting up implementation procedures for the legislation • Designation of authorities and institutions • Implementation of appropriate pre- and in-service training. 3. A specialised legal framework establishes the MACR (14 years as the absolute minimum) and ensures that administration of juvenile justice: • Promotes the child's sense of dignity and worth • Pursues an educative aim, meant to reinforce "the child's respect for the human rights and fundamental freedoms of others" • Takes into account the child's age • Facilitates "the child's reintegration and the child's assuming a constructive role in society."			

(continued)

Table 4 (continued)

	4. Legal and policy framework establishes a diversion system based on at least the following features: • Diversion applies only where there is convincing evidence that the child has committed the alleged offence and voluntarily acknowledges responsibility • Free written consent is provided by the child and their legal representative(s) • Procedures are proportionate to the child's circumstances and the offence committed • Deprivation of liberty is used as a last resort and for the shortest appropriate period (see also art. 37) • The completion of the diversion results in a definite and final closure of the case.	5. The legal framework guarantees that: • Children who commit an offence under the specified MACR cannot be formally charged or held responsible in a penal law procedure • Once a MACR is set, no exception should apply not even when serious offences are committed • If there is no reliable proof of age and it cannot be established, the child shall not be held criminally responsible and will benefit from the presumption of doubt.	6. The law ensures the following legal rights to the children alleged or accused of having committed a crime: • To benefit from the principle of the presumption of innocence • To be informed promptly and directly of their charges • To have assistance in their defence • To call witnesses 7. The law guarantees the 'principle of equality' in the justice system and the right: • To have their case determined by a competent 'independent and impartial authority or judicial body', including administrative bodies • To have the matter determined without delay, in a fair hearing according to the law • To benefit from legal assistance • To remain silent and not be obliged to give testimony • The right to free assistance of an interpreter • The right to assistance for children with disabilities • The right to appeal • The right to full respect of the child's privacy in all stages of the proceedings. 8. The law ensures children benefit from the principle of non-retroactivity of the penal law.

(continued)

Table 4 (continued)

<table>
<tr><td colspan="4">Process indicators</td></tr>
<tr><td rowspan="2">1.9. Measures for prevention of children's offending behaviour are in place.
10. Rehabilitation and integration/reintegration measures are in place for children within and exiting the judicial system.
11. Specialised authorities and institutions are in place at every stage of juvenile justice.</td><td rowspan="2">1.12. Alternatives to institutional care are in place.
13. Measures and services to avoid judicial proceedings are in place, (e.g. diversion, restorative justice measures).</td><td colspan="2">14. Regular reviews take place (as defined within juvenile justice legislation) to ensure the correct implementation of the MACR and fair trial principles.</td></tr>
<tr><td></td><td>15. A process of accreditation for specialised legal representatives is in place (e.g. lawyers, social workers).
16. Specialised child-friendly hearing systems are available before, during and after the trial (See also art. 12).</td></tr>
<tr><td colspan="2">17. A system guaranteeing regular independent inspection of places of rehabilitation, care or/and limitation/deprivation of liberty is in place.</td><td colspan="2"></td></tr>
<tr><td colspan="2">18. A child-friendly complaints system for children in places of rehabilitation, care or/and limitation/deprivation of liberty is established.</td><td colspan="2">19. A child-friendly complaints system is in place in cases of violations of the MACR and the fair trial principles.</td></tr>
<tr><td colspan="4">Outcome indicators</td></tr>
<tr><td>20. Percentage of children in conflict with the law broken down by age, sex, and type of offence.</td><td>21. Percentage of children diverted or sentenced who enter a pre-sentence diversion scheme.
22. Average duration (in weeks) of pre-sentence detentions.
23. (SDG 16.3.2 adapted) Proportion of children in pre-sentence detention (see also art. 37).
24. Percentage of children sentenced receiving a custodial sentence broken down by age, gender, and type of offence.
25. Percentage of children released from detention receiving aftercare.</td><td>26. Percentage of children illegally charged or held responsible in a formal penal law procedure under the MACR.</td><td>27. Percentage of lawyers specialised in juvenile justice accredited at the national level.
28. Average waiting times before cases come to court and average duration of the proceeding (in weeks).
29. Percentage of professional specialised interpreters in the juvenile justice system.</td></tr>
<tr><td colspan="4">30. Percentage of children in detention who have been visited by, or visited, parents, guardian, or an adult family member in the last 3 months.</td></tr>
</table>

Article 40—Guidance

The following provides guidance for the collection of data on specific indicators for Article 40. The number relates to the number of that indicator in the table above. Each indicator is identified as a Process, Structural, or Outcome Indicator, and the formula to calculate the data is described.

Indicator 20—Outcome

Percentage of children in conflict with the law disaggregated by age, sex, and type of offence.

Numerator: Number of children in conflict with the law during the past 12 months.

Denominator: Total number of children.

Formula: (numerator/denominator) × 100 (broken down by age, sex, and type of offence).

Indicator 21—Outcome

Percentage of children diverted or sentenced who enter a pre-sentence diversion scheme.

Numerator: Number of children entering a pre-sentence diversion scheme during the past 12 months.

Denominator: Total number of children diverted or sentenced during the past 12 months.

Formula: (numerator/denominator) × 100.

Indicator 23—Outcome

Proportion of children in pre-sentence detention. (SDG 16.3.2 adapted).

Numerator: Number of children in pre-sentence detention in the past 12 months.

Denominator: Total number of children accused in the past 12 months.

Formula: (Numerator/ denominator) per 100,000.

Indicator 24—Outcome

Percentage of children sentenced receiving a custodial sentence disaggregated by age, gender, and type of offence.

Numerator: Number of children sentenced to deprivation of liberty during the past 12 months.

Denominator: number of children sentenced during the same 12 months period.

Formula: (Numerator/denominator) × 100.

Indicator 25—Outcome

Percentage of children released from detention receiving aftercare.

Numerator: Number of children released from detention during a 12-month period receiving aftercare.

Denominator: Number of children released during the same 12-month period.

Formula: (Numerator/denominator) × 100.

Indicator 26—Outcome

Percentage of children illegally charged or held responsible in a formal penal law procedure under the MACR.

Numerator: Children illegally charged or held responsible in a formal penal law procedure under the MACR in the past 12 months.

Denominator: Total number of children charged or held responsible in a formal penal law procedure under the MACR in the past 12 months.

Formula: (numerator/denominator) × 100.

Indicator 27—Outcome

Percentage of lawyers specialised in juvenile justice accredited at the national level.

Numerator: Total number of lawyers specialised in juvenile justice accredited at the national level.

Denominator: total number of lawyers working in the juvenile justice system.

Formula: (numerator/denominator) × 100.

Indicator 29—Outcome

Percentage of professional specialised interpreters in the juvenile justice system.

Numerator: Number of professional specialised interpreters in the juvenile justice system.

Denominator: Total number of interpreters in the juvenile justice system.
Formula: (numerator/denominator) × 100.

Indicator 30—Outcome

Percentage of children in detention who have been visited by, or visited, parents, guardian, or an adult family member in the last 3 months.

Numerator: Number of children in detention who have been visited by, or visited, parents, guardian, or an adult family member in the last 3 months.

Denominator: Total number of children in detention.

Formula: (numerator/denominator) × 100.

Chapter 12
General Measures of Implementation

Ziba Vaghri, Roberta Ruggiero, Gerison Lansdown, Adem Arkadas-Thibert, and Christian Whalen

The articles included in this section do not add specific rights of the child. Rather, they provide guidance for states on the measures that they need to put in place in order to enable and promote the implementation of all the rights contained in the Convention:[1]

[1] For further elaboration on the implications and implementation of each of these rights, please read the relevant chapter in the companion publication to this book: Monitoring State Compliance with the UN Convention on the Rights of the Child: An analysis of attributes, Vaghri, Zermatten, Lansdown and Ruggiero, Springer, 2022.

Z. Vaghri
GlobalChild Program of Research, University of New Brunswick, Saint John, NB, Canada

R. Ruggiero (✉)
Centre for Children's Right Studies, Faculty of Law, University of Geneva, Geneva, Switzerland
e-mail: Roberta.ruggiero@unige.ch

G. Lansdown
School of Law, University College Cork, Cork, Ireland

A. Arkadas-Thibert
Independent Researcher, Specializing in International Human Rights, Marseille, France

C. Whalen
Faculty of Law, University of New Brunswick, Fredericton, NB, Canada

Z. Vaghri et al. (eds.), *Children's Rights-Based Indicators*, Children's Well-Being: Indicators and Research 28,
https://doi.org/10.1007/978-3-031-71594-5_12

- Article 1—definition of a child
- Article 4—general measures of implementation
- Article 42 and 44.6—making the Convention and the States Parties compliance widely known among children and adults.

Article 1 provides the definition as to who is a child under the terms of the Convention asserting that all the rights in the Convention apply to every child up to their eighteenth birthday. It does not suggest a point when rights commence, allowing flexibility for states to determine if they begin with conception or with birth.

Article 4 builds on earlier iterations of general implementation measures developed in the International Covenant on Economic, Social and Cultural Rights and the International Covenant on Civil and Political Rights. It provides a comprehensive and overarching framework of all the measures that States Parties must undertake to give effect to the Convention rights including reconsideration of any reservations and ratification of relevant treaties, comprehensive reviews of legislation, and remedies for violations. It involves a broad range of administrative measures including national strategies, cross-departmental coordination, transparency of budgets, the nature of engagement with the private sector and civil society, training and capacity building, monitoring, data collection, and establishment of national human rights institutions. Article 4 also affirms that social and economic rights are subject to progressive realisation, in recognition of their significant resource implications.

Article 42 impose obligations to make the provisions of the Convention widely known to children and adults alike and to disseminate their reports to the Committee on the Rights of the Child to the public. Article 44.6 requires states to make their report widely available to the public.

Overall, these articles provide the mechanisms to guide States Parties' implementation of the Convention and enable children and their families and advocates to hold those States Parties to account in meeting the obligations they have committed to respect, protect, and fulfil.

Article 1—Definition of a Child

> For the purposes of the present Convention, a child means every human being below the age of 18 years unless under the law applicable to the child, majority is attained earlier.

Table 1 Article 1 Indicator Sets

Core attributes	
Ages of majority	**Accommodation of differential ages**
Data is collected and disaggregated by prohibited grounds for discrimination including age, sex, ethnicity, disability, when applicable.	
Structural indicators	
1. In national legislation, all children under the age of 18 years are protected equally whether they reached age of majority and/or emancipation or not. 2. (SDG 5.3.1 adapted) National legislation prohibits marriage under the age of 18 years. 3. If national legislation permits emancipation under the law and prior to age 18 years as a result of marriage or leaving home voluntarily, children continue to be protected under the CRC.	

Article 4—General Measures of Implementation

> States Parties shall undertake all appropriate legislative, administrative, and other measures for the implementation of the rights recognized in the present Convention. With regard to economic, social and cultural rights, States Parties shall undertake such measures to the maximum extent of their available resources and, where needed, within the framework of international co-operation.

Table 2 Article 4 Indicator sets

Core attributes
General measures of implementation: States parties' obligations to 'undertake all appropriate, legislative, administrative, and other measures
Data is collected and disaggregated by prohibited grounds for discrimination including age, sex, ethnicity, disability, when applicable.
Structural indicators

(continued)

Table 2 (continued)

1. State party ratified CRC and all its optional protocols:
    - *Optional protocol on involvement of children in armed conflict*, 2000
    - *Optional protocol on sale of children, child prostitution and child pornography*, 2000
    - *Optional protocol on a communications procedure,* 2011
2. State party has no reservations to the CRC and its optional protocols:
    - The state party has committed to reviewing all reservations and withdrawing as necessary.
3. State party has ratified all relevant international human rights instruments including but not limited to the list provided in the general comment no 5.
4. All laws relating to children are periodically reviewed and harmonised with the CRC provisions with adequately defined key terms and mandates.
5. The CRC has a self-executing status or is fully integrated into domestic legislation giving legal effect to all CRC rights in sufficient detail to enable remedies for non-compliance to be effective.
6. Legislation is in place guaranteeing effective and child-sensitive administrative and judicial procedures for children and their representatives, including the provision of:
    - Child-friendly information
    - Advice
    - Advocacy, including support for self-advocacy (claiming their rights)
    - Access to independent complaints procedures and to the courts with necessary legal and other assistance.
7. Legislation is in place guaranteeing reparation, including compensation, to children whose rights have been violated.
8. A comprehensive child-centred national strategy is in place, and it includes at least the following features:
    - Participatory in terms of involving the competent stakeholders (included family and children in accordance with the age and maturity of the child) (see also art. 12)
    - Specific budget allocation, such as national investment funds is in place
    - Comprehensive monitoring mechanism rooted in CRC is in place.
9. An inclusive high level coordination mechanism/authority is in place:
    - To implement children's rights at all levels in accordance with the State's administrative structure
    - To allow the participation of representatives from local governments/administrations.
10. Legislation is in place regulating the private sector (businesses, non-governmental organisations and other private associations, both for profit and not-for-profit) as service provider and its indirect obligations in implementing child rights.
11. A regulatory framework is in place to:
    - Address the social and environmental responsibility of business corporations and industries, both national and international, that could prevent possible negative impacts from their activities on children.
    - Respect children's rights online to be heard, to access information, to privacy as well as to protect children from harmful content.
12. There is legislation in place requiring:
    - A child rights impact assessment procedure for any proposed law and policy initiatives affecting children and the enjoyment of their rights
    - A child rights impact assessment procedure of the actual impact of implementation of laws and policies.
13. A comprehensive disaggregated data-collection system, based on child rights indicators, is in place on the implementation of the Convention, from local to national level.
14. Information management systems are in place to regularly analyse and disseminate data collected on children's rights.
    - Appropriate child-specific provisions and resources are included in all peace and reconciliation negotiations and treaties.

(continued)

Table 2 (continued)

15. A CRC implementation tracking/monitoring system is in place for: • The allocation and use of resources needed in quantity and quality for children throughout the state budget • Impact assessments on how investments in any sector serves the best interest of the child, and addresses discrimination and participation of the child in decision-making processes • Protecting strategic budgetary lines even in situations of crisis for disadvantaged or particularly vulnerable children and for those situations that may require affirmative social measures. 16. There is a comprehensive training and capacity-building structure in place for all those working with and for children including: • Child rights education for professionals at the tertiary level • Child rights pre- and/or in-service training for professionals • Periodic evaluation of the effectiveness of child rights training. 17. Established protocols and mechanisms are in place for cooperation and collaboration with civil society in decision-making processes related to the CRC implementation, including children, non-governmental organisations, human rights organisations, child and youth-led groups, international organisations, private sector. 18. Established mechanisms exist for international cooperation: • All offered and/or sought development aid agreements have children's rights clauses to contribute to the implementation of the CRC • State party seeks technical cooperation with and advice of, among others, UNICEF, ILO, OHCHR, regional mechanism and other appropriate organisations, on implementing the CRC 19. (SDG 16.a.1) An independent human rights institution (IHRI) has been established, such as ombudsperson, child advocate, children's commissioners, in accordance with the principles relating to the status of National Institutions (the Paris principles) and in all jurisdictions with the necessary human and financial resources.
Process indicators
20. Percentage of court decisions where the CRC or its optional protocols were being directly and indirectly used in the last 12 months. 21. Percentage of local authorities that have adopted a local strategy and plan of action based on national strategy and plan of action for implementing the CRC. 22. Rate of registered non-governmental organisations involved partially or fully in the promotion and protection of the rights of the child. 23. Annual comprehensive assessment of budget and staff needs in relation to implementation of the CRC, including all services to children. 24. Percentage of central allocated budget for children spent according to strategy and plans of action of the CRC. 25. Annual comprehensive assessment of budget and staff needs of the national human rights institution on children's rights. 26. Percentage of international development assistance offered or received that is targeted to a child rights implementation framework and in compliance with the international standards.
Outcome indicators
27. Number of children being consulted in child rights impact assessments and evaluations of national laws and policies. 28. Number of complaints by children (within the last 12 months) addressed about services provided by • Public service providers • Private service providers. 29. Percentage of complaints received and addressed by the IHRI (applicable only if there is no national children's rights commissioner or ombudsman) from children, their parents and civil society organisations within the last reporting period.

Article 4—Guidance

The following provides guidance for the collection of data on specific indicators for Article 4. The number relates to the number of that indicator in the table above. Each indicator is identified as a Process, Structural, or Outcome Indicator, and the formula to calculate the data is described.

Indicator 20—Process

Percentage of court decisions where the CRC or its Optional Protocols were being directly and indirectly used in the last 12 months.

Numerator: Number of court decisions where the CRC or its Optional Protocols were being directly and indirectly used in the last 12 months.

Denominator: Total number of all court decisions involving children, as victims, plaintiffs, accused, witness, etc., in the last 12 months.

Formula: (numerator/denominator) × 100.

Indicator 21—Process

Percentage of local authorities that have adopted a local strategy and plan of action based on national strategy and plan of action for implementing the CRC.

Numerator: Number of local authorities that have adopted a local strategy and plan of action based on national strategy and plan of action for implemented the CRC.

Denominator: All local authorities.

Formula: (numerator/denominator) × 100.

Indicator 22—Process

Rate of registered non-governmental organisations involved partially or fully in the promotion and protection of the rights of the child.

Numerator: Total number registered non-governmental organisations involved partially or fully in the promotion and protection of the rights of the child.

Denominator: Total child population in the country.

Formula: (numerator/denominator) per 100,000.

Indicator 24—Process

Percentage of central allocated budget for children spent according to strategy and plans of action of the CRC.

Numerator: Amount of central allocated budget for children spent according to strategy and plans of action of the CRC.

Denominator: Total amount of budget.

Formula: (numerator/denominator) × 100.

Indicator 26—Process

Percentage of international development assistance offered or received that is targeted to a child rights implementation framework and in compliance with the international standards.

Numerator: Amount of international development assistance offered or received that is targeted to a child rights implementation framework and in compliance with the international standards.

Denominator: All international development assistance offered or received.

Formula: (numerator/denominator) × 100.

Indicator 29—Outcome

Percentage of complaints received and addressed by the IHRI (applicable only if there is no national children's rights commissioner or ombudsman) from children, their parents and civil society organisations within the last reporting period.

Numerator: Total number of complaints addressed by the IHRI from children, their parents and civil society organisations within the last 12 months.

Denominator: Total number of complaints received by the IHRI within the last 12 months.

Formula: (numerator/denominator) × 100.

Articles 42 and 44.6—Making the Convention and the States Parties Compliance Widely Known among Children and Adults

States Parties undertake to make the principles and provisions of the Convention widely known, by appropriate and active means, to adults and children alike. (A 42).

States Parties shall make their reports widely available to the public in their own countries. (A 44.6).

Table 3 Articles 42 and 44.6 Indicator sets

<table>
<tr><th colspan="2">Core attributes</th></tr>
<tr><th>Making the Convention widely known</th><th>Educating adults and children alike</th></tr>
<tr><td colspan="2">Data is collected and disaggregated by prohibited grounds for discrimination including age, sex, ethnicity, disability, when applicable.</td></tr>
<tr><th colspan="2">Structural indicators</th></tr>
<tr><td colspan="2">1. National law and sub-national law governing education services requires the teaching of children's rights in school curricula.
2. The National Strategy to promote children's rights includes provision to make the Convention widely known to adults and children throughout the national territory.
3. A lead institution, ministry or Children's Commissioner's office has a legislative mandate to make the Convention widely known to adults and children throughout the national territory.</td></tr>
<tr><td>4. Procedures are in place in to disseminate the states party report, CRC concluding observations, general comments and other material from the committee on the rights of the child.
5. Procedures are in place to translate states party reports and concluding observations into multiple languages to reach diverse populations.</td><td>6. Percentage of parenting programmes that include child rights education in their programmes.
7. Number of post-secondary courses and degree programmes for children's rights.
8. Number of students enrolled in post-secondary or degree programmes that include children's rights education.</td></tr>
<tr><th colspan="2">Outcome indicators</th></tr>
<tr><td colspan="2">9. Percentage of the general public who report being knowledgeable about the CRC and child rights, by parental status, education level and professional status and year.
10. Percentage of the general public who report being knowledgeable about the state party reports and concluding observations.
11. Percentage of front-line workers in child-serving agencies and departments who report having a good working knowledge of children's rights and how to apply them in their day-to-day work.
12. Percentage of children who report having a good understanding of their rights guaranteed under the CRC.
13. Percentage of parents who report being knowledgeable about the CRC and their child's rights.</td></tr>
</table>

Articles 42 and 44.6—Guidance

The following provides guidance for the collection of data on specific indicators for Articles 42 and 44.6. The number relates to the number of that indicator in the table above. Each indicator is identified as a Process, Structural, or Outcome Indicator, and the formula to calculate the data is described.

Indicator 6—Process

Percentage of parenting programmes that include child rights education in their programmes.

Numerator: Number of parenting programmes that include child rights education in their programmes.

Denominator: Total number of parenting programmes.

Formula: (numerator/denominator) × 100.

Indicator 9—Outcome

Percentage of the general public who report being knowledgeable about the CRC and child rights, by parental status, education level and professional status and year.

Numerator: Number of people who report being knowledgeable about the CRC and child rights, by parental status, education level and professional status and year.

Denominator: Total population within the public surveyed.

Formula: (numerator/denominator) × 100.

Indicator 10—Outcome

Percentage of the general public who report being knowledgeable about State Party Reports and Concluding Observations,

Numerator: Number of people who report being knowledgeable about the State Party Reports and Concluding Observations.

Denominator: Total population within the public surveyed.

Formula: (numerator/denominator) × 100.

Indicator 11—Outcome

Percentage of front-line workers in child-serving agencies and departments who report having a good working knowledge of children's rights and how to apply them in their day-to-day work.

Numerator: Number of front-line workers in child-serving agencies and departments who report having a good working knowledge of children's rights and how to apply them in their day-to-day work.

Denominator: Total number of front-line workers in child-serving agencies and departments.

Formula: (numerator/denominator) × 100.

Indicator 12—Outcome

Percentage of children who report having a good understanding of their rights guaranteed under the CRC.

Numerator: Number of children who report having a good understanding of their rights guaranteed under the CRC.

Denominator: Total number of children surveyed.

Formula: (numerator/denominator) × 100.

Indicator 13—Outcome

Percentage of parents who report being knowledgeable about the CRC and their child's rights.

Numerator: Number of parents who report being knowledgeable about the CRC and their child's rights.

Denominator: Total number of parents surveyed.

Formula: (numerator/denominator) × 100.

Glossary for Part III

Keyword	Meaning	Reference
Abduction	The illicit transfer and non-return of children abroad refers to the problem of the abduction of children across frontiers by one of their parents	UNICEF Office of Research-Innocenti. (2000). *Glossary*. Retrieved from https://www.unicef-irc.org/php/Thesaurus/Glossary_Display.php?THES_LANG=1&THES_SERCH=5&THES_CHAR=A
Accessibility (disability)	To enable persons with disabilities to live independently and participate fully in all aspects of life, States Parties shall take appropriate measures to ensure to persons with disabilities access, on an equal basis with others, to the physical environment, to transportation, to information and communications, including information and communications technologies and systems, and to other facilities and services open or provided to the public, both in urban and in rural areas.	CRPD, Article 9

Z. Vaghri et al. (eds.), *Children's Rights-Based Indicators*, Children's Well-Being: Indicators and Research 28,
https://doi.org/10.1007/978-3-031-71594-5

Keyword	Meaning	Reference
Accessibility (education)	Educational institutions and programmes must be accessible to everyone, without discrimination, within the jurisdiction of the State Party. Accessibility has three overlapping dimensions: • Non-discrimination—education must be accessible to all, especially the most vulnerable groups, in law and fact, without discrimination on any of the prohibited grounds • Physical accessibility—education must be within safe physical reach, either by attendance at some reasonably convenient geographic location (e.g. a neighbourhood school) or via modern technology (e.g. access to a "distance learning" programme) • Economic accessibility—education must be affordable to all. This dimension of accessibility is subject to the differential wording of Article 13 (2) in relation to primary, secondary, and higher education: whereas primary education shall be available "free to all", States Parties are required to progressively introduce free secondary and higher education.	*CESCR General Comment No. 13: The Right to Education* (Art. 13), para. 6

Keyword	Meaning	Reference
Accessibility (health)	The element of accessibility has four dimensions: (a) Non-discrimination: Health and related services as well as equipment and supplies must be accessible to all children, pregnant women. And mothers, in law and in practice, without discrimination of any kind (b) Physical accessibility: Health facilities must be within accessible distance for all children, pregnant women, and mothers. Physical accessibility may require additional attention to the needs of children and women with disabilities. The committee encourages states to prioritise the establishment of facilities and services in under-served areas and to invest in mobile outreach approaches, innovative technologies, and well-trained and supported community health workers, as ways of reaching especially vulnerable groups of children (c) Economic accessibility/affordability: Lack of ability to pay for services, supplies or medicines should not result in the denial of access. The committee calls on states to abolish user fees and implement health-financing systems that do not discriminate against women and children on the basis of their inability to pay. Risk-pooling mechanisms such as tax and insurance should be implemented on the basis of equitable, means-based contributions (d) Information accessibility: Information on health promotion, health status and treatment options should be provided to children and their caregivers in a language and format that is accessible and clearly understandable to them.	*Convention on the Rights of the Child*, CRC/GC/145,2013, para. 14
Best interest	The principle of best interests of the child is a threefold concept: "(a) A substantive right: The right of the child to have his or her best interests assessed and taken as a primary consideration … and the guarantee that this right will be implemented whenever a decision is to be made concerning a child… (b) A fundamental, interpretative legal principle: If a legal provision is open to more than one interpretation, the interpretation which most effectively serves the child's best interests should be chosen. … (c) A rule of procedure: Whenever a decision is to be made that will affect a … child, the decision-making process must include an evaluation of the possible impact (positive or negative) of the decision on the child or children concerned…."	United Nations Committee on the Rights of the Child (2013). *General Comment No. 14 on the Right of the Child to Have His or Her Best Interests Taken as a Primary Consideration* (art. 3, para. 1) (29 May 2013) UN Doc CRC/C/GC/14, para. 6. Retrieved from https://www.refworld.org/docid/51a84b5e4.html

Keyword	Meaning	Reference
Best interest assessment and determination	The "best interests assessment" consists in evaluating and balancing all the elements necessary to make a decision in a specific situation for a specific individual child or group of children. It is carried out by the decision-maker and his or her staff—If possible, a multidisciplinary team—And requires the participation of the child. The "best interests determination" describes the formal process with strict procedural safeguards designed to determine the child's best interests on the basis of the best interests assessment.	CRC/C/GC/7,2005, para. 4
Child and youth-led organisations	A child or youth-led organisation is one which is autonomous and independent of adults and governments, and free of political control or manipulation which enables children to organise among themselves to identify those issues of concern to them and to determine how to take action to address them.	Lansdown, G. (2011). *Every Child's Right to be Heard. A resource guide on the UN Committee on the Rights of the Child General Comment No.12*. Retrieved from https://www.unicef.org/french/adolescence/files/Every_Childs_Right_to_be_Heard.pdf
Child friendly	A child-friendly approach is one rooted in children's rights to deliver better outcomes. It involves seven core principles including participation, non-discrimination, best interests, life, survival and development, dignity, transparency and accountability, interdependence and indivisibility of rights. It takes into account the need for systems to be sensitive to the evolving capacities and developing maturity of the child, and to their enhanced need for protection.	https://www.unicef.org.uk/child-friendly-cities/crba/; Law Insider, accessed 16/11/23
Child labour	The term "child labour" is often defined as work that deprives children of their childhood, their potential and their dignity, and that is harmful to physical and mental development. It refers to work that: • Is mentally, physically, socially, or morally dangerous and harmful to children; and • Interferes with their schooling by • Depriving them of the opportunity to attend school, obliging them to leave school prematurely, or requiring them to attempt to combine school attendance with excessively long and heavy work.	UNICEF Office of Research-Innocenti. (2000). *Glossary*. Retrieved from https://www.unicef-irc.org/php/Thesaurus/Glossary_Display.php?THES_SERCH=1&THES_CHAR=C

Keyword	Meaning	Reference
Child Rights Impact Assessment (CRIA)	Child Rights Impact Assessments (CRIA) predict the impact of any proposed law, policy or budgetary allocation which affects children and the enjoyment of their rights.	UN Committee on the Rights of the Child. (2003). *General Comment No. 5: General measures of implementation of the Convention on the Rights of the Child (arts. 4, 42 and 44, para. 6) para. 45*. Retrieved from Refworld website: https://www.refworld.org/docid/4538834f11.html
Child-friendly justice	Child-friendly justice refers to "justice systems which guarantee the respect and the effective implementation of all children's rights at the highest attainable level, bearing in mind the principles listed below and giving due consideration to the child's level of maturity and understanding and the circumstances of the case. It is, in particular, justice that is accessible, age appropriate, speedy, diligent, adapted to and focused on the needs and rights of the child, respecting the rights of the child including the rights to due process, to participate in and to understand the proceedings, to respect for private and family life and to integrity and dignity."	The Council of Europe. (2011). *Guidelines of the Committee of Ministers of the Council of Europe on child-friendly justice*. Retrieved from https://rm.coe.int/CoERMPublicCommonSearchServices/DisplayDCTMContent?documentId=090000168045f5a9
Competent adoption authorities	A 'competent authority' in the context of adoption is an adoption agency that is a properly licensed by the law of the state, complies with minimum standards and is established, authorised and supervised by the state to undertake the role of approving applications to adopt.	Adapted from: *Hague Convention on Private International Law*. (1993). *The Implementation and Operation of the 1993 Hague Intercountry Adoption Convention: Guide to Good Practice*. Guide No. 2. Retrieved from https://assets.hcch.net/docs/7ea29e33-b8e6-49de-8d3b-89864d72584f.pdf

Keyword	Meaning	Reference
Contracting state	A contracting state is a state that has expressed its consent to be bound by a treaty whether or not the treaty has not yet entered into force	See Article 2 (1) (f) of the *Vienna Convention* 1969. (UN, 2012). United Nations. (2012). *Treaty Handbook*. Prepared by the Treaty Section of the Office of Legal Affairs. Retrieved from https://treaties.un.org/doc/source/publications/THB/English.pdf
Country of origin	In the migration context, a country of nationality or of former habitual residence of a person or group of persons who have migrated abroad, irrespective of whether they migrate regularly or irregularly.	International Organization for Migration (n.d.) *Key Migration Terms*. Retrieved from https://www.iom.int/key-migration-terms
Demobili-sation	The term 'demobilisation' refers to ending a child's association with armed forces or groups. The terms 'release' or 'exit from an armed force or group' and 'children coming or exiting from armed forces and groups' rather than 'demobilised children' are preferred. Child demobilisation/release involves removing a child from a military or armed group as swiftly as possible. This action may require official documentation (e.g. issuing a demobilisation card or official registration in a database for ex-combatants) to confirm that the child has no military status.	United Nations. (2006). Glossary: Terms and Definitions. Retrieved from https://www.unddr.org/uploads/documents/IDDRS%201.20%20Glossary.pdf
Deprivation of liberty	Deprivation of liberty: any form of detention or imprisonment or the placement of a person in a public or private custodial setting, from which this person is not permitted to leave at will, by order of any judicial, administrative, or other public authority;	*Convention on the Rights of the Child, General Comment on children's rights in the child justice system*, para. 6, CRC/C/GC/ 24, 2019
Direct discrimination (associated term: direct)	Direct discrimination occurs when a child is treated worse than another person or other people because: • They have a protected characteristic (such a religion, race, or disability) • They are thought to have that protected characteristic (known as discrimination by perception) • They are connected to someone with that protected characteristic (known as discrimination by association)	Adapted from: United Nations Economic and Social Council. (2009). *General Comment No. 20, Non-discrimination in economic, social and cultural rights (art.2, para. 2)*, E/C.12/GC/20. Retrieved from https://www.refworld.org/docid/4a60961f2.html
Diversion	Diversion refers to measures referring children away from the judicial system, any time prior to or during the relevant proceedings	*Convention on the Rights of the Child* /C/GC/24, Sept 2019, para. 13

Keyword	Meaning	Reference
Emanci-pation	Emancipation means a child is no longer under the financial, legal, or physical control of their parent or legal guardian. Minors get emancipated for a variety of reasons, including the desire to be independent, to escape an abusive or neglectful household, or even to access more financial support. Emancipation does not, necessarily mean 'legal majority', and may be granted earlier (when the minor is at least sixteen years old, living apart from the parents with their consent, have a legal source of income and able to manage their finances) or at a later age, (for instance when the child is mentally or physically challenged and unable to support themselves or make decisions)."	*The Law Dictionary*, https://thelawdictionary.org/article/what-does-emancipation-mean/. Accessed 6th Nov 2023
Evolving capacity of the child	Evolving capacities is defined as an enabling principle that addresses the process of maturation and learning through which children progressively acquire competencies, understanding and increasing levels of agency to take responsibility and exercise their rights.	Adapted from: Committee on the Rights of the Child. (2016). *General comment No. 20 (2016), para 18, on the implementation of the rights of the child during adolescence*. Retrieved from https://www.refworld.org/pdfid/589dad3d4.pdf Committee on the Rights of the Child. (2005). *General Comment No. 7 (2005), para 17, Implementing Child Rights in Early Childhood.* Retrieved from https://www.refworld.org/docid/460bc5a62.html
Family reunification	The process of bringing together families, particularly children and elderly dependents with previous care providers for the purpose of establishing or re-establishing long-term care. Separation of families occurs most often during armed conflicts or massive displacements of people.	United Nations High Commissioner for Refugees. (2006). *Master glossary of terms*. Refugees. Retrieved from https://www.refworld.org.es/cgi-bin/texis/vtx/rwmain/opendocpdf.pdf?reldoc=y&docid=5d82b8fa4
Financial inducement	A financial inducement represents a payment that a person is able to make in order to 'purchase' a child, or influence an adoption proceeding, thus reducing the child to the status of a commodity. The Convention is explicit that "no one shall derive improper financial or other gain from an activity related to intercountry adoption and that central authorities must take all appropriate measures to prevent this practice."	Hague Convention on Private International Law. (1993). *The Implementation and Operation of the 1993 Hague Intercountry Adoption Convention: Guide to Good Practice*. Guide No. 1. Retrieved from https://assets.hcch.net/docs/bb168262-1696-4e7f-acf3-fbbd85504af6.pdf

Keyword	Meaning	Reference
Forced labour	Forced or compulsory labour is: "all work or service which is exacted from any person under the threat of a penalty and for which the person has not offered himself or herself voluntarily."	*ILO Forced Labour Convention*, 1930, Article 2, (No. 29)
Grooming	Grooming is when someone builds a relationship, trust and emotional connection with a child or young person so they can manipulate, exploit, and abuse them. Children and young people who are groomed can be sexually abused, exploited, or trafficked. Anybody can be a groomer, no matter their age, gender, or race. Grooming can take place over a short or long period of time—From weeks to years. Groomers may also build a relationship with the young person's family or friends to make them seem trustworthy or authoritative	National Society for the Prevention of Cruelty to Children. (2019). *Grooming*. Retrieved from https://www.nspcc.org.uk/what-is-child-abuse/types-of-abuse/grooming/#what-is
Human rights education	Human rights education should provide information on the content of human rights treaties. But children should also learn about human rights by seeing human rights standards implemented in practice, whether at home, in school, or within the community. Human rights education should be a comprehensive, lifelong process and start with the reflection of human rights values in the daily life and experiences of children.	CRCGC//2001, 2001, para. 15
Inclusion	Inclusion is the process of taking necessary steps to ensure that every child is given an equality of opportunity to develop socially, to learn and to enjoy community life. Promoting inclusion necessitates the removal of the barriers (including physical, communication, transport, legislation and policy, attitudinal and cultural barriers) to enable opportunities to participate in society on an equal basis with others. Inclusive education is where students of all abilities learn together in the same classroom environment. This means students with and without disabilities. It involves creating an education system where everyone can learn together and have their individual needs met.	*CRPD General Comment on Inclusive Education*, CRPD/C/GC/4, 2016, para. 11
Indirect discrimination (associated term: indirect)	Indirect discrimination arises when a child is treated in the same way as someone else, but this treatment has a negative effect on them because of a protected characteristic such as disability, sex, ethnic status, or religion. An example of indirect discrimination would be to ban children from adopting certain hairstyles in school, when the prohibition would only effectively apply to one particular racial group	Adapted from: United Nations Economic and Social Council. (2009). *General Comment No. 20, Non-discrimination in economic, social and cultural rights (art.2, para. 2)*, E/C.12/GC/20. Retrieved from https://www.refworld.org/docid/4a60961f2.html

Keyword	Meaning	Reference
Informational privacy	Children's informational privacy means privacy relating to personal information belonging to them or about them. Children's communications privacy is threatened where their posts, chats, messages, or calls are intercepted by governments or other actors, and children's informational privacy can be put at risk when children's personal data are collected, stored or processed whether in school records, health records, other public records, financial records, family photo albums, or registration information or material they produced as members of clubs, camps or other associations	UNICEF. (2018). *Industry toolkit: Children's online privacy and freedom of expression*. Retrieved from https://www.unicef.org/csr/files/UNICEF_Childrens_Online_Privacy_and_Freedom_of_Expression(1).pdf
Kinship care	Kinship care: Family-based care within the child's extended family or with close friends of the family known to the child, whether formal or informal in nature;	*Guidelines for the Alternative Care of Children*, para. 29(c)(1), A/RES/64/142, 24 Feb 2010
Leisure	"Leisure refers to the time in which play or recreation for children can take place. It is defined as free and unobligated time that does not involve formal education, work, home responsibilities, performance of other life sustaining functions or engaging in activity directed from outside the individual. In other words it is largely discretionary time to be used as the child chooses."	United Nations Committee on the Rights of the Child. (2013). *General comment No. 17 (2013) on the right of the child to rest, leisure, play, recreational activities, cultural life and the arts (art. 31)* (CRC/C/GC/17). Retrieved from https://www.refworld.org/docid/51ef9bcc4.html
Minimum age of criminal responsibility	The minimum age below which the law determines that children do not have the capacity to infringe the criminal law.	CRC/C/GC/24, 2019, para. 8
Minority	"A minority is a group of people in minority within the territory of a State. Under Article 30 of the CRC those States Parties in which ethnic, religious, or linguistic minorities exist shall not deny a child belonging to such a minority the right, in community with other members of their group, to enjoy their own culture, to profess and practise their own religion, or to use their own language"	UNICEF Office of research-Innocenti. (2000). *Glossary*. Retrieved from https://www.unicef-irc.org/php/Thesaurus/Glossary_Display.php?GLOSS_ID=303&PoPuP=No
Narcotic drugs	According to the UN Convention Against Illicit Traffic in Narcotic Drugs and Psychotropic Substances (1988), "'Narcotic Drug' means any of the substances, natural or synthetic, in Schedules I and II of the Single Convention on Narcotics Drugs (1961), and the 1972 Protocol amending this latter convention. Control is exercised over 134 narcotic drugs"	United Nations. (1988). *United Nations Convention Against Illicit Traffic in Narcotic Drugs and Psychotropic Substances*, 1988. Retrieved from http://www.incb.org/documents/PRECURSORS/1988_CONVENTION/1988Convention_E.pdf

Keyword	Meaning	Reference
Positive discrimination	Specific measures not to be regarded as discrimination are positive or affirmative measures that aim to accelerate or achieve de facto equality of persons with disabilities. Such measures are mentioned in other international human rights treaties, such as Article 4 of the *Convention on the Elimination of All Forms of Discrimination against Women* or Article 1 (4) of the *International Convention on the Elimination of All Forms of Racial Discrimination*, and entail adopting or maintaining certain advantages in favour of an underrepresented or marginalised group. They are usually temporary in nature, although in some instances permanent specific measures are required, depending on context and circumstances, including by virtue of a particular impairment or the structural barriers of society. Examples of specific measures include outreach and support programmes, allocation and/or reallocation of resources, targeted recruitment, hiring and promotion, quota systems, advancement, and empowerment measures, as well as respite care and technological aids.	CRPD/C/GC/6, 2018, para. 28
Poverty line	The poverty line measures the threshold below which an individual lacks access to economic resources (income) to satisfy basic material needs. A person (or household) is considered poor if the person's (or household's) income cannot acquire the basket of goods and services used to define a threshold for poverty.	https://devinit.org/wp-content/uploads/2016/07/Definitions-and-measures-of-poverty.pdf, taken from World Bank
Principle of sufficiency	The concept of play sufficiency is one that involves a commitment to assessing and securing sufficient play opportunities for children in an area. It represents the 'quantity and quality of opportunities for children to play'. The aim of the concept is to make real and meaningful changes that support children's right to play as well as providing them with a wealth of opportunity and experience.	*Convention on the Rights of the Child General Comment Convention on the Rights of the Child* CRC/GC/17 para. 58a, 2013
Prohibited grounds	The term 'grounds' refers to the criteria or circumstances against which it is prohibited to discriminate in Article 2 of the convention. They are race, colour, sex, language, religion, political or other opinion, national, ethnic, or social origin, property, disability, birth or other status. The inclusion of "other status" indicates that this list is not exhaustive and other grounds may be incorporated in this category	Adapted from: United Nations Economic and Social Council. (2009). *General Comment No. 20, Non-discrimination in economic, social and cultural rights (art.2, para. 2)*, E/C.12/GC/20. Retrieved from https://www.refworld.org/docid/4a60961f2.html

Keyword	Meaning	Reference
Psychotropic substances	Psychoactive substances are substances that, when taken in or administered into one's system, affect mental processes, e.g. cognition or affect. This term and its equivalent, psychotropic drug, are the most neutral and descriptive term for the whole class of substances, licit and illicit, of interest to drug policy	World Health Organization. (n.d.). *Management of substance abuse: Psychoactive substances*. Retrieved from https://www.who.int/substance_abuse/terminology/psychoactive_substances/en/
Ratification	Ratification refers to the act whereby the competent authorities of the state express their consent to be bound by an international treaty.	United Nations (1969). *Vienna Convention on the Law of Treaties. Article 2(1)(b)*. Retrieved from https://treaties.un.org/doc/Publication/UNTS/Volume%201155/volume-1155-I-18232-English.pdf
Reasonable accommodation	Necessary and appropriate modification and adjustments not imposing a disproportionate or undue burden, where needed in a particular case, to ensure to children with disabilities the enjoyment or exercise on an equal basis with others of all human rights and fundamental freedoms"	CRPD, Article 2
Recreation	"Recreation is an umbrella term used to describe a very broad range of activities, including, inter alia, participation in music, art, crafts, community engagement, clubs, sports, games, hiking and camping, pursuing hobbies. It consists of activities or experiences, chosen voluntarily by the child, either because of the immediate satisfaction provided or because he or she perceives that some personal or social value will be gained by accomplishing them. Recreation often takes place in spaces specifically designed for it. While many recreational activities may be organised and managed by adults, recreation should be a voluntary activity. Compulsory or enforced games and sports or compulsory involvement in a youth organisation, for example, do not constitute recreation."	*General comment No. 17 (2013) on the right of the child to rest, leisure, play, recreational activities, cultural life and the arts (art. 31)* (CRC/C/GC/17).
Refugee children	Refugees are defined and protected in international law. The 1951 Refugee Convention is a key legal document and defines a refugee as: "someone who is unable or unwilling to return to their country of origin owing to a well-founded fear of being persecuted for reasons of race, religion, nationality, membership of a particular social group, or political opinion."	*Refugee Convention* 1951

Keyword	Meaning	Reference
Reintegration	Taking all appropriate measures to promote physical and psychological recovery and social reintegration of a child victim of any form of abuse, neglect, exploitation, torture, armed conflict, or any other form of cruel, inhuman or degrading treatment or punishment	UNICEF Innocenti Research Centre. (2000). *Glossary*. Retrieved from https://www.unicef-irc.org/php/Thesaurus/Glossary_Display.php?THES_STR=recovery+and+reintegration
Reservation	Reservation means a unilateral statement, however phrased or named, made by a state, when signing, ratifying, accepting, approving, or acceding to a treaty, whereby it purports to exclude or to modify the legal effect of certain provisions of the treaty in their application to that state.	United Nations (1969). *Vienna Convention on the Law of Treaties*. Article 2(1)(d). Retrieved from https://treaties.un.org/doc/Publication/UNTS/Volume%201155/volume-1155-I-18232-English.pdf
Restorative justice	Restorative justice is an approach in which the victim/survivor and offender, and in some cases other persons affected by a crime, "participate actively together in the resolution of matters arising from the crime, generally with the help of a facilitator." Restorative justice is a way of responding to criminal behaviour which emphasises repairing the harm caused by the crime and 'restoring' harmony as much as possible between offender, victim/survivor and society.	UNICEF. (2010). *Toolkit on diversion and alternatives to detention*. Retrieved from https://www.unicef.org/tdad/index_56040.html
Right to be forgotten	The right to be forgotten appears in Recitals 65 and 66 and in Article 17 of the GDPR. It states, "The data subject shall have the right to obtain from the controller the erasure of personal data concerning him or her without undue delay and the controller shall have the obligation to erase personal data without undue delay" if one of a number of conditions applies. The right to be forgotten dovetails with people's right to access their personal information in GDRP Article 15. The right to control one's data is meaningless if people cannot take action when they no longer consent to processing, when there are significant errors within the data, or if they believe information is being stored unnecessarily. In these cases, an individual can request that the data be erased.	European Union. (n.d.). *Everything you need to know about the "Right to be forgotten"*. Retrieved from https://gdpr.eu/right-to-be-forgotten/
Safe third country	A country in which an asylum-seeker could have had access to an effective asylum regime, and in which he/she has been physically present prior to arriving in the country in which she/he is applying for asylum.	United Nations High Commissioner for Refugees. (2006). *Master glossary of terms*. Refugees. Retrieved from https://www.refworld.org.es/cgi-bin/texis/vtx/rwmain/opendocpdf.pdf?reldoc=y&docid=5d82b8fa4

Keyword	Meaning	Reference
Sale	Sale of children means any act or transaction whereby a child is transferred by any person or group of persons to another for remuneration or any other consideration	*Article 2, Optional Protocol to the Convention on the Rights of the Child on the sale of children, child prostitution and child pornography*, resolution A/ RES/54/263 25 May 2000
Social protection	Social protection covers the range of policies and programmes needed to reduce the lifelong consequences of poverty and exclusion. Programmes like cash transfers—Including child grants, school meals, skills development and more—Help connect families with health care, nutritious food, and quality education to give all children, no matter what circumstances they are born into, a fair chance in life.	Retrieved from https://www.unicef.org/social-policy/social-protection, 10/11/23
Social protection floors/ systems	Social protection floors are nationally defined sets of basic social security guarantees that should ensure, as a minimum that, over the life cycle, all in need have access to essential health care and to basic income security which together secure effective access to goods and services defined as necessary at the national level.	International Labour Organization. (n.d.). *Social protection floor*. Retrieved from https://www.ilo.org/secsoc/areas-of-work/policy-development-and-applied-research/social-protection-floor/lang%2D%2Den/index.htm
Trafficking	"Trafficking in persons" shall mean the recruitment, transportation, transfer, harbouring or receipt of persons, by means of the threat or use of force or other forms of coercion, of abduction, of fraud, of deception, of the abuse of power or of a position of vulnerability or of the giving or receiving of payments or benefits to achieve the consent of a person having control over another person, for the purpose of exploitation. Exploitation shall include, at a minimum, the exploitation of the prostitution of others or other forms of sexual exploitation, forced labour or services, slavery, or practices similar to slavery, servitude or the removal of organs…	*Protocol to Prevent, Suppress and Punish Trafficking in Persons Especially Women and Children, supplementing the United Nations Convention against Transnational Organized Crime*, UNGA Resolution, 55/25–15.11.2000
Trauma informed care	Trauma-sensitive approaches takes into consideration the impact of trauma when gathering information from trauma survivors, analysing that information and take corrective action to redress human rights violations.	United Nations Office of the High Commissioner for Human Rights. (2011). *Manual on human rights monitoring*: Chapter 12 Trauma and self-care. Retrieved from https://www.ohchr.org/Documents/Publications/Chapter12-MHRM.pdf

Keyword	Meaning	Reference
Unaccom-panied minor	Children who are not in the company of parents or another adult caregiver (UNHCR, 2005).	United Nations High Commissioner for Refugees (UNHCR). (2005). UNHCR global report: *Glossary*. Retrieved from https://www.unhcr.org/449267670.pdf
Universal design	"'Universal design"'means the design of products, environments, programmes and services to be usable by all people, to the greatest extent possible, without the need for adaptation or specialised design. 'Universal design' shall not exclude assistive devices for particular groups of persons with disabilities where this is needed."	CRPD, Article 2
Unpaid household services	"Unpaid household services, or household chores, refer to the production of domestic and personal services by a household member for consumption within their own household. Children might be involved in household activities while they attend school, while they are involved in employment, or while they perform both or neither of these additional activities. Household chores include caring for siblings, sick, infirm, disabled or elderly household members; cleaning and minor household repairs; cooking and serving meals; washing and ironing clothes; and transporting or accompanying family members to and from work and school."	*Unpaid household services and child labour Working Paper*, March 2013, International Labour Office. 19th International Conference of Labour Statisticians Geneva, 2–11 October 2013, Unpaid household services and child labour.
Worst forms of child labour	"The worst forms of child labour comprises: (a) all forms of slavery or practices similar to slavery, such as the sale and trafficking of children, debt bondage and serfdom and forced or compulsory labour, including forced or compulsory recruitment of children for use in armed conflict (b) the use, procuring or offering of a child for prostitution, for the production of pornography or for pornographic performances (c) the use, procuring or offering of a child for illicit activities, in particular for the production and trafficking of drugs as defined in the relevant international treaties (d) Work which, by its nature or the circumstances in which it is carried out, is likely to harm the health, safety or morals of children."	International Labour Organization (ILO). (1999). *Worst Forms of Child Labour Convention*, C182, 17 June 1999, C182. Retrieved from https://www.refworld.org/docid/3ddb6e0c4.html

Appendix for Part I

Attributes Article 16—Right to Privacy[1]

Attribute One: Interference with Privacy

Privacy is vital for children's agency, dignity, and safety, and for the exercise of their rights (Innocenti, 2017; Kaye and UN Human Rights Council, 2018; UN General Assembly, 2019). One of the core values protected by the right to privacy is the right to be left alone, or the right to solitude. Janusz Korczak, for example, highlighted that even children in an orphanage, with dormitories and very limited privacy, need a private space, be it a drawer or a suitcase to keep their more prized possessions, a place that would be only theirs (2009, p. 25).[2] Courts sometimes distinguish personal privacy from informational or spatial privacy.[3] The closer an intrusion comes to the biographical core of a child's privacy, the higher the onus against interference will be. National constitutional courts and regional human rights bodies have developed a clear jurisprudence in relation to privacy rights, placing strict limits on state intrusions on a child or any citizen's privacy. They insist that the law must protect against privacy infringements that are:

[1] Extract from Monitoring State Compliance with the UN Convention on the Rights of the Child: An Analysis of Attributes, ed. Vaghri, Zermatten, Lansdown and Ruggiero, Springer, 2022, pp. 93–102.

[2] The Human Rights Committee also describes this right to solitude when it insists that 'competent public authorities should only be able to call for such information relating to an individual's private life the knowledge of which is essential in the interests of society': (United Nations, 2006, p. 18).

[3] For example, see *R. v. Dyment* [1988] 2 S.C.R. 417 (http://canlii.ca/t/1ftc6) and R. v. Plant [1993] 3 S.C.R. 281 (http://canlii.ca/t/1fs0w).

Z. Vaghri et al. (eds.), *Children's Rights-Based Indicators*, Children's Well-Being: Indicators and Research 28,
https://doi.org/10.1007/978-3-031-71594-5

- Not sanctioned by law
- Arbitrary (in the sense that they must be carried out in the pursuit of legitimate state aims)
- Unnecessary. It must be shown that the privacy infringement was not disproportionate to the legitimate aims sought and constituted the least intrusive means of securing those legitimate aims (Electronic Frontier Foundation, 2014).

The Convention also requires that States Parties take measures to protect children's privacy from the intrusion by non-state actors. Violations of a child's intimacy, through relentless bullying, luring, or unwanted attention or touching, infringe Article 16 (UN Committee on the Rights of the Child, 2014). Similarly, non-consensual collection of a child's biological data, through blood samples, voice-prints, and fingerprints, may constitute infringements (Global Privacy Assembly, 2008). Consent-based schemes to collect such data may also infringe on privacy.[4] Threats to privacy are often online. Data mining and targeted marketing to children based upon their web-surfing activities, and the use of embedded sensors in toys and clothes connected to automated systems, often lack transparency and may constitute violations of the child's right to be let alone (Milkaite & Verdoodt, 2017). School video surveillance also intrudes upon children's privacy and can only be justified if the interference is neither unlawful nor arbitrary (Information and Privacy Commissioner of Ontario, 2015; Office of the Privacy Commissioner of Canada, 2012).

Attribute Two: Interference with Family, Home, or Correspondence

Article 16 also deals with spatial or territorial privacy and informational privacy which is given a very broad reading by the Committee, as it is in other constitutional law texts and human rights treaties (Hodgkin et al., 2007, pp. 210–211). The text is broad enough to encompass a trespass to property or to a family member, and although the Convention does not establish property rights for children, the privacy protections do afford children a certain right to exclusive enjoyment of their property and protection against the interference of others (Kilkelly, 2001, pp. 59–62). It also protects their relationships with family. For example, attempts at alienating a child from one of their parents or siblings could constitute a privacy rights violation (Kilkelly, 2001, pp. 50–54). In jurisdictions subject to the *European Convention on Human Rights*, the privacy rights of children are frequently invoked in child protection matters. However, most privacy infractions today are in relation to informational privacy, and increasingly in respect of the digital environment, for example, breaches of confidentiality, personal health information leaks, and surveillance. In many cases, intrusions into children's personal information that would be

[4]As, for instance, when young internauts provide online consent to unscrupulous internet service providers or online game services through privacy policies that take unfair advantage or are couched in terms that children will not clearly understand (Lawford et al., 2008, p. 19).

unacceptable for adults are justified for children in terms of their protection and best interests. However, any such intrusions must be valid and justified, considering children's own views and their evolving capacities (Tobin & Field, 2019, p. 570).

Attribute Three: Unlawful Attacks on Honour and Reputation

Privacy experts maintain that we are moving from an information age to an economy founded on reputation (Lessig, 2010; Swallow, 2013). Article 16 rights protect children from traditional harms such as libel, slander, and misappropriation of their image. The Committee, for example, has pointed to the vulnerability of street children to unlawful attacks on their honour and reputation (2017, paras. 27, 43, 60). The Committee has also argued that children's honour and reputation can be abused as a group, for example, by the media denigrating them and their behaviour based merely on their age.[5] However, in the era of social media, where children are increasingly engaged in activities without parental supervision, children are particularly at risk of various online harms to their honour and reputation (Nyst, 2017). Increasingly, the attacks on honour and reputation are distribution of sexts, cyber bullying, child pornography, and the unauthorised use of children's images online.

To constitute a violation, an attack must be intentional and contain untruthful statements (Tobin & Field, 2019, p. 594). The Human Rights Committee has argued that States Parties must balance the rights embodied in Article 16 with the right to freedom of expression, but at the same time they also have an obligation to enable individuals to protect themselves from unlawful attacks and to have an effective remedy against those responsible (UN Human Rights Committee, 2011, para. 37; United Nations, 2006, p. 181).

Attribute Four: Protection of the Law Against Unlawful Interference or Attacks

Data monitoring and measurement of child privacy standards requires more than the simple proclamation of the rights to privacy. There must also be programmes to dissuade the public from these practices, to sanction them, and to provide recourses and remedies to victims of bullying and other privacy violation (United Nations, 2006, p. 182). Surveillance of children, together with any associated automated processing of personal data, must not be conducted routinely or indiscriminately, and not without children's knowledge (UN General Assembly, 2019). States Parties should review their own procedures regarding the collection and processing of children's personal data and correspondence to ensure they respect children's right to privacy, including in governmental decision-making and within the criminal justice

[5] See, for example, *Concluding Observations for Nicaragua* (UN Committee on the Rights of the Child, 1995, paras. 17, 34).

system (UN General Assembly, 2019). Furthermore, any restrictions or intrusions on the child's right to privacy must be prescribed by law, necessary, and proportionate (UN Human Rights Council, 2017, para. 2; UN Office of the High Commissioner for Human Rights (OHCHR), 2014, para. 23). States Parties should also ensure the implementation of effective data protection legislation, and take other measures as necessary to prevent arbitrary or unlawful interference with children's privacy, family, home, or correspondence in relation to the digital environment (Albania et al., 2018; Nyst, 2017; UN General Assembly, 2019).

References

ACPF (African Child Policy Forum). (2018). *The African report on child wellbeing 2018: Progress in the child-friendliness of African governments*. ACPF.

Albania, Argentina, Australia, Austria, Belgium, Bosnia & Herzegovina, et al. (2018). *The promotion, protection and enjoyment of human rights on the Internet: Draft resolution, 2018, A/HRC/38/L.10/Rev.1*. UN. Accessed October 25, 2020, from http://digitallibrary.un.org/record/1639844

Banisar, D. (2011). *The right to information and privacy: Balancing rights and managing conflicts (SSRN Scholarly Paper No. ID 1786473)*. Social Science Research Network. https://doi.org/10.2139/ssrn.1786473

Beco, G. (2013). Human rights indicators: From theoretical debate to practical application. *Journal of Human Rights Practice, 5*(2), 380–397.

Ben-Arieh, A., Casas, F., Frønes, I., & Korbin, J. E. (2014). Multifaceted concept of child well-being. *Handbook of Child Well-being, 1*, 1–27.

Better Care Network/UNICEF. (2009). *Manual for the measurement of indicators for children in formal care*. Better Care Network/UNICEF. Available from https://resourcecentre.savethechildren.se/sites/default/files/documents/5016.pdf.

Bradshaw, J., & Richardson, D. L. (2009). An index of child well-being in Europe. *Child Indicators Research, 2*, 319–351. https://link.springer.com/article/10.1007/s12187-009-9037-7

Casas, F. (1997). Children's rights and children's quality of life: Conceptual and practical issues. *Social Indicators Research, 42*, 283–298.

Chapman, A. (2007). Development of indicators for economic, social and cultural rights: The rights to education, participation in cultural life and access to the benefits of science. In Donders, Y./Volodin, V. (Eds.), *Human rights in education, science and culture. Legal developments and challenges*. UNESCO Publishing, 111–151.

Child Rights Connect. (2023). *2022 in review*. https://childrightsconnect.org/2022-in-review-new-spaces-opened-for-children-to-voice-their-views-engage-adults-and-act-for-what-they-believe-in/

CoE. (2016a). *Child participation assessment tool*. Council of Europe Children's Rights Division and Youth Development. https://rm.coe.int/16806482d9

CoE. (2016b). *Child participation assessment tool: Implementation Guide*. Council of Europe Children's Rights Division and Youth Development. https://rm.coe.int/CoERMPublicCommonSearchSer-vices/DisplayDCTMContent?documentId=09000016806482da

Z. Vaghri et al. (eds.), *Children's Rights-Based Indicators*, Children's Well-Being: Indicators and Research 28,
https://doi.org/10.1007/978-3-031-71594-5

CoE (Council of Europe). (2012). *Council of Europe Recommendations of the participation of children and young people under the age of 18*. https://rm.coe.int/168046c478

Dawes A., Bray R., & Van der Merwe, A. (2007). *Monitoring child well-being: A South African Rights-based approach*. https://resourcecentre.savethechildren.net/node/6046/pdf/6046.pdf

de Beco, G. (2008). Human rights indicators for assessing state compliance with international human rights. *Nordic Journal of International Law, 77*(1–2), 23–49.

de Beco, G. (2009). *Right to education indicator based on the 4 A framework: Concept paper*. Right to Education Project. https://www.right-to-education.org/sites/right-to-education.org/files/resource-attachments/RTE_RTE_indicators_Concept_Paper_De%20Beco_2010.pdf.

Dejene, N. (2018). *Child friendliness index-score*. The African Child Policy Forum. http://data.africanchildinfo.net/bfhyjkg/child-friendliness-index-score

Detrick, S., Abel, G., Berger, M., Delon, A., & Meek, R. (2008). *Violence against children in conflict with the law: A study on indicators and data collection in Belgium, England and Wales, France and the Netherlands*. Defence for Children International. https://howardleague.org/wpcontent/uploads/2016/05/DCI-Violence-Engels-2007-LR.pdf

Detrick, S., Doek, J. E., & Cantwell, N. (1992). *The United Nations convention on the rights of the child: A guide to the "Travaux Préparatoires"*. Martinus Nijhoff Publishers.

Doek, J. E. (2011). The CRC: Dynamics and directions of monitoring its implementation. In A. Invernizzi (Ed.), *The human rights of children: From visions to implementation* (pp. 99–116). Routledge. https://doi.org/10.4324/9781315557007

Dünkel, F. (2016). Recent developments of juvenile justice legislation and practice in Europe. In T. R. Birckhead & S. Mouthaan (Eds.), *The future of Juvenile justice procedure and practice from a comparative perspective* (pp. 3–36). Carolina Academic Press.

Electronic Frontier Foundation. (2014). *Necessary & proportionate: International principles on the application of human rights to communications surveillance*. https://www.ohchr.org/Documents/Issues/Privacy/ElectronicFrontierFoundation.pdf

Equality and Human Rights Commission. (2017). *Measurement framework for equality and human rights*. https://www.equalityhumanrights.com/sites/default/files/measurement-framework-interactive.pdf

European Union-UNICEF. (2014). *Child rights toolkit: Integrating child rights in development cooperation*. UNICEF. http://www.childrightstoolkit.com/wp-content/uploads/toolkit/English/Child-Rights-Toolkit-Web-Links.pdf

Feinberg, J. (1980). The child's right to an open future. In W. Aiken & H. Lafollette (Eds.), *Whose child?: Children's rights, parental authority, and state power* (pp. 124–153). Littlefield Adams.

Foresti, M., Smith, H. B., & Jones, H. (2009). *Towards a suite of tools for ex ante child rights impact assessment: Concept note for UNICEF*. Overseas Development Institute. http://criacommunity.org/wp-content/uploads/gravity_forms/1-1baf9042c4fceeee12b9dcd57a5f0b68/2015/10/Ex-ante-CRIA.pdf

FRA. (2010). Fundamental rights indicators. https://europa.eu/capacity4dev/sites/default/files/learning/Child-rights/docs/developing_indicators_for_the_protection_respect_and_promotion_of_the_rights_of_the_child_in_the_european_union.pdf

FRA (European Union Fundamental Rights Agency). (2011). *Fundamental rights indicators*. https://fra.europa.eu/en/project/2011/fundamental-rights-indicators.

Gadda, A., Harris, J., Tisdall, E. K. M., Millership, E., & Kilkelly, U. (2021). *Human rights monitoring and implementation: How to make rights 'real' in children's lives*. Routledge.

Girls Not Brides/Aspen Planning and Evaluation Program. (2014). *Preliminary list of recommended indicators for the Girls not Brides (GNB) partnership*. https://www.girlsnotbrides.org/wpcontent/uploads/2014/09/APEP-Preliminary-List-of-Recommended-Indicators-8-29-14.pdf

Girls Not Brides/Aspen Planning and Evaluation Program. (2015a). *Measuring progress: Recommended indicators for Girls not Brides members working to address child marriage*. https://www.girlsnotbrides.org/wp-content/uploads/2015/08/GNB_Full-List-of-Indicators_August-2015_Final.pdf

Girls Not Brides/Aspen Planning and Evaluation Program. (2015b). *Measuring progress: Recommended indicators for Girls not Brides members working to address child marriage: A user's guide*. https://www.girlsnotbrides.org/wp-content/uploads/2014/12/GNB_Indicators-Users-Guide_August-2015_Final1.pdf

Girls Not Brides/Aspen Planning and Evaluation Program. (2015c). *Measuring progress: Recommended indicators for Girls not Brides members working to address child marriage. Indicators for Outcomes and Results on Establish and Implement Laws and Policies*. https://www.girlsnotbrides.org/wp-content/uploads/2015/08/GNB_Full-List-of-Indicators_August-2015_Final.pdf

Global Child Forum. (2015). *Setting a children's rights benchmark for the corporate sector*. https://globalchildforum.org/benchmarks/

Global Privacy Assembly. (2008). Resolution on children's online privacy – Adopted at the 30th International Conference for Data Protection and Privacy Commissioners—Strasbourg, France 2008. Accessed October 25, 2020, from http://globalprivacyassembly.org/wp-content/uploads/2015/02/Resolution-on-Childrens-Online-Privacy-.pdf

Hammarberg, T. (2001). Searching the truth: The need to monitor human rights with relevant and reliable means. *Statistical Journal of the United Nations Economic Commission for Europe, 18*(2/3), 131–140.

Hazel, N. (2008). *Cross-national comparison of youth justice*. https://dera.ioe.ac.uk/id/eprint/7996/1/Cross_national_final.pdf

Hoffman, S. (2020). Ex-ante children's rights impact assessment of economic policy. *The International Journal of Human Rights, 24*(9), 1333–1352. https://doi.org/10.1080/13642987.2020.1819798

Information and Privacy Commissioner of Ontario. (2015). *Guidelines for the use of video surveillance*. Accessed October 25, 2020, from https://www.ipc.on.ca/wp-content/uploads/Resources/2015_Guidelines_Surveillance.pdf

Innocenti, U. O. of R. (2012). *Child safety online: Global challenges and strategies. Technical Report*. Accessed October 25, 2020, from https://www.unicef-irc.org/publications/652-child-safety-online-global-challenges-and-strategies-technical-report.html

Innocenti, U. O. of R. (2017). *Child privacy in the age of Web 2.0 and 3.0: Challenges and opportunities for policy*. Accessed October 25, 2020, from https://www.unicef-irc.org/publications/926-child-privacy-in-the-age-of-web-20-and-30-challenges-and-opportunities-for-policy.html

Joyce, N. (2011). An analysis of the extent of the Juvenile offender's right to privacy: Is the child's right to privacy circumvented by public interest? *European Journal of Crime, Criminal Law and Criminal Justice, 19*(2), 113–124. https://doi.org/10.1163/157181711X566335

Kälin, W. (2012). Examination of state reports. In H. Keller & G. Ulfstein (Eds.), *UN human rights treaty bodies: law and legitimacy. Studies on human rights conventions* (pp. 6–72). Cambridge University Press. https://doi.org/10.1017/CBO9781139047593.003

Karp, J. (2000). Reporting and the committee on the rights of the child. In A. Bayefsky (Ed.), *The UN human rights treaty system in the 21 century* (pp. 35–44). Brill Nijhoff. https://doi.org/10.1163/9789004502758_007

Kaye, D., & UN Human Rights Council. (2018). *Promotion and protection of the right to freedom of opinion and expression: report of the Special Rapporteur, A/73/348*. UN. Accessed October 24, 2020, from http://digitallibrary.un.org/record/1643488

Kilkelly, U. (2001). *The right to respect for private and family life: A guide to the implementation of Article 8 of the European Convention on Human Rights* (2003rd ed.). Council of Europe Publishing. Accessed October 25, 2020, from https://rm.coe.int/090000168007ff47

Korczak, J. K. (2009). *Janusz Korczak: The child's right to respect - Lectures on today's challenges*. Council of Europe Publishing. https://rm.coe.int/09000016807ba985

Landman, T., & Schwarz, K. (2022). Chapter 16: Human rights indicators and implementation. In *Research handbook on implementation of human rights in practice*. Edward Elgar Publishing.

Lansdown, G., (2018). *National human rights institutions (NHRIs)* Series: Tools to support child-friendly practices. Presentation of the tool kit and child rights approach, UNICEF ECARO.

Lansdown, G., & O'Kane, C. (2014). *A Toolkit for monitoring and evaluating children's participation*. Booklet no. I, Save the Children.

Lansdown, G., et al. (2017). *UNICEF child friendly cities and communities initiative: Toolkit for national committees*. https://s25924.pcdn.co/wp-content/uploads/2018/03/CFCI_TOOLKIT_24.02.17.pdf

Lawford, J., Taheri, M., & Public Interest Advocacy Centre (Canada). (2008). *All in the data family: children's privacy online*. Accessed October 25, 2020, from http://epe.lac-bac.gc.ca/100/200/300/public_interest_advocacy/children_final/children_final_small_fixed.pdf

Lessig, L. (2006). *Code: And other laws of cyberspace, Version 2.0*. Basic Books.

Lessig, L. (2010, January 17). Sharing economies. *The mindful word*. Accessed October 25, 2020, from https://www.themindfulword.org/2010/sharing-economies-lawrence-lessig

Lundy, L. (2020). *The rights of child human rights defenders: Implementation guide*. Child Rights Connect. https://www.childrightsconnect.org/wp-content/uploads/2020/12/final-implementation-guide-the-rights-of-child-human-rights-defenders-forweb.pdf

Lundy, L., & McEvoy, L. (2012). Childhood, the United Nations convention on the rights of the child and research: What constitutes a 'rights-based' approach? In M. Freeman (Ed.), *Law and childhood: Current legal issues* (Vol. 14, pp. 75–91). Oxford University Press.

Mekınen, Y. (2010). Measuring government performance in realising child rights and child wellbeing: the approach and indicators. *Child Indicators Research, 3*(2), 205–241. https://rd.springer.com/article/10.1007/s12187-009-9047-5

Merry, S. E. (2011). Measuring the world. Current anthropology. In D. J. Partridge, M. Welker, & R. Hardin (Eds.), (Supplement to April 2011) *Corporate lives: New perspectives on the social life of the corporate form* (*Current anthropology*, Vol. 52, No. S3) (pp. S83–S95).

Merry, S. E. (2014). The problem of human rights indicators. In M. Goodale (Ed.), *Human rights at the crossroad*. Oxford Scholarship. https://doi.org/10.1093/acprof:osobl/9780199376414.003.0010

Milkaite, I., & Verdoodt, V. (2017). *The General Data Protection Regulation and children's rights: Questions and answers for legislators, DPAs, industry, education, stakeholders and civil society*. Better Internet for Kids. Accessed October 25, 2020, from https://www.betterinternetforkids.eu/documents/167024/2013511/GDPRRoundtable_June2017_FullReport.pdf

Mukherjee, S., Pothong, K., & Livingstone, S. (2021). *Child Rights Impact Assessment: A tool to realize child rights in the digital environment*. 5Rights Foundation.

Mwanza, I. (2002). *How nations misbehave: Compliance with human rights treaties in commonwealth Africa*. A dissertation submitted to the Johns Hopkins University in conformity with the requirements of the degree of the Doctor of Philosophy, Baltimore, Maryland.

Nyst, C. (2017). *Privacy, protection of personal information and reputation rights*. UNICEF. https://www.unicef.org/csr/css/UNICEF_CRB_Digital_World_Series_PRIVACY.pdf

OECD (Organisation for Economic Co-operation and Development). (2008). *Handbook on constructing composite indicators – Methodology and user guide*. http://www.oecd.org/std/leadingindicators/42495745.pdf

Office of High Commissioner on Human Rights (OHCHR). (n.d.). *Human rights indicators – Main features of OHCHR conceptual and methodological framework*. Accessed February 14, 2019, from https://www.ohchr.org/EN/Issues/Indicators/Pages/framework.asp

Office of the Privacy Commissioner of Canada. (2012). *Surveillance technologies and children*. Accessed October 25, 2020, from https://www.priv.gc.ca/media/1751/opc_201210_e.pdf

Office of the UN High Commissioner for Human Rights (OHCHR). (2006a). *Report on indicators for monitoring compliance with international human rights instruments*. Report prepared for the 18th meeting of the chairpersons of the human rights treaty bodies. 11 May. HRI/MC/2006/7.

Office of the UN High Commissioner for Human Rights (OHCHR). (2006b). *Report on indicators for promoting and monitoring the implementation of human rights.* Report prepared for the seventh inter-committee meeting of treaty bodies. 6 June. HRI/MC/2008/3.

OHCHR. (2012). *Human rights indicators: A guide to measurement and implementation of human rights.* http://www.ohchr.org/Documents/Publications/CoI_Guidance_and_Practice.pdf.

Payne, L. (2017). Child Rights Impact Assessment (CRIA): *A review of comparative practice across the UK.* UNICEF UK. https://www.unicef.org.uk/publications/unicef-uk-cria-2017/

Payne, L. (2019). Child Rights Impact Assessment as a policy improvement tool. *The International Journal of Human Rights, 23*(3), 408–424. https://doi.org/10.1080/13642987.2018.1558989

Payne, L. (2020a). *ENOC Synthesis Report: Child Rights Impact Assessment.* European Network of Ombudspersons for Children (ENOC). http://enoc.eu/wp-content/uploads/2020/12/ENOC-Synthesis-Report-on-CRIA-FV.pdf

Payne, L. (2020b). *Common framework of reference on Child Rights Impact Assessment: A guide* on how to carry out CRIA (p. 36). European Network of Ombudspersons for Children (ENOC). http://enoc.eu/wp-content/uploads/2020/12/ENOC-Common-Framework-of-Reference-FV.pdf

Prosser, W. L. (1960). Privacy. *California Law Review, 48*(3), 383–423. https://doi.org/10.2307/3478805

Rishmawi, M., & Keable-Elliott, C. (2012). *Right to education project indicators stocktaking report.* Right to Education Project. https://www.right-to-education.org/sites/right-to-education.org/files/resource-attachments/RTE_Indicators_Stocktaking_Report_2012.pdf

Save the Children. (2015). *Child protection outcome indicators.* https://resourcecentre.savethechildren.net/library/child-protection-outcome-indicators.

Sedletzk, V. (2017). *The child-friendly city initiative in France.* UNICEF. https://s25924.pcdn.co/wp-content/uploads/2017/10/CFCI-Case-Study-France.pdf.

Swallow, E. (2013, October 9). The rise of the reputation economy. *Forbes.* Accessed October 25, 2020, from https://www.forbes.com/sites/ericaswallow/2013/10/09/reputation-economy/

Tobin, J. (Ed.). (2019). *The UN convention on the rights of the child: A commentary.* Oxford University Press.

Tobin, J., & Field, S. M. (2019). Article 16: The right to protection of privacy, family, home, correspondence, honour, and reputation. In J. Tobin (Ed.), *The UN convention on the rights of the child: A commentary* (pp. 551–599). Oxford University Press.

Tobin, J., & Read, C. (2019). Article 40: The rights of children in the Juvenile justice system. In J. Tobin (Ed.), *The UN convention on the rights of the child: A commentary* (pp. 1597–1665). Oxford University Press.

UN Committee on Economic, Social and Cultural Rights. (1998). *State obligations, indicators, benchmarks and the right to education.* Background paper submitted by Paul Hunt. 16 July. E/C.12/1998/11.

UN Committee on the Rights of the Child. (1995). *Concluding observations: Nicaragua, June 20, 1995, CRC/C/15/Add.36.* Accessed October 11, 2020, from https://digitallibrary.un.org/record/191818?ln=en

UN Committee on the Rights of the Child. (1996). *Day of general discussion: The child and the media.* UN. Accessed October 25, 2020, from https://www.ohchr.org/EN/HRBodies/CRC/Pages/DiscussionDays.aspx

UN Committee on the Rights of the Child. (2006). *General Comment No. 7 (2005) Implementing child rights in early childhood, September 20, 2006, CRC/C/GC/7/Rev.1.* Accessed October 12, 2020, from https://digitallibrary.un.org/record/584854?ln=en

UN Committee on the Rights of the Child. (2007). General Comment No. 8 (2006) The right of the child to protection from corporal punishment and other cruel or degrading forms of punishment (arts. 19; 28, para. 2; and 37, inter alia), March 2, 2007, CRC/C/GC/8. Accessed October 12, 2020, from https://digitallibrary.un.org/record/583961?ln=en

UN Committee on the Rights of the Child. (2009). *General Comment No. 12 (2009) The right of the child to be heard, July 20, 2009, CRC/C/GC/12*. Accessed October 12, 2020, from https://digitallibrary.un.org/record/671444?ln=en

UN Committee on the Rights of the Child. (2014). *Day of General Discussion: Digital media and children's rights*. UN. Accessed October 24, 2020, from https://www.ohchr.org/EN/HRBodies/CRC/Pages/Discussion2014.aspx

UN Committee on the Rights of the Child. (2017). *General Comment No. 21 (2017) on children in street situations, June 21, 2017, CRC/C/GC/21*. Accessed October 12, 2020, from https://digitallibrary.un.org/record/1304490?ln=en

UN General Assembly. (2019). *The right to privacy in the digital age: Resolution adopted by the General Assembly, 2019, A/RES/73/179*. UN. Accessed October 25, 2020, from http://digitallibrary.un.org/record/1661346

UN Human Rights Committee. (2011). CCPR General Comment No. 34 (2011) Article 19, Freedoms of opinion and expression, September 12, 2011, CCPR/C/GC/34. https://digitallibrary.un.org/record/715606?ln=en

UN Human Rights Council. (2017). The right to privacy in the digital age: Resolution adopted by the Human Rights Council on 23 March 2017, A/HRC/RES/34/7. UN. Accessed October 25, 2020, from http://digitallibrary.un.org/record/1307661

UN Office of the High Commissioner for Human Rights (OHCHR). (2012). *Human rights indicators: A guide to measurement and implementation*, HR/PUB/12/5. Accessed October 11, 2023, from https://www.refworld.org/docid/51a739694.html

UN Office of the High Commissioner for Human Rights (OHCHR). (2014). The right to privacy in the digital age: report of the Office of the United Nations High Commissioner for Human Rights, 2014, A/HRC/27/37. UN. Accessed October 25, 2020, from http://digitallibrary.un.org/record/777869

UNESCO. (2019). From access to empowerment: UNESCO strategy for gender equality in and through education 2019–2025. https://unesdoc.unesco.org/ark:/48223/pf0000369000

UNESCO (United Nations Educational, Scientific and Cultural Organization). (2015). *Education for all 2000–2015: Achievements and challenges*. UNESCO. https://en.unesco.org/gem-report/report/2015/education-all-2000-2015-achievements-and-challenges

UNESCO Institute for Statistics. (2014). *Medium-term strategy 2014-2021*. UNESCO Institute for Statistics. http://uis.unesco.org/sites/default/files/documents/uis-medium-termstrategy-2014-2021-en.pdf

UNICEF. (2006a). *Manual for the measurement of indicators of violence against children*. https://www.unicef.org/violencestudy/pdf/Manual%20Indicators%20UNICEF.pdf

UNICEF. (2006b). *Indicators on violence against children: Guidelines for Field Testing*. UNICEF Child Protection Section, Programme Division, New York. https://www.unicef.org/violencestudy/pdf/Guidelines%20Indicators%20UNICEF.pdf

UNICEF. (2007). *Implementation handbook for the Convention on the Rights of the Child* (3rd ed.). UNICEF. Accessed September 21, 2020, from https://digitallibrary.un.org/record/620060?ln=en

UNICEF. (2016). *Statistics and monitoring: Core indicators in depth*. https://www.unicef.org/statistics/index_24296.html

UNICEF. (n.d.). *Element 7: CRC reporting process*. https://www.unicef.org/pacificislands/Element_7.pdf

United Nations. (2006). Compilation of General Comments and General Recommendations adopted by human rights treaty bodies, HRI/GEN/1/Rev. 8. UN. Accessed April 19, 2020, from http://digitallibrary.un.org/record/576098

United Nations (UN) Commission on Human Rights. (2006). *Report of the Special Rapporteur on the right of everyone to the enjoyment of the highest attainable standard of physical and mental health*, Paul Hunt. 3 March. E/CN.4/2006/48.

United Nations Children's Fund. (2012). *Measuring and monitoring child protection systems: Proposed core indicators for the East Asia and Pacific Region*. Strengthening Child Protection: Indicator 1.2 (Series No. 3), Bangkok: UNICEF EAPRO.

United Nations Committee on the Rights of the Child. (1989). *Convention on the rights of the child*. https://www.ohchr.org/en/professionalinterest/pages/crc.aspx

United Nations Committee on the Rights of the Child. (2003). *General Comment No. 5 (2003) on general measures of implementation of the Convention on the Rights of the Child (arts. 4, 42 and 44, para. 6)*, CRC/GC/2003/5. https://www.refworld.org/docid/4538834f11.html

United Nations Committee on the Rights of the Child. (2006). *General Comment No 7, Implementing Child Rights in Early Childhood*, CRC/C/GC/2006/7. https://www.refworld.org/legal/general/crc/2006/en/40994

United Nations Committee on the Rights of the Child (2013). *General comment No. 14 (2013) on the Right of the Child to Have His or Her Best Interests Taken as a primary consideration*, CRC/C/GC/14. https://www.refworld.org/docid/51a84b5e4.html

United Nations Committee on the Rights of the Child. (2023a). *Concluding observations on the combined third to fifth periodic reports of the Democratic Republic of the Congo*, CRC/C/AND/CO/3-5.

United Nations Committee on the Rights of the Child. (2023b). *Combined fifth and sixth periodic reports submitted by Sao Tome and Principe under article 44 of the Convention*, due in 2018, CRC/C/STP/CO/5-6.

United Nations Committee on the Rights of the Child. (2023c). *Concluding observations on the combined fifth and sixth periodic reports of Azerbaijan*, CRC/C/AZE/CO/5-6.

United Nations Committee on the Rights of the Child. (2023d). *Concluding observations on the combined third and fourth periodic reports of Liechtenstein*, CRC/C/LIE/CO/3-4.

United Nations Committee on the Rights of the Child. (2023e). *Concluding observations on the combined fifth and sixth periodic reports of Togo*, CRC/C/TGO/CO/5-6.

United Nations Committee on the Rights of the Child. (2023f). *Concluding observations on the sixth periodic report of the Dominican Republic*, CRC/C/DOM/CO/6.

United Nations Committee on the Rights of the Child. (2023g). *Concluding observations on the combined fifth and sixth periodic reports of Albania*, CRC/C/ALB/CO/5-6.

United Nations Committee on the Rights of the Child. (2023h). *Concluding observations on the combined fifth and sixth periodic reports of the Plurinational State of Bolivia*, CRC/C/BOL/CO/5-6.

United Nations General Assembly. (1989). *The convention on the rights of the child*. Accessed February 28, 2024, from https://www.ohchr.org/en/professionalinterest/pages/crc.aspx

United Nations Office of High Commissioner of Human Rights. (2012). *Human rights indicators: A Guide to measurement and implementation*. https://www.refworld.org/reference/themreport/ohchr/2012/en/97602

United Nations Office of the High Commissioner for Human Rights (UNHCR). (2013). *General comment No. 16 on the State obligations regarding the impact of the business sector on children's rights*. United Nations Committee on the Rights of the Child.

United Nations Office of the High Commissioner of Human Rights. (2015). *Who will be accountable? Human Rights and the Post-2015 Development Agenda*. https://www.ohchr.org/sites/default/files/Documents/Publications/WhoWillBeAccountable_summary_en.pdf

United Nations/Inter-agency and Expert Group on Sustainable Development Goal Indicators. (2016). *Final list of proposed sustainable development goal indicators*. https://sustainabledevelopment.un.org/content/documents/11803Official-List-of-Proposed-SDG-Indicators.pdf

UNODC & UNICEF. (2006). *Manual for the measurement of juvenile justice indicators*. https://www.unodc.org/pdf/criminal_justice/Manual_for_the_Measurement_of_Juvenile_Justice_Indicators.pdf

UNODC (United Nations Office on Drugs Crimes). (2009). *International framework for action to implement the trafficking in persons protocol*. https://www.unodc.org/documents/human-trafficking/Framework_for_Action_TIP.pdf

Vaghri, Z. (2018). *Piloting the early childhood rights indicators in British Columbia: Protection against violence*. https://onlineacademiccommunity.uvic.ca/globalchild/wpcontent/uploads/sites/2048/2018/12/BC-ECRI-Pilot-Report.pdf

Vaghri, Z., Arkadas, A., Hertzman, C. Krappmann, L., Gertsch, L., Cabral de Mello, M., Ulkuer, N., & Kikuchi-White, A. (2010). *Manual for early childhood rights indicators*. https://resource-centre.savethechildren.net/node/6717/pdf/6717.pdf

Vaghri, Z., Arkadas, A., Kruse, S., & Hertzman, C. (2011). CRC general Comment 7 indicators framework: A tool for monitoring the implementation of child rights in early childhood. *Journal of Human Rights, 10*(2), 178–188. https://doi.org/10.1080/14754835.2011.568916

Vaghri, Z., & Erdemli, I. (2019). A desk top review of the existing indicators on articles and general comments of the united nations convention on the rights of the child. *Zeitschrift für Menschenrechte, Journal for Human Rights, 13*(1), 94–117. https://www.zeitschriftfuermenschenrechte.de

Vaghri, Z., Krappmann, L., Arkadas, A., Hertzman, C., & Fenn, C. (2011). *Piloting the Indicators of General Comment (GC7): Implementing child rights in early childhood. Final Report submitted to UNICEF (Tanzania) and the government of the United Republic of Tanzania.*

Vaghri, Z., Krappmann, L., Arkadas, A., Hertzman, C., Fenn, C., & Diaz, C. (2013). *Piloting the Indicators of General Comment (GC7): Implementing child rights in early childhood. Final report submitted to UNICEF (Chile) and the Government of Chile.*

Vaghri, Z., Krappmann, L., & Doek, J. (2019). From the indicators of General Comment 7 to globalchild: A decade of work to enhance state parties' accountability to children. *International Journal of Children's Rights, 27*(4), 821–851. In press.

Vaghri, Z., Zermatten, J., Lansdown, G., & Ruggiero, R. (Eds.). (2022). *Monitoring state compliance with the UN convention on the rights of the child* (Children's well-being: Indicators and research, vol. 25). Springer. https://doi.org/10.1007/978-3-030-84647-3

Vuckovic-Sahovic, N., Doek, J., & Zermatten, J. (2012). *The rights of the child in international law: Rights of the child in a nutshell and in context-all about children's rights*. Stämpfli.

Westin, A. F. (1967). *Privacy and freedom*. Atheneum.

WHO (World Health Organization). (2018). *2018 global reference list of 100 core health indicators (plus health-related SDGs)*. WHO.

William, S. C., & Baker, T. (2016). *Right to education index pilot report*. Right to education index. https://www.results.org/wp-content/uploads/RTEI_Pilot_Report.pdf

MIX
Papier aus verantwortungsvollen Quellen
Paper from responsible sources
FSC® C105338

If you have any concerns about our products,
you can contact us on
ProductSafety@springernature.com

In case Publisher is established outside the EU,
the EU authorized representative is:
Springer Nature Customer Service Center GmbH
Europaplatz 3, 69115 Heidelberg, Germany

Printed by Libri Plureos GmbH
in Hamburg, Germany